How to Make It Big in the Seminar Business

Paul Karasik

D0970629

McGraw-Hill

New York   St. Louis   San Francisco   Auckland   Bogotá
Caracas   Lisbon   London   Madrid   Mexico City   Milan
Montreal   New Delhi   Paris   San Juan   São Paulo
Singapore   Sydney   Tokyo   Toronto

Library of Congress Cataloging-in-Publication Data

Karasik, Paul
   How to make it big in the seminar business / Paul Karasik.
      p.   cm.
   Includes index.
   ISBN 0-07-033185-5 (hc)   ISBN 0-07-034120-6 (pbk.)
   1. Seminars–Planning–Handbooks, manuals, etc.   1. Title.
AS6.K26   1992
658.4'56–dc20   91-41689
                                            CIP

McGraw-Hill

A Division of The McGraw-Hill Companies

      6 7 8 9 0 DOC/DOC 9 7 6 5 (HC)
9 10 11 12 13 DOC/DOC 0 5 4 3   (PBK)

ISBN 0-07-033185-5 (HC)
ISBN 0-07-034120-6 (PBK)

*The sponsoring editor for this book was James H. Bessent, Jr., the editing
supervisor was Jane Palmeri, and the production supervisor was Pamela
Pelton. It was set in Baskerville by McGraw-Hill's Professional book Group
composition unit.*

Printed and bound by R. R. Donnelley & Sons Company.

This book is printed on recycled, acid-free paper containing a
minimum of 50% recycled de-inked fiber.

To Saul Ellenbogen, Alan Gompers, Moss Jacobs, Marilyn Portnoy, and Gary Karasik, my best friends. You always had faith in me and the work. And to all those who want to improve the lives of others through education.

Contents

Part 2. How to Make Big Money in the Seminar Business

Part 3. How to Hold Your Audience in the Palm of Your Hand

Part 4. The Seminar Business Yellow Pages

Preface

It was a warm August afternoon when I walked into my boss's office to drop the bomb. Commencement day had finally arrived. The words were simple and direct, "I quit." The implications for both my boss and myself were not.

For me, leaving my well-paying position was the biggest professional risk I had ever taken. I had spent two years building an extremely profitable division of his company and I would be giving up a great deal of security. For my boss, my leaving meant the loss of considerable revenue. Although he mouthed the words, "Good luck," I knew his heart was saying, "Paul, are you sure you know what you're doing?"

Neither friends nor family could believe I was leaving a secure job to pursue seminar leadership professionally. In fact, most of them didn't know what a professional seminar leader was.

It Started on a Dare

The path that led me to the seminar business actually began about 22 years before, when I was 15 years old and became a professional musician. This was when I first experienced the exhilaration of applause and accolades from an audience.

The love of performance and the media led me to pursue a major in communications at Temple University. But after college, I found myself pursuing music again.

This was during the early 1970s and the "personal-growth" seminar trend was taking hold throughout America. Thanks to a friend who was promoting speakers, seminars, and personal-growth conferences in New York City, I began to subsidize my music career with talks and seminars on personal-development topics. I thoroughly enjoyed delivering these seminars, but the idea of doing it full-time never occurred to me.

Although I sold a number of my songs to major publishers, signed a modest recording contract, and produced a moderately successful record, enduring success proved elusive. Making it in the music business was far more difficult than I had imagined.

My desire for a more stable lifestyle and steady income led me to pursue sales and marketing. For the next five years I achieved financial success, but felt something was missing. I did not have any passion for what I was doing day to day.

Coincidentally, at this time, my friend Jennifer invited me to accompany her to a seminar. At first I refused. "I know all that stuff," I told her, "I used to give those seminars myself a few years back." She insisted, so finally I caved in and went to the seminar.

Soon after it began, the seminar leader asked if anyone in the audience wanted to do something different with their life. She then looked at *me* and said, "What do *you* want to do?" Without missing a beat—and without thinking—I jokingly said, "I want to do what you do."

Not to be outdone, the seminar leader said, "Then why don't you come up here and do it."

Accepting her challenge, I said, "OK, I will!"

The audience of more than 500 people gasped in unison as I made my way to the front of the room. The seminar leader stood on the side and watched with delight as I answered questions from the audience, which seemed somewhat intoxicated by the sight of one of their own fulfilling his dream right there. After about ten minutes, I thanked the seminar leader for the opportunity and returned to my seat. I sat down knowing what I needed to do. My personal mission became totally clear. It was that evening that I heard my "calling" to be a seminar leader.

Growth as a Seminar Leader and the Launching of the American Seminar Leaders Association

Since that auspicious moment, I have delivered hundreds of seminars and speeches throughout the world. Many times, before I am about to walk up to the front of a room and stand before an audience, I am overwhelmed with the deepest sense of gratitude. I feel blessed to have found a profession that allows me to help others while receiving so much inner satisfaction and financial reward.

The seminar business is a creative wonderland. It offers unlimited opportunities to design and deliver new programs, as well as create profitable products such as books and audio and video programs.

In just the few short years I have been in this business, I have created 12 seminars, 8 different audio programs, 2 video programs, and authored 2 other books. My most recent book, *Sweet Persuasion*, has been published by Simon & Schuster and is being distributed worldwide. In addition, Simon & Schuster purchased the film rights and released a training film by the same name.

I have had the honor of appearing on programs with such notable people as ex-President Ronald Reagan, Dr. Norman Vincent Peale, and many of the gurus from the world of business. In fact, I feel that in a sense, I am a guru of sorts. My specialty is a motivational program called "Winning." It is a unique multimedia program with music, a customized slide show, humor, and strategies and techniques for achieving peak performance. Recently I had the unique pleasure of presenting this "Winning" program as a one-man show on Broadway in New York City.

I truly believe that what I have achieved is attainable for you too, for almost anyone. The purpose of this book is to guide you toward success in the seminar business.

Soon after entering the seminar business, I began to tell others about all the rewards it offered. Often I would spend hours offering advice to individuals who had an interest in pursuing seminars. Then, in order to help others more efficiently, I organized the information into a program called, "How to Create Your Own Successful Seminar/Workshop Business." It has been extremely successful and I continue to present it on a regular basis throughout America.

At the end of this program participants would often ask for a follow-up seminar or meeting. To fill this need, I sent out an announcement to all the alumni of the seminar inviting anyone who was seriously interested in the seminar business to attend. About 20 people showed up and we made a commitment to meet monthly.

The meeting in New York became the first official gathering of what soon came to be known as the American Seminar Leaders Association or ASLA. We agreed on a mission statement. "ASLA is an organization of professional seminar and workshop leaders who seek to enhance their professional skills and market their services and products more successfully."

ASLA has grown rapidly and currently provides a national newsletter, books, tapes, regional and national educational programs, certification for seminar leaders, and professional services that produce brochures and audio and video products for seminar leaders.

How This Book Evolved and How It Will Benefit You

How to Make It Big in the Seminar Business is a natural continuation of my national seminar and the work of the American Seminar Leaders Association. It is in the true spirit of my role as an "information entrepreneur."

Before I wrote this book, I carefully evaluated hundreds of "how-to" books to determine the approach and format that would be most useful to both the entry-level and the advanced seminar leader. In addition, I reviewed any existing material that related to the seminar business. My aim was to create the most comprehensive and beneficial book ever written on this subject.

In order to achieve that aim, I have provided you with the rules, strategies, techniques, guidelines, and methodologies that will make your journey to success as problem-free as possible. None of the information contained in this book is theoretical. Instead, I have provided you with information that works when applied. Throughout the book and in the Yellow Pages section, you are provided with resources and specific contacts that will connect you to the business of developing, marketing, and presenting seminars.

We have entered the information age. There are unlimited opportunities for qualified seminar leaders. By helping you I help myself. As the seminar business grows and the quality of seminar leaders improves, there will be more and more opportunities for everyone.

Ultimately the role of the seminar leader is to help others, to educate them, and to make the world a better place to live. There can never be too many competent and inspired presenters, as long as the information is needed. It is in this spirit that I offer you this book.

May your continued success be filled with joy, satisfaction, and unlimited financial rewards.

Acknowledgments

J. B., Rob Gibert, Jeff Herman, Donna Libby, Lynne Lindahl, Lisa Merrill, Deirdre MacLean, and Marsha Tolkin. You helped by planting the seeds, cultivating the soil, carrying the water, and shedding the light that produced this beautiful flower.

Paul Karasik
Weehawken, N.J.

PART 1

How to Put Together a Dynamic Seminar

Introduction

Welcome to the Profitable World of Seminars

You probably already have some idea of the rewards available in doing seminars if you are reading this book. You may even be sharing in these rewards already. Just in case you are not familiar with the scope of the seminar business, let's take a minute to expand your view of this incredible business.

According to *Training* magazine, a periodical of the corporate seminar business, American businesses currently spend more than $44 billion a year on educational programs. In addition to that, the personal-growth seminar market is estimated to be between $10 to $20 billion a year. In the United States today, there are thousands of seminar companies and countless seminar leaders who are sharing a piece of the seminar pie.

If you possess knowledge or information that can be of value to someone else, then you qualify to share in the profits currently being reaped in the seminar business. Whether you decide to go into seminars part time or full time, the good news is that you can become part of this profitable business starting right now.

Besides money, you will receive recognition, perhaps even fame. Yes, the seminar business has its stars too. By choosing to become a seminar leader, you will gain attention, respect, and recognition from others. By positioning yourself as the expert in your field, you will become the guru that others admire. There is a feeling of intoxication that comes with this territory, a kind of addiction that develops once you have a taste of what it's like to be an information entrepreneur.

The third reward you will reap from the seminar business occurs on an inner level. Each of us has the capacity to fulfill a deeper purpose, to make a contribution to this world, and to help others enjoy a better life.

The seminar business offers a direct way to share a part of yourself and to influence the lives of others in a positive manner.

As Ralph Waldo Emerson said, "It is one of the most beautiful compensations of this life, that no man can sincerely try to help another without helping himself." Although there may be many endeavors that are more altruistic in nature, giving seminars provides the opportunity to help others and thereby to help yourself.

What Exactly Is a Seminar?

A seminar is an exchange of information that is confined to a specific topic. This information answers questions and usually solves specific problems. It can affect the personal or professional life of the participants. Seminars generally last from one hour to a few days in length. They don't usually take as long or go into the same depth as a college course.

There are a few similar kinds of information exchanges worth noting for comparison:

A *speech* is a session that usually lasts for less than two hours and can be used to inform, inspire, or entertain.

A *workshop* is similar to a seminar, although it is more likely to involve some hands-on experience. For example, a computer software workshop might include sitting down at the computer and actually using the software.

A *training program* is a seminar designed to develop specific skills that are applied in a business or professional setting to increase effectiveness or productivity.

For the sake of simplicity, I will refer to any short, concise, benefit-oriented program as a seminar.

What Are the Two Major Seminar Markets?

The seminar business can be divided into two markets. It is important for anyone trying to break into the seminar business to become familiar with each and to understand their similarities and differences. You should also know their advantages and disadvantages, so you can decide which one is best for you.

Public Seminars

First let's examine the *public* seminar market. This is the market with which people are most familiar. A public seminar refers to any seminar that is given in a public gathering place, such as a hotel, and can be attended by anyone willing to pay the seminar tuition. There are numerous public seminar companies that offer programs nationwide on a variety of topics. Some of the most popular public seminar companies include: American Management Association, Dun & Bradstreet, Career-Track, Keye Productivity Center, and National Seminar Group. In Part 4, "The Seminar Business Yellow Pages," you will find a list of public seminar companies.

Many public seminars are on a general topic, such as management skills for the new manager or selling skills. In many cases these seminars are focused on special interest groups, such as bankers, insurance agents, or accountants, and the participants are sent by their employer or perhaps by an organization to which they belong.

The most popular form of promotion for the public seminar is direct mail, although there are certain kinds of seminars that lend themselves to newspaper advertisements or radio spots.

Public seminars have the potential for enormous profits, but they require a substantial investment for promotion. In addition, the potential for mistakes in choosing the correct mailing lists or advertising vehicles makes the public seminar a high-risk venture.

The specific strategies for marketing public seminars with the least amount of risk are discussed in detail in later chapters of this book that focus on marketing techniques.

One example of an extremely successful public seminar is Dr. Norman Vincent Peale's program. His organization consistently sells 1000 or more seats in each of the cities he visits regularly.

There are a few reasons for Dr. Peale's success. First, he has had a number of best-selling books, including the classic, *The Power of Positive Thinking*. This book positioned him as an authority and gives him celebrity status.

Second, he works with highly skilled promoters. A direct mail campaign is launched about a month before the seminar. In addition, the promoters initiate a telemarketing campaign. They telephone the recipients of the brochure and personally invite them to the seminar. Finally, teaser ads are run in the major local newspaper about a week before the seminar. These ads are inquiry generators and result in additional registrations.

In most cases a minimum of a few thousand dollars is required for the promotion of a public seminar. On the other hand, if you win, you stand a chance to win big. Public seminars can be powerful income generators. In addition, income from selling books, tapes, and other spin-off products can add up to a small fortune in a multicity rollout of a good seminar. In fact, public seminars are often loss leaders for the "real money" that is generated from "back-of-the-room sales." The art of back-of-the-room sales is discussed in detail in Chapter 16.

In-House Seminars

The second market is the *in-house* seminar. This is the hidden seminar market. An in-house seminar is sponsored by one organization — a corporation, a professional association, or a nonprofit group, such as a church, synagogue, civic club, chamber of commerce, and so forth. The seminar is focused on providing benefits to the members of the sponsoring organization. The organization usually pays the seminar leader a set fee and pays the marketing expenses. This program is not open to the general public, and many times it is delivered on location, hence the name *in-house* or *on-site*.

An example of an in-house seminar is a selling skills seminar for salespeople at a company that manufacturers copiers. The company might have 20 salespeople in a given office. The seminar will be delivered at the company's office, and only those 20 salespeople will be invited.

Another example of an in-house program is a seminar at a multiday conference for chiropractors on techniques for building a professional practice. The professional association of chiropractors provides the city, the room, and the audience. The seminar leader merely shows up, delivers the seminar, and gets paid.

Other examples of in-house, or sponsored, programs are corporate training programs for the development of employees and adult education evening classes at a local college.

The primary disadvantage of developing, promoting, and delivering in-house programs is that there is usually a ceiling on your income as a seminar leader. Although in many cases you can prearrange for additional money if the program draws more than a certain number of participants, generally your fee will be predetermined.

The good news is that your fee can be more than generous if you are able to provide immediate solutions to an organization's problems. While you might deliver an evening seminar for an adult education program and receive a few hundred dollars, a similar program for a corporation or a trade or professional association can be worth a few thousand dollars. In addition, you might be able to profit further from the sale of books and tapes if you have them.

The greatest advantage of in-house seminars is that there is little risk involved in promoting them. Low-cost marketing techniques are employed, and there is no major investment needed.

By focusing your energies on providing a special interest group with information that will contribute to the success of its members, you can begin to make money in the seminar business immediately.

In the beginning you need to establish your credibility, but once you have a track record, you will be able to market your program easily and inexpensively. Chapter 13 is devoted to marketing in-house seminars.

There are some companies that specialize in providing in-house programs. These companies are listed in Part 4 under "Corporate Training Companies."

To Sponsor or Not to Sponsor Seminars

How to Make It Big in the Seminar Business is designed to give you all the information you need to understand the opportunities, challenges, and rewards of the seminar business.

Do you want to sponsor your own public seminars? Or would you rather market in-house programs to corporations and other organizations?

Or perhaps you might like to get a job delivering a program for one of the major seminar companies. You will find a list of public seminar companies and corporate training companies in Part 4. Chapter 15, "How to Get a Job with a Seminar Company," explains the steps you must take to land a job with one of these companies.

You might want to investigate all of these opportunities and then make your decision based upon your investigation. This book provides the information you need to be successful, regardless of the path you choose.

The Two Secrets for Success in the Seminar Business

In public and in-house seminars alike, your ultimate success will be guaranteed if you devote your efforts to mastering both ends of the business: the "front end" and the "back end."

The front end involves standing in front of a room full of people. It includes the program itself (its content and structure) and your delivery of it. It is always far easier to sell quality. Ultimately the most effective marketing strategy is to design and deliver a fantastic seminar. If you do so, your reputation will precede you. Quality will earn you sponsors, seminar registrants, repeat business, and referrals.

The back end of the business includes everything involved in getting you to the front of the room. It is the marketing of the seminar. The greatest seminar in the world is worthless if there is nobody in the room to receive the information.

You must make a commitment to mastering this back end of the seminar business. Initially, you must focus your efforts equally on front-end and back-end issues. If you correctly and diligently follow the "front-end/back-end" philosophy, you are assured a piece of the seminar pie and will have no trouble making it big in the seminar business.

How to Use This Book

The purpose of this book is provide you with opportunity to achieve success in the seminar business. *How to Make It Big in the Seminar Business* is based upon two proverbs. The first is knowledge is power. To this end, Parts 1 and 3 provide the information you need to design and deliver a money-making seminar. Part 2 focuses on seminar marketing strategies and techniques.

The second proverb this book is based upon is it's not what you know, it's who you know. To address this issue in a comprehensive way, important contacts are provided throughout this book. In addition, Part 4 is a Yellow Pages for the seminar business. No other book on the seminar business has as many contacts as you will find in *How to Make It Big in the Seminar Business*.

A conscientious effort has been made to make sure all addresses and phone numbers are up to date. However, because of constant changes in the business world, there are bound to be some that are inaccurate. These inaccuracies are beyond our control, and we apologize. Future editions will be updated to keep *How to Make It Big in the Seminar Business* the classic how-to business book that it is meant to be.

1

How to Choose
a Winning Topic

A winning seminar topic is one that will attract lots of people who are willing to spend their time and money to attend your seminar.

The Four Critical Features of a Winning Topic

Choose a Topic That You Love

What do you love to talk about? What is your passion? What topic do you find fascinating? What valuable information would you love to share with others?

The eminent educator Dale Carnegie addressed this aspect of the business well: "You never achieve real success unless you like what you're doing."

It is important for you to choose a topic that excites you. No one else will get excited about your topic unless and until you do. When you get excited, your enthusiasm becomes infectious and your program much more motivational. Motivation is an essential ingredient of any truly dynamic seminar and will usually make the difference between just good evaluations and excellent ones.

!!! **Caution.** Ultimately it is the public, not you, who decides if a seminar topic is good or not.

Related to choosing a topic that you love is teaching what you yourself want to learn. When you approach your topic with curiosity, you will naturally stay current and well informed about it. When you are well

9

informed, you will deliver your seminar in a more relaxed and confident manner. The result will be a relaxed, receptive audience that will be inspired by your program.

Choose a Topic That Provides Hard-to-Find Information That Can Be Applied Immediately

We live in an age and culture in which the speed at which information is distributed continues to accelerate. Fax machines, modems, computers, cellular phones, voice mail—all have created an atmosphere of instant information in our society.

People will pay big money for immediate answers and instant relief to their problems.

There is one simple measure of a winning topic: Are people willing to pay to attend a seminar on your topic? You must be able to answer this question with a resolute yes. If you can't, you probably have a marketing problem on your hands.

If you don't know, do some research. Are there similar seminars currently being presented? Have there been seminars presented on your topic in the past? Is it a topic of current interest that is receiving a lot of media attention?

Chances are, if the program has been delivered successfully in the recent past, it can be presented again with similar success.

Choose a Topic That Has a Laser Beam Focus

You have two ways in which you can focus your seminar: by topic and by audience. You can focus by topic alone, by audience alone, or by topic and audience. For example, let's assume you have decided you would like to do a financial-planning seminar. This is a broad topic.

Now, let's see how the audience can be focused by topic and by audience. To focus your financial-planning seminar by topic, choose only one aspect of financial planning, such as tax planning or retirement planning. To focus by audience, you might choose women. A more focused audience might be recently divorced or widowed women. A laser beam focus might be recently widowed or divorced women under the age of 35 who earn $50,000 or more a year and have one or two children.

If you have already decided whom you would like to market your seminar to, one of the easiest ways to focus your topic and organize your seminar is by using a questionnaire or survey. If you have an idea for a seminar, ask a sampling of your prospective audience if they would attend a seminar on this topic. If you need an idea for a seminar, ask your prospective audience what kind of seminar they would be willing to attend.

Figure 1-1 is an example of a survey you might want to customize for your audience.

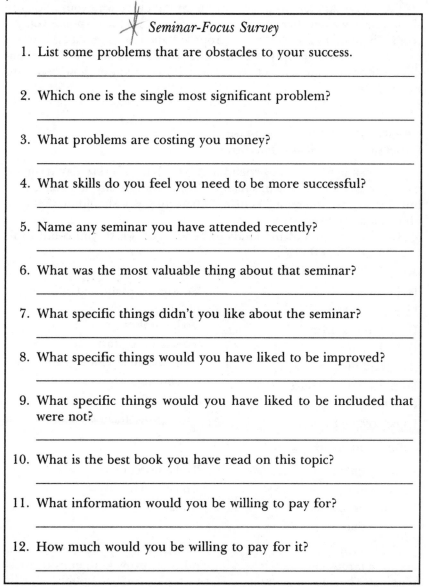

Seminar-Focus Survey

1. List some problems that are obstacles to your success.

   _____

2. Which one is the single most significant problem?

   _____

3. What problems are costing you money?

   _____

4. What skills do you feel you need to be more successful?

   _____

5. Name any seminar you have attended recently?

   _____

6. What was the most valuable thing about that seminar?

   _____

7. What specific things didn't you like about the seminar?

   _____

8. What specific things would you have liked to be improved?

   _____

9. What specific things would you have liked to be included that were not?

   _____

10. What is the best book you have read on this topic?

    _____

11. What information would you be willing to pay for?

    _____

12. How much would you be willing to pay for it?

    _____

Figure 1-1. A questionnaire will help you focus your seminar on the needs of the audience.

Aside from helping you identify your topic, a seminar questionnaire provides you with valuable marketing information. The questionnaire enables you to discover specific needs and to uncover problems you will want to address in your seminar. Take care of the needs of your audience, and your audience will take care of you.

If you have an idea for a seminar but are not sure who your audience should be, try a few direct mail tests. Judging from the response you get from a mailing to a few of your proposed audience members, you will quickly and fairly cheaply determine if you have identified a good audience for your seminar. There is more information on how to do this in Chapter 9.

Choose a Topic That Provides Substantial Perceived Benefits

People seek benefits. They spend a greater part of every day trying to gain rewards or avoid punishment. People do not buy seminars; they buy the benefits the seminars offer. Therefore, you should market benefits, not seminars.

Here are samples of the kinds of benefits on which you could focus your marketing efforts.

Rewards people want to gain:

To be loved	To win the praise and admiration of peers
To make money	
To gain recognition	To be healthy
To feel secure	To live in comfort
To advance in their careers	To maintain a positive self-image
To experience pleasure	To save time
To achieve success	To have fun
To be accepted socially	To improve themselves

Punishments people want to avoid:

To feel pain	To be insecure
To be unhealthy	To be lonely
To waste or lose money	To die
To waste time	

The bottom line is that you must correctly identify the specific benefits your target audience is seeking and then provide them with those benefits. The most commonly offered topics for both public and in-house seminars are listed in Figures 1-2 and 1-3.

Business and Professional Topics

Accounting
Affirmative Action
Alcoholism
Assertiveness
Assessment
 (Employee)
Attitude Automation
Behavioral Theories
Body Language
Brain Theory
Budgeting
Career Development
Change
Chemical Dependency
Clerical Skills
Counseling Skills
Computers
Conflict Management
Creativity
Credit
Crime in the Work-
 place
Crisis Management
Cross-Cultural Skills
Customer Service
Data Processing
Delegation
Disabilities
Discipline
Drug Abuse
Engineering
Ergonomics
Ethics

Executive Develop-
 ment
Family
Financial Planning
First Aid
Future Trends
Goal Setting
Graphic Design
Group Dynamics
Hiring
Health Issues
Industrial Relations
Interviewing
Inventory Control
Labor Relations
Language (Foreign)
Legal Issues
Leadership
Listening Skills
Management Skills
Marketing
Mathematics
Media Relations
Meeting Planning
Memory Development
Mergers/Acquisitions
Motivation
Needs Analysis
Negotiation
Nutrition
Office Automation
OSHA

Outplacement
Performance
 Appraisal
Problem Solving
Productivity
Project Management
Public Relations
Public Speaking
Purchasing
Quality
Reading (Remedial)
Retirement
Robotics
Safety
Sales Management
Sales Training
Security
Sensitivity Training
Sexual Harassment
Statistical Analysis
Strategic Planning
Stress Management
Succession Planning
Supervising
Team Building
Technical Skills
Telemarketing
Telephone Skills
Time Management
Women's Issues
Word Processing
Writing Skills

Figure 1-2. Listing of the most commonly offered business and professional seminar topics.

Personal-Development Topics

Acting	Dance	Losing Your Foreign
Art	Desktop Publishing	Accent
Body Building	Drawing	Meeting People
Body Massage	Fencing	Modeling
Bridge	Finding a Mate	Photography
Calligraphy	Flirting	Procrastination
Career Alternatives	Flower Arranging	Psychic Development
Charisma	Gift Baskets	Real Estate Investing
Classical Music	Home Repair	Reflexology
Clutter	Horseback Riding	Scuba Diving
Color Analysis	Hypnosis	Self-Esteem
Comedy	Ice Skating	Swimming
Creative Visualization	Image	Taxes
Creative Writing	Jewelry Making	Voice
Credit	Karate	Weight Control
Cross-Country Skiing	Knitting	Wine Tasting

Figure 1-3. Listing of the most commonly offered personal-development seminar topics.

2

What You Need to Succeed in the Seminar Business

There are three prerequisites for success in the seminar business. You will need knowledge, the right attitude, and skills. In some of these areas you might have the necessary qualifications. The purpose of this chapter is to help you make an honest self-assessment. Let's look at each prerequisite in more detail.

Knowledge

You must know your subject completely. In fact, you must be able to position yourself as one of the leading authorities on your particular topic. To put it bluntly, *do your homework*.

Although you probably have direct experience and possibly all the right credentials, you must work continually to expand your frame of reference. You must become a veritable repository of information on your topic. As a seminar leader, you are an information entrepreneur. You must keep updating your stock. There are six simple steps you must take to become a true authority:

1. Identify the top 10 books written on your topic and read them. Make sure to include all of the classics in your field.

2. If there are any audio or video cassettes available, listen to and watch them.

3. Locate any seminars on your topic and go to them. You can learn a lot from your colleagues and competitors.

4. Subscribe to any periodicals that have up-to-date information on your topic.

5. Join any organizations that focus on your topic. For example, if your topic is computers, there are a number of professional associations to which computer consultants belong.

6. Position yourself as one of the experts. Personally introduce yourself to as many notable people in your field, both locally and nationally, as you can. You'll be amazed how quickly and easily you'll be received by the so-called gurus on your topic. The "great ones" always seem to want to help those who are sincerely interested and dedicated to the topic. After all, teaching or mentoring is a large part of what being a guru means. Remember that. You may be a guru yourself someday.

As an illustration of step 6, let me share a personal experience.

Not too long ago, I was consulting for an individual who wanted to give seminars on stress management. She came to my office holding a book that she felt contained the most valid and essential information on this topic. The author was a personal idol of hers.

Although she was thoroughly knowledgeable about her topic, she had not yet empowered herself as an authority. I asked her if she would like to become a colleague of the author. She replied, "Of course." I looked up the author's telephone number, picked up the phone, and dialed it. When he answered, I handed the phone to my client.

She almost panicked, but she took the phone. She apologized for bothering him, nervously introduced herself, and subsequently had a long conversation that initiated a relationship that, to my knowledge, is still alive today.

Now when my client is delivering her seminar, she refers to the well-known author as a personal friend and associate. She also has developed a very real and direct connection to one of the most respected people in her field and a pipeline to the most current information on her topic.

When you give a seminar, you will invariably be asked a variety of questions. If you do your homework, you will always be able either to answer the question, fully or in part, or, at the very least, to provide direction to where the questioner might find the answer.

!!! **Contacts.** See the Yellow Pages in this book under "Professional Associations for Networking and Education."

Attitude

There are six essential personal qualities that winners possess. You probably possess all of them to one degree or another, but there is no one who can't benefit from improvement in one or several of these areas. Identify the traits or qualities you need to enhance or develop.

1. *Commitment.* As in all areas of endeavor, until you commit yourself—in this case to the seminar business—you will achieve very little. You will lack effectiveness. Commitment helps you overcome any fears or misgivings you might have. Commitment is the mind-set, the wellspring for the resources and creative ideas, that is so essential in the seminar business.

Regardless of the professional path you choose to take in the seminar business, commitment will help you overcome the obstacles that are bound to occur.

2. *Confidence.* Confidence is not only a feeling but also the outward expression of commitment. Whether you are promoting or presenting, exhibiting confidence is critical in gaining the support of others.

It is not always possible to feel confident, but it is always possible to exhibit confidence. An excellent exercise is to practice exhibiting confidence under all conditions. To do this, you reverse cause and effect, working backward from the outward manifestation to the feeling itself. You'll be amazed what happens. In many cases, the result is that you will feel confident!

3. *Sense of mission.* When you feel a sense of mission, or purpose, you will automatically possess the positive mental attitude you need to create, market, and present your program. Speakers with a mission are charismatic and almost always effective. If you feel that presenting seminars is a way to help others and that it is, therefore, more of a calling than a job, your potential for achieving success is unlimited.

4. *Persistence.* Let's face it, everything is not going to go your way all the time. Sure, you're likely to catch a lot of breaks along the way, but you're also likely to catch an equal number of challenges. If you can't accept failure, you've got a big problem. Every new undertaking requires the ability to bounce back and stay on course with positive expectancy. As Calvin Coolidge said,

> Nothing in the world can take the place of persistence.
> Talent will not; nothing is more common than unsuccessful
>   men with talent.
> Genius will not; unrewarded genius is almost a proverb.
> Education will not; the world is full of educated derelicts.
> Persistence and determination are alone supreme.

5. *Goal orientation.* If you don't know what you want, you're not very likely to get it. It is important to make goal setting a habit, not just an occasional practice. Your goals should be divided into three categories: short-term, medium-range, and long-term. Setting goals means writing them down, with target dates for achieving them. Start right now if you haven't already.

Here is an example of short-term, medium-range, and long-term goal setting.

Long-Term Goal
Sell 50,000 copies of my book to target market   5 years

Medium-Range Goals
Complete the writing of the book   2 years
Secure a publishing contract   1 year

Short-Term Goals
Complete the book proposal   90 days
Write two or three sample chapters   60 days
Begin to outline the book   30 days

In this case, your long-term goal might be to sell 50,000 books to your target market. Completing the book is a necessary step toward achieving this goal. Breaking this goal into bite-sized pieces makes success not only possible but also probable.

6. *High energy (enthusiasm).*   The seminar business requires energy, lots of it, and in many forms.

Creative energy is needed to put your program together. Good seminar programs are continually updated and revised to keep them current for the audience and interesting for you as a presenter.

Mental energy is needed to research and replenish your information pool, as well as to market your program and run your business.

Physical energy is needed to keep up hectic travel schedules and to present your seminar enthusiastically. Success requires stamina to endure long hours on your feet and many long hours in preparation.

Emotional energy is needed to really care about the participants who have spent their time and money to attend your program. You will also need emotional strength to deal with the successes and disappointments that come with the turf.

Skills

Although you might have the luxury of hiring others with the following five skills, more than likely you will need to develop them personally. All of these skills range from necessary to highly desirable if you are to achieve your greatest potential as a seminar leader.

Writing Skills

Although the spoken word is your basic communicating and money-making tool in the seminar business, writing skills are also needed if you want to ease your path to glory. You needn't be a Hemingway, but you will need effective business writing skills.

If you don't already possess the ability to write persuasively and you want to develop better writing skills, start by reading one of the many good books available on the topic or by attending classes at your local college or university. Classes in business and professional writing are proliferating currently. Your options have never been better.

But the real secret to becoming an effective writer is *to write*. Start writing now. As with most skills, you will improve faster with practice.

Our culture practically worships the written word. Therefore, you will gain respect and influence people if your letters, workbooks, resource guides, articles, and proposals are powerful, clear, and of high quality. Ultimately, you will *want* to be the person who "*wrote* the book."
Chapter 16 provides valuable information and resources to help you get out your written word.

Telephone Skills

The most valuable business tool of the twentieth century remains the telephone. You need to be able to secure speaking opportunities and enroll participants using the convenience of the telephone. Even if you are already comfortable and fairly proficient doing business on the phone, work to increase your effectiveness. It will increase your profits. There are three key principles to remember when using the telephone.

1. Always set measurable goals for yourself when you use the telephone. For example, if you are marketing your in-house seminar, you can set a goal of 10 calls per day to prospective organizations.

2. Always develop a script from which to work in order to keep control of the conversation. This script should include your opening and closing, as well as answers to possible questions you might be asked.

3. Never sound as though you are using a script. Each call should maintain a conversational tone. Even though you might be answering the same question for the one hundredth time, it should sound fresh. This might be difficult at first, but you will quickly master it if you make this one of your skill development goals.

Selling Skills

Your ability to sell your program will largely determine your success, like it or not. You will be selling your seminar, your books, your tapes, your ideas, and, of course, yourself. As I have already mentioned, the greatest seminar in the world is of no value without people in the room.

Selling is a learned discipline, but it is simple once you know how.

You should never have to use a hard sell. In fact, the hard sell will do you and your business more harm than good. As a first step, you must learn the art of selling as a way of serving. If you believe in your seminar and your products, you will find this kind of selling a very simple and natural process.

There are a few important ideas to always keep in mind when you sell.

1. Take the time to develop rapport and establish a relationship with the person to whom you are selling. In this way, you will always be setting up long lasting relationships. Once you have sold yourself as a resource, the chances are excellent the person will come back.

2. Identify the needs of the person you are selling to, and sell the benefits that relate to those needs. For instance, let's say you want to enroll someone in your time-management seminar. If you determine that your prospect is seeking to achieve more balance between his or her business and personal life, focus your sales presentation on how your seminar will provide answers to this specific problem.

3. Never forget to ask for exactly what you want If you want the people in your seminar to purchase your book or tapes, say clearly, "My books and tapes are on sale in the back of the room. I accept all major credit cards." There have been numerous studies done of professional salespeople in which a large percentage of them never asked for the order. Don't forget to ask for the order!

!!! **Resource.**   An excellent and inexpensive publication designed to help you develop effective selling skills is a bimonthly magazine, *Personal Selling Power*. It is well written, educational, and motivational as well.

Personal Selling Power
P.O. Box 5467
Fredericksburg, VA 22403-9904
(800) 752-7355

Presentation Skills

Your ability to present information effectively is a necessary skill. One of your most powerful marketing strategies is repeat business and referrals. In order to get this business, you need highly evolved speaking skills.

Professional presentation skills in the seminar business go beyond standing in the front of the room and delivering a lecture like a college professor. You need to add humor, audiovisuals, and a level of drama to the presentation.

Perhaps you possess very good speaking skills already. That's fine, but don't stop with very good. Make one of your goals to improve continually as a speaker, to set yourself far above the crowd.

Computer Skills

The primary need for computer skills is to take advantage of the computer's word processing capabilities. There are letters to write, proposals to generate, and lots of handouts and workbooks to create. The computer will save you time and money in the long run. Along with the computer, you need basic typing skills.

!!! **Contacts.** Two organizations will provide you with invaluable assistance in developing your professional skills. They both offer books, tapes, seminars, newsletters, networking opportunities, and lots of other resources.

American Seminar Leaders
 Association
899 Boulevard East
Weehawken, NJ 07087
(800) 735-0511

National Speakers Association
3877 N. 7th St., No. 350
Phoenix, AZ 85014
(602) 265-1001

3
How to Design a Money-Making Seminar

In order to create a truly successful seminar, you must follow Karasik's axiom.

> Focus on the needs of your audience, and your audience will focus on you.

Strategies for Putting Your Seminar Together

Designing a great seminar is simple if you follow this three-part process.

1. *Focus on where your participants are right now.* What is their level of expertise on the topic before taking your seminar: beginner, intermediate, or advanced? Among the most common mistakes a seminar leader makes is to create a seminar that is either too elementary or too advanced. In either case, your participants do not get what they came for or what they need.

For example, if you are delivering a sales seminar to brand-new salespeople, your content should be very broad. They need an understanding and an overview of the selling process itself, the basics. On the other hand, if your audience consists of experienced salespeople, they will be bored with material they've heard before.

2. *Focus on where they want to go.*   Focus on the benefits your participants expect. In the case of the sales seminar, the participants will probably want to make more money by closing more sales. If you construct a seminar that focuses on helping them achieve their goals, you are guaranteed rave reviews.

3. *Focus on what your audience needs to learn to get where they want to go.*   Again, using the example of the sales seminar, the audience might want to learn how to prospect for new clients, how to handle objections, and how to prequalify leads. The information or skills your audience needs are known as objectives. By achieving the objectives above, the salespeople will get where they want to go—they will make more money.

The One Technique Essential for a Perfect Seminar

The first step you must take in creating a perfect seminar for your participants is to *ask them what they need to know.* You can accomplish this with a written questionnaire or by interviewing on the telephone.

If you are designing a new seminar and have identified your target audience, you can reach them easily enough. For example, if your seminar is for secretaries, you can call up a few secretaries at random, tell them what you're doing, and ask them for a few minutes of interviewing time.

Another good technique for finding out the needs of your potential audience is to call an association made up of your potential audience. For example, let's say your target audience is nurses. There are 54 national nursing associations you can contact to pinpoint the problems they would like you to solve. You can locate the names and telephone numbers of the associations that would be helpful to you by referring to the pages in Chapter 13 that deal with trade and professional associations.

Once you have begun to deliver your program, you will be able to refine the design of your seminar with the information you receive from participants. You get this information from informal interviews conducted after each program and from formal written evaluations filled out after the seminar.

Whether you are asking your audience on the phone, in person, or by means of a written questionnaire, the answers to the following two questions will become the basis for your seminar:

1. What three things would you most like to see covered in this seminar?

2. If you could have only one of these covered, which would it be?

The answers to these two questions will provide you with your seminar modules. It's almost as if you've created a series of miniseminar topics. Designing a comprehensive seminar becomes much easier when you break your seminar down into bite-sized pieces.

Answers to the second question will help you prioritize your modules. By knowing which modules are most important to your audience, you will be able to devote the appropriate amount of time to each module.

Why Use the Modular Design Approach (MDA)?

The quick answer to this question is very simple. You use it because it works. But here are several of the reasons why it works so well.

1. It allows you to arrange or rearrange the flow of the seminar easily and quickly.

2. You can customize your seminar according to the specific needs of a given group. For example, if your sales group does not need information on prospecting, it becomes very simple to drop this module without affecting the integrity of the rest of the seminar.

3. Researching your material is much easier when you have organized your seminar in a modular fashion. If you develop each module as if it were a miniseminar, your seminar will be filled with lots of variety. Each module will have its own opening, middle, and closing.

4. It makes it easier to transpose your seminar into other media. For example, the modules can easily become a series of printed monographs, chapters of a book, or sections in an audio or video program.

5. You will be able to create spin-off programs based on the needs of your audience. For example, a time-management module could be expanded into a full stand-alone seminar, such as time-management techniques for salespeople.

6. Participants appreciate the feeling of completion as you progress from one module to the next. Because modules make it possible to digest larger bodies of information, attendees literally get more for their money using an MDA. Think of it this way: Most of us cut up our food and chew it a while before we swallow it.

If you have identified the needs of your audience and designed modules to address those needs, your seminar is practically guaranteed to be effective.

An Example of MDA

Let's say you have decided to do a three-hour seminar called "How to Run Your First Marathon without Killing Yourself." Here is a step-by-step application of the MDA in putting together an effective seminar.

The first step is to interview members of the local running clubs who are training for a marathon, members of the local track team, Sunday joggers, or anyone else who might be interested in running a marathon. Ask them what a person needs to know to run his or her first marathon. Have them identify the one thing with which they are most concerned.

Let's say you get a random list that looks like this:

- Type of shoes to train in
- Foods to eat during training and marathon
- Training schedule
- Clothes to wear during marathon
- Time needed to train for the marathon
- What to do on marathon day
- How to choose the best marathon to run
- Protection from getting injured
- How to stay motivated
- How to avoid "hitting the wall"
- Special running gear
- Pain and difficulty in running a marathon

Suppose you found that the topic people identified most as their first priority was training.

With this information in hand, the modules for your seminar would be arranged as follows:

A. How to choose the best marathon to run

B. Shoes and running gear

C. Training schedule for your first marathon

D. Injuries, how to avoid them, and what to do

E. Peak performance and self-motivation techniques

F. What to do the day of the marathon

As you can see, these modules are the logical building blocks for the seminar. You can research each topic independently and develop each module with appropriate case studies, stories, participatory exercises, and so forth. For example, Module F could be broken down like this:

F. What to do the day of the marathon
   1. Wake-up time
   2. Physical and mental preparation
      a. Participatory exercise
   3. Pacing yourself correctly
      a. The first few miles
      b. Predicting your finishing time
   4. How to avoid "hitting the wall"
      a. Personal story
      b. Precautionary technique
      c. What to do if you do "hit the wall"
      d. Walking, water, and stretching
   5. Recovering after the run

As you can see from this example, the modular design approach makes building a comprehensive and effective seminar a simple process. Master the MDA methodology, and you will be able to create new seminars quickly and easily.

!!! Resource. If you want to deliver an outstanding seminar that has been designed and packaged with workbooks, visuals, and a step-by-step leaders guide, you might want to become a member of the Performax Learning Network. You can choose from a wide variety of business and personal development topics. Optional programs are held throughout the country to teach you how to deliver the seminars.

To obtain more information on these quality "prepackaged" seminars, call or write:

Sandy Karn
Creative Results Sources, Inc.
P.O. Box 405
Wheaton, IL 60189
(708) 668-2726 (Ask for Dept. 101 for special discounts.)

PART 2

How to Make Big Money in the Seminar Business

4

Your Passport to Marketing Success—TADA

Most seminar marketing plans don't work for one simple reason: failure to define accurately the target market. When I ask a potential seminar leader or promoter who his or her audience is, and that person replies, "Everybody," I know we're in big trouble. In most cases, marketing a program to *everybody* presents a monumental, usually insurmountable problem.

TADA—The Magic Marketing Formula

TADA stands for target audience design approach. TADA is the guiding light for successful seminar marketing. It is the reference point for developing a marketing plan. TADA will help you make decisions such as site selection, workbook design, fees, refreshments, advertising methods, brochure style, mailing-list selection, and practically anything else.

Successful program marketing depends upon making correct decisions, not arbitrary ones. Using your target audience as a reference point, you will automatically make the right choices.

It is easy to design a concise and efficient marketing plan based upon your target audience. For example, let's say you have a seminar called "How to Hire the Right People." It would be safe to say that the human resources department of small- to medium-sized companies would be the market. Since the average salary of a director of human resources for a company of this size is not in a high range, traveling from a great distance to attend this seminar is unlikely. Because of the nature of the seminar, industries that have a high employee turnover rate, such as retail sales, might be good candidates.

In the above example, the target audience was defined by a number of factors: industry, company size, department, position, and salary range.

How to Use the Target Audience Design Approach

With the above information in hand, you can now make educated marketing decisions. Using TADA, you can easily locate mailing lists of directors of human resources of large retail operations.

You might also examine the possibility of using advertising vehicles, such as trade magazines that your prospective audience might read. (In this case, you would use the trade magazine of the National Retail Merchants Association.) Of course, your seminar brochure would be designed with your target audience in mind, written in the language of the retail industry.

When you apply TADA to market your seminar, you spend your marketing dollar wisely. Use TADA to make all marketing decisions, and you can't lose.

Creating a Ten-Factor Profile of Your Target Audience

Here are 10 criteria by which you can define your audience. For each category, try to think of the requirements that need to be met when pitching your seminar.

1. *Sex.*   You will want to identify the ratio of men to women. If your audience is all or primarily men, an advertisement in the sports section of the Sunday newspaper might be an effective marketing vehicle. Similarly, if you are marketing a weight loss seminar to an audience that is primarily women, the life-style section of the newspaper would be the proper place for an ad.

2. *Age.*   What age group are you targeting? When you are writing copy for your brochure, certain words and phrases will mean different things to different age groups. What might be perfect for baby boomers could be totally ineffective with the generation that precedes them.

3. *Place of residence.*   Where does your target audience live? If your audience is urban, posters put up around town could work well. This marketing strategy would be much less effective in the suburbs.

4. *Industry.*   Specific industries require specific seminars. A great example of this is the overnight shipping industry. Because of the con-

stant time pressure employees feel, companies such as Federal Express provide an assortment of stress management seminars. Industries such as this might also be a fertile market for seminars on similar topics, such as time management.

5. *Occupation.* Some occupations require specific ingredients in order to be successful. For example, seminars for CEOs might require exotic locations, such as Bermuda or Hawaii. Similarly, seminars for law enforcement officers might do best broken up into small segments or held on weekends.

6. *Education.* Although you might possess an MBA from Harvard Business School, your target audience might not have more than a high school diploma. Sometimes marketing material completely misses its mark because it fails to speak the language of the target audience.

7. *Position.* If you can identify the exact position of your target audience, you will be able to pinpoint the correct and most profitable mailing lists. For example, if you have a seminar for reducing business overhead, purchasing agents of large companies might be the mailing list to purchase.

8. *Income level.* Lots of seminar leaders who give programs on financial investment want to market their seminar to very wealthy people. The problem is that few people in this income group attend public seminars. Therefore, if you are seeking to market to this target audience, you must develop more creative strategies. One seminar leader on this topic travels to the various high-price health spas and does his program on this topic for "free." He walks away with valuable clients, which pays huge dividends.

9. *Career experience.* Is your program for entry-level employees or for those with more experience? One of the popular programs the American Management Association offers is geared for the newly appointed manager. By focusing their program on a specific experience level, they have tapped a lucrative market.

10. *Career skill needed for professional success.* Perhaps you know your market is for receptionists. Market telephone skills, and you will hit a valuable marketing "hot" button.

In many cases, one or two of these factors will weigh more heavily than the others. Use any or all, but make sure you use the laser beam marketing strategy of TADA.

$$$ **Saver.** Your most important money-saving strategy is TADA. With it you will avoid wasting marketing dollars. You will minimize risk when you advertise or use direct mail. In general, you will be able to make the best choices when it comes to promoting your seminar.

5
Choosing the Best Month, Day, and Time

It is crucial for you to choose the date and time for your seminar very carefully. Timing will have an immense impact on the attendance of your seminar.

Rules of Thumb When Choosing Your Month and Day

Although there are exceptions to every rule, follow these general guidelines when you are planning dates for your seminar.

1. *Avoid holidays of any kind.* This includes both national and religious holidays, as well as the vacation periods that normally fall around them. People get wrapped up in the preparations for holidays, are distracted by them, or travel to visit friends and family during holiday periods. For example, you should avoid the Friday after Thanksgiving and the days before Christmas and just after New Year's Day.

2. *Avoid major national events.* Although many of these events are of no interest to you personally, they preoccupy many members of your potential audience. Some examples of this type of event are the Super Bowl, the World Series, political conventions and elections, and even TV broadcasts like the Academy Awards.

3. *Avoid major local events.* Don't try to compete with such local events as county fairs and festivals and local sporting events. If a home-

town college football team is playing a big game, be careful; you don't want to compete with this type of event.

4. *Be careful about weather conditions.*   Winter months, especially in certain regions, can pose threats to the success of your seminar. Particularly in urban areas, snow is seen as a major obstacle. It can cause a poor turnout of preregistered participants and wipe out most of your on-site registrations. To avoid a case such as this, you might want to schedule your event before or after the time period when you are most likely to get snow storms.

5. *Remember TADA.*   Timing should take into account the requirements of your target audience as defined in the preceding chapter. For example, if you are planning a seminar for doctors, make sure the American Medical Association is not holding a convention or major meeting at the same time. Similarly, don't plan a seminar for accountants during the first part of April.

The Best (and Worst) Months of the Year to Hold and Promote Your Seminar

If you are promoting seminars, there are a few important guidelines to consider when choosing the date.

1. September and October are generally the best attended months for seminars. Perhaps it is a holdover from the school-year schedule that seminars seem to do best in the fall, the back-to-school time of year.

2. Early November works well, but be careful to avoid the week of Thanksgiving for reasons already explained.

3. The winter months of January, February, and March are good, except where weather conditions could make travel difficult. As mentioned, in areas such as the Northeast there is often hesitation, cancellation, or drop-off due to bad weather. Also, avoid the beginning of January, since it falls right after a holiday.

4. April and May are also generally good months for promoting seminars. There are no major holiday conflicts except for Memorial Day and Easter.

5. June, July, and August are not the best months for promoting seminars because many people take their vacations during these months.

6. Although very early December can work well, December is the least favorable month because of the preoccupation with the Christmas holiday.

The Best Days of the Week to Hold and Promote Your Seminar

In addition to the considerations already mentioned, here are guidelines for choosing the best day of the week to promote your seminar.

1. Tuesday, Wednesday, and Thursday are generally very good days to give seminars of any kind. The primary reason is that people often take three-day weekends and might be unavailable on Mondays and Fridays. Chances are good most people will be available during the heart of the workweek.

2. Friday is an excellent day to promote business seminars, especially if the fee is paid by the participant's business. Seminar registrants usually take advantage of a Friday seminar schedule to make their weekend begin early.

3. Saturday is an excellent day for personal-development seminars, since it avoids conflicts with business hours.

4. Sunday tends to be considered a family day or "day of rest" for many people. It can work for personal-development seminars, but the better choice is Saturday.

5. Monday is a get-back-to-work day. Most time-management research has proven that Mondays are stress filled and very busy. Consequently, you should avoid trying to put one more item on people's agendas. As a general rule, avoid Monday if you can.

Guidelines for Choosing the Best Time of Day

One final bit of fine tuning is in order when thinking about optimal timing. There are a few basic guidelines for choosing the time of the day to hold your seminar.

1. Traffic patterns must be considered. Make allowances for rush hour in major metropolitan areas.

2. Remember TADA. For example, if your audience consists of secretaries or receptionists, an 8 a.m. start is feasible, since they are accustomed to this hour. If your audience consists of homemakers with children, a 9 a.m. start would probably fit into their schedule more conveniently. They need the early morning hours to get children off to school and complete daily household chores.

3. Half-day seminars should be scheduled between the hours of 8 a.m. and 12:30 p.m. or 12:30 p.m. and 5 p.m.

4. Full-day seminars should start no later than 9 a.m. and end preferably before 5 p.m. People like to get a jump on traffic. Starting at about 4 p.m. they begin to fidget in their seats or apologetically start to leave early, no matter how good you are.

5. If you are promoting a multiday program, there will probably be participants using air transportation. You can end the first day between 4 p.m. and 5 p.m., but plan to end the final day by 4 p.m. at the latest so that people will have time to get to the airport and make their plane connections.

6. Evening seminars should be scheduled between 6 p.m. and 10 p.m. The best hours in the evening are between 6:30 p.m. and 9:30 p.m. Most people need time to grab some dinner after work and travel to the seminar location and would prefer not returning home too late in the evening.

7. It is always preferable to reduce the number of days for which a program is scheduled and extend the hours. There are two reasons for this strategy. First, many participants find it difficult to devote a number of days to attending a seminar. Second, you will want to use your time efficiently. Whether you spend 2 hours or 6 hours on a given day at a seminar, you essentially spend the whole day. Therefore, two 6-hour days is more efficient than four 3-hour days.

8. If you are presenting your seminar to a local audience and your TADA profile reveals that participants will not be traveling great distances, do not present multiday evening seminars on consecutive nights. If you do, there is an increased chance that participants will have schedule conflicts. Book your seminar on alternate weekday evenings or on the same day on consecutive weeks.

9. Personal-development seminars are best presented in the evening hours to avoid conflicts with work. Your participants are less likely to get time off for a seminar that is not work related.

10. Finally, schedule business seminars to end early in the afternoon. For those who are busy and conscientious, they will have time to get back to their office or job. For those who are looking for a reason to end the day a little early, your seminar might be just the right ticket.

6

How to Choose the Best Seminar Site

The All-Important Question

What site will increase your attendance or make your seminar most profitable?

Here we come back to TADA. Choose a site with your target audience in mind. Are your attendees high-level executives who not only can afford but also expect to spend their time in an attractive, upscale, possibly exotic location? Are you marketing a seminar to an audience who would be more likely to attend if your program was conveniently located in the center of the city? Or would your audience be more drawn to a beautiful, natural setting?

Assuming you are familiar with your target audience, you probably have some good ideas about what type of location would be most likely to appeal to them.

!!! **Contacts.** The Yellow Pages of this book contains a list of over 500 hotels in major seminar markets that are equipped for seminars. They have facilities that are designed to accommodate your needs.

Most seminars are held in meeting rooms at hotels throughout the world, but some seminars are routinely held at resort settings such as Club Med, on Caribbean cruise ships, and at retreat centers in mountain wilderness areas. To find out about these exotic sites, you might have to do some research at the library.

In the past twenty years, a new type of seminar location has evolved — the conference center. These facilities are specially built to accommodate meetings and seminars. They have been designed to maximize program effectiveness and convenience. The accommodations, business services, audiovisual equipment, and facility location provide the perfect environment for holding seminars.

!!! **Contact.** For a list of conference centers and for more information on the conference center concept, you can contact:

The International Association of Conference Centers
900 South Highway Dr.
Fenton, MO 63026
(314) 349-5576

Criteria for Choosing a Seminar Location

1. *Population.* As in any form of marketing, you want to choose locations with significant populations. There is no magic size for a city to qualify as a good location for a seminar, but generally any city with a population of a million or more is a viable site.

Of course, there are many excellent cities for seminars that have populations of fewer than a million. Usually these cities draw from a greater metropolitan area. San Francisco and northern New Jersey are good examples of densely populated areas that fit this description.

2. *Accessibility to transportation.* If your audience will be arriving by plane, it is important to choose a city with daily, nonstop flights. Air access is especially important if you have to attract an audience from diverse parts of the country. However, surveys show that the majority of seminar participants travel 100 miles or less. Therefore, you should consider locations that have easy and convenient access by car or public transportation.

3. *Economic conditions.* Although you might choose an area or city that has a substantial population, it is important to consider the community's economic base. The presence of the following institutions or conditions are favorable signs: Fortune 500 companies, large universities and colleges, a wide variety of first-class hotels, an active chamber of commerce and/or convention center, and low unemployment.

4. *Charisma.* Ask yourself this question, "When I think of this city what do I think of?" Your answer to this simple question will give you a good idea of what others will think when you advertise your seminar in this location. Bayonne, New Jersey, is my hometown, but, although it is quite a beautiful place, thanks to lots of Johnny Carson jokes very few people view it as such. Similarly, cities such as Miami or Las Vegas evoke

images that will have either a positive or negative effect on your marketing efforts, depending on your target audience. Availability of entertainment, such as sporting events, theater, and other cultural activities, contribute to the charisma of a city and should also be considered when choosing a city as a seminar location.

Guidelines for Evaluating a Facility

The seminar facility you choose can help to make or break the success of your seminar. You will want to choose a location that will provide your participants with a location that is both convenient and comfortable. In addition, you will want to choose a facility that is cost-effective without sacrificing quality. The simplest way to evaluate and choose a facility for your seminar is to ask the following questions.

Site Location

1. How far is the facility from the airport, both in traveling time and in distance? If people will be flying from other cities to attend your seminar, you will want to choose a facility that is easy to reach from the airport where they will arrive. (See the Yellow Pages of this book for locations close to the airports in most of the major seminar cities across the United States.)

2. Is direct transportation available to the facility from the airport? Many hotels and conference centers will provide shuttle service to the facility free of charge. When you are calling or visiting a location, be sure to ask if they provide this service. It may help you to make your final decision.

3. Is there convenient and adequate on-site parking available? If people will be driving to the location, you will want to provide easy parking. Although many facilities will provide parking, many do not. If on-site parking is not adequate, you will need to direct your participants to nearby, reasonably priced parking.

Site Facilities and Services

4. Is there an adequate number of sleeping rooms available? If your seminar site is a meeting room in a hotel, there will probably be lots of sleeping rooms. However, if there is another big meeting at the hotel or if there is a major convention in town, there may be no rooms available. In these instances, you might not be able to accommodate the people who will be attending your event. Find out.

5. Does the facility have recreational facilities, such as a pool, health club, golf course, and tennis courts, to help attract participants? Many people view seminars as an opportunity to get away from work, and they look forward to spending some fun time while they are away. All other things being equal, a facility that offers these activities is preferred.

6. Are the sleeping rooms well furnished and do they have room to spread out? Many hotels that cater to business groups have rooms large enough for spreading out papers or provide a desk area where work can be done. If your seminar is a multiday program with homework, room size might be important.

7. Is room service available? If your participants will be arriving late in the evening after the restaurants are closed, this can be especially important. Also, many people prefer room service when they are traveling alone.

8. Are the public areas neat and clean? Like it or not, the cleanliness of the facility is a reflection on you. Often, participants will spend more time in the public areas than in their sleeping rooms. When you are performing a site inspection, observe these public areas carefully.

9. Are the front desk personnel and bellhops courteous and efficient? Once again, the staff members at the site location are part of your team. Make sure they reflect positively on you.

10. Are the elevators quick and large enough? Elevators that are slow or inadequate could result in delays that affect your program schedule.

11. Are there other events, seminars, or conferences scheduled before, during, or after your program? A very busy seminar site can put a strain on the overall service.

12. Is the sales or banquet office service-oriented and, in general, helpful? You will be able to get a good idea of the kind of overall service available by the way the people you contact at the sales office treat you.

13. Are there a variety of meeting rooms to choose from? If you get a larger number of registrants than you projected, it is comforting to know that there will be a larger meeting room available.

14. Is there storage available if you want to ship materials ahead? If you have a considerable amount of material to ship ahead, make sure the facility has adequate storage space.

The Meeting Room

15. Are the heating and cooling systems in the meeting rooms efficient? Find out how the temperature is controlled. Make sure it is easy to adjust the temperature, if necessary.

16. Are the meeting rooms sufficiently soundproof? The easiest way to check this out is to turn on a portable radio or tape player in the meeting room adjacent to the one you are considering for rental. You'll know how soundproof your room is by listening to the volume level from your room.

17. Are the ceilings high enough in the meeting rooms? Meeting rooms with low ceilings can be claustrophobic, especially if there will be a large group of people attending your program.

Audiovisual Equipment

18. What audiovisual equipment is included with the room rental? Many meeting facilities provide some simple audiovisual equipment with the room. Ask before you rent the room. This complimentary equipment can result in hundreds of dollars of savings to you.

19. Does the facility provide its own audiovisual equipment, or do they use an outside vendor? If the facility provides the equipment, it will be easier to make last-minute changes in equipment. In some cases, rentals can be less expensive when the facility provides the equipment.

20. What is the full menu of audiovisual equipment available on-site, and what are the charges? Ask for a complete price list for equipment rental. Certain equipment, such as video projectors, might be extremely expensive. In such cases, it might be more cost-effective to bring your own.

Additional Amenities

21. Are any added conveniences, such as pencils, pads, water setups, and mints, provided in the meeting rooms? Sometimes it's the little things that make the big impression.

22. What specific food and beverages are available for meals and breaks, and what are the costs? You will need to know what is available and the costs in order to budget your expenses.

23. Does the facility have a good restaurant on-site, or are some located nearby? This is especially important if your program is one day or more in length.

24. Do the meeting rooms have comfortable chairs and well-designed tables for working on and taking notes?

25. Is there easy access to telephones and other business equipment, such as fax and copy machines?

What About Meals and Refreshments?

There is no conclusive evidence that including meals or refreshments will increase registrations. But there are some general guidelines that can help you make your decision.

1. If networking and sharing are important to the participants, including lunch or dinner could increase the profitability of the seminar.

2. People expect coffee and tea at seminars that start first thing in the morning. It is best to include these beverages. Be sure to mention it in your brochure.

3. Order your coffee by the gallon; it will save you money.

4. If you order soft drinks or juices for afternoon refreshments, asked to be charged by consumption.

5. Making meals an option may work the best. Some people would rather use lunch to make telephone calls, take a walk, or spend one-on-one time with another participant.

6. Lunch generally costs between $15 and $20. If you decide to include lunch, make the proper adjustments when you are pricing your program.

7. When you are ordering food of any kind, give regard to the current trends in eating habits. In general, people are eating with more attention to health and nutrition. Many people are vegetarians, avoid soft drinks, and drink decaffeinated coffee. When you order food of any kind, include the healthy alternatives. If you don't, resentments can develop.

Rules to Guarantee the Best Meeting Room Price

1. *Follow the principle of buy small, sell big.* This rule says that when you are buying a product or service, you should always appear small while negotiating for the best price. Don't puff yourself up or try to impress the hotel or facility staff when you are reserving space. Instead, say "Well, I'm planning a little meeting. I'm not really sure how many people we're going to get...." On the other hand, when you are selling your seminar, emphasize your credibility and how big you are.

2. *Emphasize the fact that if things go well, you will be a repeat customer.* Although staff members at many hotels constantly change, the fact that they might be able to book you again will appeal to them and give them the justification they need to reduce the rate.

3. *Utilize the sleeping rooms and catering department at the hotel.* Your leverage will increase if you rent sleeping rooms or buy food. The more you spend in these two areas, the lower your room rental will be. In fact, it is not unusual to get your meeting room *free of charge* if your expenditures in these other areas are significant. If you know your group will be occupying a considerable number of rooms, open your negotiations with this fact.

4. *Remember, there is no set price.* There is an old adage that says that you can negotiate anything. In the business of contracting a facility for your seminar, this is the rule, not the exception. In most cases, the facility would rather reduce the room rental rate than leave the rooms empty. Correspondingly, during a busy period, you will have less room to negotiate.

!!! Resources.   The following two resources are excellent sources for information on new sites and on developments in the meeting industry.

Meeting Planners International
1950 Stemmons Freeway
Dallas, TX 75207
(214) 746-5248

Successful Meetings
Bill Publications
633 Third Ave.
New York, NY 10017
(212) 983-6930

Meeting Planners International (MPI) is an organization of professional meeting planners. It provides a wide variety of educational programs and an extremely sophisticated magazine. There is an annual national convention, and local chapters exist in all major cities.

Successful Meetings is a monthly publication that provides valuable current information relevant to the meeting industry.

After You Have Booked Your Meeting Room

You will want to send out a confirmation agreement to describe and confirm the arrangements you have made on the phone. In addition, it is a good idea to include a simple layout of the exact setup you would like. See Figure 19-1 in Chapter 19 for an example of a sample layout.

Figure 6-1 illustrates a basic confirmation form. This form will act as a letter of agreement. It will eliminate any chance for confusion in your verbal negotiations and can help minimize problems the day of your event. You can customize this agrement to suit your specific needs.

Meeting Facility Confirmation
(Your Letterhead)

To: _____(Contact name)_____

_____(Facility)_____

_____(Address)_____

_____

Meeting date(s) _____

Meeting hours _____

List meeting as _____

Food and beverage service:

Date	Time	Refreshment	Quantity
_____	_____	_____	_____
_____	_____	_____	_____
_____	_____	_____	_____

Please refresh the water and the room at _____(Time)_____.

Please set up the room for _____ people. (See attached diagram for the setup.)

Please provide the following audiovisual equipment.

No.   Description

____ Microphone _____

____ Overhead projector _____

____ Slide projector _____

____ Flipchart _____

____ 16mm projector_____

____ Screen_____

____ Video monitor _____

____ Audiocassette monitor _____

____ Other _____

As per our agreement, charges will be:

Room rental $_____

Food and beverage service $_____

Audiovisual $_____

Guest room rental $_____

Please feel free to call me with any questions.

Thank you.

Sincerely,

Figure 6-1. Sample of a meeting facility confirmation letter.

7

How to Set Your Fee and Get It

Guidelines for Setting Your Fee

Here are the basic factors you must consider when you set your fee. Of course, with experience, your fee can easily be adjusted and fine-tuned for optimum profitability.

1. *Research the competition.* Identify seminars that are being offered to the same target audience or on the same topic as yours. Study their pricing schedules. Do as many comparison studies as you can. Make sure you are using established seminars. Otherwise, it might be a case of the inexperienced leading the inexperienced.

2. *Give perceived value.* If you are offering enough perceived added value, you can increase your fee proportionately. You can add value with take-home manuals, reference materials, books, tapes, and follow-up consulting.

3. *Use the target audience design approach.* Consider the financial situation of your target audience. For example, if you are promoting seminars on telephone skills for receptionists, you might not be able to charge as much as you could if you are promoting seminars on the development of an international marketing plan for business executives.

4. *Establish the participant-to-profitability factor.* Let's say your seminar fee is $50 and you attract 100 people. If you increase your fee to $100, you attract only 60 people. Even though you have reduced the

number of participants by 40 percent, your gross has increased by 20 percent. In this case, it would be more profitable to double the fee.

5. *Play the numbers game.* Sometimes the number of participants is more important than seminar fee profits. If your real profits come from spin-off products and services, it would be better to lower the seminar fee. The game of selling is largely a numbers game. If you are selling books, tapes, consulting service, or more intensive seminars, you'll want to play the numbers game.

Many seminar leaders conduct introductory seminars for free or for $10 or $20 and use that technique to introduce themselves and their program to their target audience. At the introductory event, they offer another more intensive — and usually more expensive — program. In effect, they are marketing one seminar with another seminar. The introductory event is an investment for the second seminar. (There is more about this two-step promotion strategy in Chapter 12.)

6. *Test your price.* Try two different prices for your seminar and see which price works better. It's easy to do. First print two sets of brochures that are identical except for the price. Then mail to your target audience using different mailing lists, or use the same mailing list and distinguish among the different zip codes. Use the results of this test to help determine your fee.

7. *Measure success by the ratio of return on your marketing dollar.* Your fee and your gross receipts are important, but they do not measure your profitability. Your success is determined by the ratio of return on your marketing dollar. A return of $3 for every $1 spent is considered good. A return of $4 is great.

Group Discounts

Group discounts are excellent incentives for increasing seminar enrollment. Here are a few ways to take advantage of this strategy:

- Offer a discount to participants when they enroll in groups of two or more. For example, if the seminar fee is $100 and two people sign up together, you can drop the tuition to $90 per person.
- Offer one free registration to any organization or individual who signs up three or more people. In effect, you are offering a scholarship program. In doing so, you are creating an incentive program for seminar enrollment.
- When appropriate, offer discounts to couples.

Don't Forget Early Bird Specials

The best way to start seeing a quick return on your investment is to offer discounts for early registration. It will be well worth the 10 percent or 15 percent off to get some money coming back to you as soon as possible. For example, if your registration fee is $195, offer it for $175 to anyone who registers two weeks or more in advance.

Using the Magic-9 Technique

Have you ever wondered why so many products and services are priced at $9.95, $99, or $195? The answer is simple. It works.

Human behavior is fascinating to study. Just think how different you feel about these two numbers: $99.95 and $100.10. Marketing research has proven a substantially larger number of people will buy at the $99.95 price. The difference is only 15 cents, but the cost is perceived to be more than that.

It's a good idea to price your seminar using the magic-9 technique.

Special Pricing Issues for In-House Seminars

Setting fees for in-house seminars is really a matter of what the traffic will bear. Corporations, businesses, and large organizations generally pay between $1500 and $3500 for a full-day seminar. Local adult education programs are accustomed to paying considerably less, usually a few hundred dollars.

Sometimes an organization will promote your seminar, but they are unsure how successful it will be. In these cases you can ask for a minimum payment with the stipulation that you will get a bonus if the seminar draws *more than* a certain number of participants. To determine the fee you will be able to charge there are three helpful questions you can ask the sponsor.

1. "How many people will be attending?" Generally, the larger the anticipated audience, the bigger the budget is likely to be.

2. "What have you paid your seminar leaders in the past?" Whatever people have paid in the past they are likely to pay again in the future.

3. "What are the participants paying for the program?" If the organization sponsoring the seminar is charging a fairly high fee, it will

likely mean more money for you. Conversely, if you have been asked to speak at a local chapter of a professional association, the fee is more likely to be modest.

How to Negotiate the Highest Fee for Your In-House Seminar

You should have a published fee schedule. The published fee is the price you charge to give your seminar.

The price for a full-day seminar and a half-day should not be that far apart. For example, you might charge $3000 for a half-day seminar and $3500 for a full-day seminar. The logic for this close pricing is very simple. If you do a half-day seminar in Columbus, Ohio, it is unlikely you will be able to deliver another program that day. Even though you have only spoken for a half day, your whole day has been consumed.

You need a second published price for local programs. For programs you can drive to and return home the same day, a price schedule might be $2000 for a half-day seminar and $2500 for a full-day seminar. You can afford to charge less for local programs because you will not have to spend as much time traveling. You also avoid the inconvenience of air travel.

Sometimes the organization that wants you to speak will pay the fee without hesitation, and other times they will be unable to pay your fee. Expect both reactions.

When they can't pay your published fee, ask, "What are you prepared to pay?" At this point negotiations have begun, and you will have to decide how much you want to take the assignment. Until you are established, it is always best to try to take every program you possibly can.

As your reputation and credibility grow, you will negotiate less often and receive your published fee on a more regular basis.

Aside from the fee, make sure the sponsoring organization pays for all travel expenses. *Fees should always be separate from your expenses.* The reason is very simple. You can quickly lose a large share of your fee if you are paying your own way.

When delivering an in-house seminar, you can add profits by charging for your workbooks. Depending upon the quality of your materials, you can charge anywhere from $10 to $100 per person. If you have a book available, you can offer to provide it to all the participants as seminar materials. Even a small markup of $2 or $3 can add up to $500 or $1000 for the day if there are 200 or 300 participants at your program.

If you have a handout of a few pages, the best policy is to offer the masters to the program director and allow the organization to reproduce the handout at their cost.

After you have agreed upon all the financial details, send a contract or letter of agreement. Figure 7-1 illustrates a sample letter of agreement that works well.

Company and Personal Checks

It is difficult, if not impossible, to be in the seminar business without taking checks. Many times you will not be able to wait for them to clear. In most cases this will not be a problem; the vast majority of checks will be fine.

If businesses are sending people to your seminar, you will probably have to bill them and wait. Although sometimes it seems like forever, you will usually get your check within 30 to 60 days. If you don't, give them a call. Your billing or your check probably got lost somewhere, possibly in the mail.

Why You *Must* Take Credit Cards

Statistics show that as much as 50 percent of your registrations may be paid by credit cards. As a general rule, accepting credit cards will increase your enrollments by up to 20 percent. You cannot afford not to take credit cards.

Credit cards will also help you capture much of the spin-off business in products and services at the seminar itself, when participants are most inspired to make purchases. Many participants attend a seminar without their checkbooks, but few will be there without their credit cards.

Another advantage of accepting credit cards is that they serve as a guarantee for check payments. When you take a check, write the applicant's credit card number on it.

The most common credit cards are Visa, MasterCard, and American Express. The advantage of Visa and MasterCard is that you pay no fees when participants pay using these cards. When American Express cards are used, you lose a few percentage points from each purchase. This money goes back to American Express as a service charge.

Opening a Credit Card Merchant's Account—It's Simple

In order to take credit card payments, you will need to open a merchant's account. For Visa and MasterCard, first check with your local

LETTER OF AGREEMENT
Between
Paul Karasik Associates and XYZ Company

Dear _____ :

Subject: Sweet-Persuasion Selling Seminar

Paul Karasik will speak to your group on _____. The location
(Date)
will be _____ in _____ , _____ .
(Hotel or training facility)   (City)   (State)
This presentation will be _____ in length. It will
begin at _____ and end at _____ .

The fee for this presentation will be _____ plus expenses, which include round-trip air fare from Newark International Airport in Newark, New Jersey (it may not be necessary to include the state); hotel; meals; and ground transportation.

You will receive one master copy of the handout material, which will be tailored to your organization's program. This will be mailed 30 days prior to the program date. This master copy will then be reproduced by you in sufficient number for each participant to receive one copy.

Paul Karasik Associates reserves the right to make available for sale books and learning cassette programs.

No tape recorder, audio or visual, may be used without the expressed, prior written permission of Paul Karasik.

Upon receipt of a 10 percent deposit of ____ and this signed letter, the proposed date will be reserved for you.

The balance of ____ will be given to Paul Karasik prior to the presentation. All expenses will be billed.

Paul Karasik Associates   XYZ Company

By: _____ Pres. By: _____
                          Dated: _____

Figure 7-1. This example shows an agreement used by the author and is for illustrative purposes only. To ensure maximum protection, you should seek professional legal help in drafting an agreement that best covers your specific needs.

bank. Many banks have been the victims of credit card fraud and consequently are reluctant to give you a merchant's account. You might have to get on the phone and start checking around at other banks. Each bank has its own criteria for determining whether you qualify.

One important criteria for determining whether or not you qualify to receive a merchant's account is that you do no mail-order business. I repeat *no mail order*. Mail order has been one of the major areas the credit card companies have been ripped off and don't want to get burned any more.

!!! **Contacts.**   If you have had no success getting a merchant's account for Visa and MasterCard (or other credit cards) from banks here are two excellent contacts that specialize in helping businesses get their merchant accounts:

Credit Flow Corporation   National Association of Credit
(201) 445-7196   Card Merchants
                                                   (407) 737-7500

To get a merchant's account with the other major credit card companies, call them directly at the numbers shown here:

American Express   Discover Card
(800) 528-5200   (800) 347-6673

Diner's Club and Carte Blanche
(800) 525-7376

Each credit card company sets its own criteria for allowing you to open a merchant's account.

Unless you are doing heavy volume with credit cards at the seminar, you really don't need to carry the credit card machine with you. Keep it simple. Create a form on which you can write the person's name and their credit card number and expiration date. When you get home, you can manually enter their purchases on credit card forms and mail them.

If people want to register for the seminar by telephone with a credit card, it's very simple. Take their name and credit card number and expiration date. Write the words *telephone order* where their signature would normally be.

8

How to Create
a Winning Brochure

Regardless of the type of program you are marketing, a printed promotional announcement of your program is necessary. This could be
anything from a simple flyer or letter format to a multicolor, multipage
booklet. For the sake of simplicity, let's refer to your printed marketing
piece as your brochure.

The First Step Is Easy

The easiest way to create a winning brochure is to first collect a lot of
other brochures. Most successful seminar companies have developed
their brochure as a result of many years of trial and error or by spending thousands of dollars on market research studies or both. Why not
save your money and reap the benefits of their efforts?

$$$ Saver. You can refer to the list of public seminar companies in
the Yellow Pages of this book. Here are a few good companies to start
with. Ask to be put on their mailing list.

American Management Association
(518) 891-0065

Keye Productivity Center
(800) 821-3919

CareerTrack Seminars
(303) 447-2300

Padgett Thompson Seminars
(800) 255-4141

Dun & Bradstreet Seminars
(212) 312-6880

Using the TADA Strategy

You can put the target audience design approach strategy to work again when creating your brochure. For example, let's say you're marketing a program to lawyers. This is a very conservative profession. Lawyers are in the business of both the written and the spoken word. Much of the material that comes across the desk of a lawyer is in black and white, or perhaps pastel green. The type style is usually Times Roman or Helvetica.

Brochure copy addressed to lawyers must be precise, and any claims must be substantiated with facts or proof. A brochure for lawyers should be written in their language and appropriate to their sensibilities. All creative design decisions should be based on the fact that the target audience is lawyers.

On the other hand, in accordance with the TADA strategy, if you are offering an expensive seminar to a very select group at an exotic location, it would be important to invest in an impressive marketing piece. For example, if you are offering a medical seminar to doctors on a new procedure or technical development at a resort in Hawaii, it might be appropriate to develop an expensive, high-quality, multicolor brochure.

Don't forget to focus on the benefits your target audience will receive when they attend your seminar. Include any and all specific information that will attract your target audience.

Speak the verbal language of your target audience, and visually present the information in a manner that makes them feel comfortable. Your brochure should make the recipient feel that "you are one of them." The target audience should conclude from your brochure that you know them, you know their problems, and you will provide the answers to those problems at your seminar.

The Big-Six Brochure Questions

1. *What kind of paper?* Glossy or plain?   Heavy-weight or standard bond? White or colored? Paper comes in a wide range of thicknesses, colors, and styles. Standard bond (regular typewiter paper) is the least expensive and works well in most cases. On the other hand, if your seminar is a corporate program, glossy paper might be a better choice. If you come across a particular paper you like, bring it to your printer and ask for a quote. Be aware that special paper can add considerably to your printing costs.

$$$ Saver.   You can often get a discount on high-quality paper if you ask the printer to let you know if he or she will be making any big pur-

chases of such paper for other jobs. By tacking your order onto another job, you will get a quantity discount. This strategy for saving money works when you want to use paper of a higher quality than your printer normally stocks.

!!! **Resource.** Here is a book to answer everything you ever wanted to know about paper for printing:

Papers for Printing: How to Choose the Right Paper at the Right Price for Any Printing Job by Mark Beach and Ken Russon (Coast to Coast Books, 2934 NE 16th St., Portland, OR 97212)

2. *How many colors of ink?* One color, two colors, or four colors? The addition of each color will increase your overhead costs. If you intend to use one color and have photographs in your brochure, use black ink. Whenever possible, however, use two colors. Two colors add a lot to the overall look of your brochure.

If you will be using your brochure to market to high-level corporate executives or to an upscale audience, or if you want to impress the person who receives the brochure, using lots of color can be very effective.

3. *How big should it be?* 8 by 10 in or 11 by 17 in? Should it be one, six, or eight pages? How will it be folded? Again, economics will play a part in your decision. Each additional page will add to the typesetting, printing, and mailing costs.

4. *What kind of typeface is optimal?* There are many type styles. Before you choose a printer, make sure he or she has a variety of available type styles from which to choose. Ask for samples.

Choose a typeface that is simple and easy to read. Figure 8-1 shows some typefaces that are excellent for brochure copy.

5. *What is the best visual style?* Should you use graphics? Should you use photographs or illustrations? Should there be lots of text or lots of white space?

Graphic design is an art in itself. You have two choices. You can do it yourself or hire a professional. With a little study and a simple straight-

---

This is an example of Helvetica typeface.
This is an example of Times Roman typeface.
This is an example of Souvenir typeface.
This is an example of Bookman typeface.
This is an example of Century Old Style typeface.

Figure 8-1. Samples of different styles of typefaces that could be used for brochure copy.

forward approach based upon professional brochures you have collected, you will be able to design your own brochure. The books listed at the end of this chapter will help you do this.

$$$ Saver. The printing business is fiercely competitive. Many printers have creative design capabilities on-site and will be willing to help you make layout and design decisions for no additional charge.

On the other hand, if you have an adequate budget, your other choice is to hire a professional. Many printers have a design department on-site. If your printer doesn't offer design and layout services, the chances are good you will be referred to a graphic designer. If all else fails, the yellow pages of the telephone book provide many choices.

6. *Will you be using an envelope or a self-mailer?* If your brochure is going to be designed as a multipage letter, an envelope is perfect. An envelope gives your mailing a more personal touch.

A self-mailer will save you money. The cost of envelopes can add up quickly when you are mailing thousands of brochures. You will also have to pay your mailing house additional money for stuffing envelopes.

Figure 8-2 illustrates the most common designs for self-mailer brochures.

Principles for Writing Sensational Copy

The basic principles for writing brochure copy are very simple.

1. *Keep your benefits and objectives specific and straightforward.* If you will be teaching 12 ways to save time, say that. If you will be teaching people 17 ways to make money in real estate, say it.

2. *Write copy that is short and snappy.* People do not think or speak in complete sentences. The purpose of your brochure is to persuade people to attend your seminar. For this purpose, a conversational tone works best. The best example of persuasive copy can be found in advertising copy. Study the short, precise style you see in advertisements in newspapers and magazines. Use this style as a model for your brochure.

3. *Repeat your benefits throughout your brochure.* Remember, you are selling information that will help make people's lives better. This is

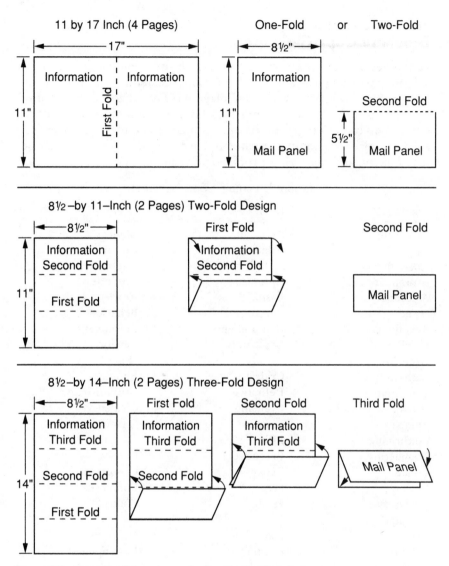

Figure 8-2. Examples of three types of self-mailer brochure designs.

the reason they are willing to pay for your seminar. They are not particularly interested in hearing you speak, no matter how eloquent you are. Put your benefits on the brochure cover, and repeat them as often as possible throughout the brochure.

4. *Use powerful, action-oriented words.* The best words are ones that sell. The Instant Brochure Copy Generator that follows is a gold mine of "power-speak."

How to Use the Instant Brochure Copy Generator

If you get bogged down trying to describe your seminar, you can consult the following Instant Brochure Copy Generator. The verbs and verb forms in column A are action oriented. The adjectives in column B are benefit oriented. The nouns in column C are implicitly results oriented. You can put together dynamic phrases by combining words from each column, for example, create effective attitudes, achieving competitive quality, and mastering professional relationships.

Instant Brochure Copy Generator

Column A	Column B	Column C
Achieving	Accessible	Abilities
Alert	Administrative	Advances
Answering	Authoritative	Alternatives
Anticipating	Automatic	Attidudes
Assessing	Basic	Awareness
Avoid	Careful	Behavior
Benefiting	Comprehensive	Benchmarks
Building	Competitive	Benefits
Capitalize	Creative	"Bible"
Cash-in	Critical	Blunders
Centering	Definitive	Breakthroughs
Clarify	Dramatic	Challenges
Compare	Dynamic	Change
Confirming	Effective	Climate
Conquering	Executive	Clues
Create	Expansive	Competence
Dealing	Free	Consensus
Demystify	Fresh	Control
Detailing	Full	Culprit
Diagnose	Hands-on	Decisions
Eliminate	Hidden	Development
Evaluating	High-level	Diagnostics
Expanding	Human	Direction
Explode	Immediate	Education
Exploring	Incisive	Effectiveness
Expose	Incremental	Evaluation
Facilitating	Individual	Feedback
Focusing	Individualized	Focus
Gain	In-house	Frontiers
Grasp	Intelligent	Fulfillment
Guarantee	Intensive	Fundamentals
Highlighting	Interpersonal	Gain

Instant Brochure Copy Generator (*Continued*)

Column A	Column B	Column C
Implementing	Key	Goals
Increase	Latest	Growth
Influencing	Lucid	Highlight
Initiate	Mutual	Impact
Integrating	New	Interaction
Investing	No-nonsense	Intervention
Learn	Nuts-and-bolts	Keys
Mastering	Organizational	Kit
Maximize	Original	Landmark
Measuring	Penetrating	Mastery
Monitoring	Personal	Measures
Motivating	Powerful	Mine fields
Negotiating	Practical	Models
Optimize	Professional	Needs
Pinpoint	Proven	Nightmares
Planning	Safe	Objectives
Preclude	Self	Performance
Preempt	Shrewd	Pipeline
Probe	Simple	Planning
Profile	Sophisticated	Potential
Providing	Sound	Power
Receive	Special	Practices
Rethinking	Staff	Prerequisites
Revealing	State-of-the-art	Principles
Sharpen	Step-by-step	Priorities
Shatter	Straight	Problems
Short-circuit	Strategic	Process
Stimulate	Supervisory	Productivity
Strengthening	Targeted	Quality
Survey	Team	Relationships
Tackle	Tested	Research
Tap	Timely	Resources
Target	Tough	Results
Test	Unprecedented	Revelations
Uncover	Vital	Secrets
Understanding	Winning	Skills
Unlocking	Workable	Strategies
Zero in		Styles
		Target
		Techniques
		Theory
		Time

Twenty-Two-Point Brochure Checklist

The easiest way to construct an effective brochure is to break it down into small modules. If you take your time to build each component well, the end result will be a first-class brochure. Here is a list of the necessary components.

☐ *Title.*   Choose a title that is clear and direct. A title that starts with "How to..." can work well in a wide variety of situations. Of course, it's always best to convey the benefit of your seminar in the title whenever possible. Some examples of simple and effective titles for business-sector audiences are "Managing Multiple Priorities," "Stress Management Seminar for Secretaries," "How to Handle Difficult People," and "How to Take Control of Your Workday."

☐ *Hook.*   Like the title, the hook should focus the reader on the benefits. Here are some examples of titles with hooks.

Title: "How to Supervise People"
Hook: Learn techniques to get results through people.

Title: "Successful Selling Techniques"
Hook: Learn how to close more sales.

Title: "How to Manage Your Advertising"
Hook: Make your advertising really contribute to profits.

Title: "How to Enter the World of Professional Speaking"
Hook: Begin a profitable and exciting career now.

☐ *Date, time, and location(s).*   Believe it or not, many brochures have been printed without this information.

☐ *Benefits.*   The best place to put your benefits is everyplace. Start right on the front page, and continue on throughout the copy. People must be reminded about how much better they'll feel, how much money they'll make, or how their professional or personal life will improve, thanks to your program.

☐ *Who should attend?*   Identify the exact audience that will profit from your program. This lets readers know the program will be geared to their particular needs. After a title such as "How to Give Telephone Customer Service," you might include the following:

Who Should Attend?   Receptionists, Administrative Assistants, and Customer Service Representatives

In some cases, it might even be useful to start the copy of a brochure by targeting the intended audience. For example:

Attention: Separated, Divorced, or Widowed Men and Women

Then continue with the title, "Letting Go of a Relationship."

□ *What your participants will learn.*   In this portion you list the specific topics that will be addressed in the program. This section is straightforward. Use action verbs, and list the specific strategies, techniques, skills, and measurable results the participants will receive from your seminar. Use the Instant Brochure Copy Generator to help you write this section.

□ *Program schedule.*   Although it is not essential, you might want to list the complete agenda of what will be covered during the day. For example:

9:00 a.m.– 10:30 a.m.	Personal writing evaluations
10:30 a.m.–10:45 a.m.	Coffee break
10:45 a.m.–12:00 noon	Creative writing techniques
12:00 noon–1:00 p.m.	Lunch
1:00 p.m.–2:30 p.m.	How to overcome writer's block
2:30 p.m.–2:45 p.m.	Afternoon break
2:45 p.m.–4:00 p.m.	How to market your writing
4:00 p.m.–4:10 p.m.	Break
4:10 p.m.–5:15 p.m.	Goal-setting module

□ *Program methodology.*   Are there unique participatory activities or exercises that will help fill seats? Will the attendees actually taste wines at your wine lover's workshop? Will the participants of your how-to-make-a-speech program actually deliver a speech? Will they actually write advertising copy at the seminar on success in advertising? This kind of information should be included.

□ *Client list.*   Credibility is important for any marketing effort. Your client list helps to establish credibility. A simple direct approach works best. Here is an example:

Here is a Partial List of Our Clients:
American Heart Association
American Red Cross
Federal Express
Hallmark Cards
Marriott Corporation
Xerox

Expand and update this list any time you reprint your brochure.

□ *Endorsements.*   An effective endorsement should have four components: name, profession or business, title, and specific benefit the participant received. For example, "Thanks to the sales techniques I learned at Carol Jones's seminar, I was able to earn 20 percent more in commissions for the year." Paul Stuart, Sales Consultant, Atlantic Insurance Company.

If your program is brand-new, you might have to get creative. Ask friends or associates to give you some positive comments you can print. After you have completed a few programs, you will acquire many more endorsements that can be printed in subsequent brochures. See Chapter 18 to find out how to get endorsements the day of your seminar.

Most people who have benefited from your seminar will be more than happy to provide you with endorsements. All you have to do is ask. Be sure to ask for endorsements on the participant's professional letterhead. That way you will have the option of reducing it and including it on future promotional material.

□ *Seminar leader bio.* A short bio about the seminar leader (you) should be included. Be sure to give your experience with the subject matter. The bio should focus on answering the question, What makes you qualified to present this seminar or workshop?

Other information could include experience as a professional speaker, educational background, honors or recognition you have received pertinent to your topic, and names of associations that you belong to which certify your professionalism. For example, if you belong to the American Seminar Leaders Association or National Speakers Association, be sure to mention them.

Remember, include only information that is relevant to the topic and audience you are addressing. For example, if you are doing a program on stress management, it might be relevant to say you are a certified yoga instructor. If you are doing a program on how to be an entrepreneur, it would be important to include any information on successful businesses you have created.

□ *Your photograph.* Although it is not essential, in many cases you will want to include your photograph in the brochure. You need a professional quality, black-and-white, promotional head shot.

□ *Methods of payment.* Who should checks be made out to? List the credit cards you accept. In addition, you might want to use the credit card logos of the cards you accept.

□ *How to register.* Clearly print this information in one area of the brochure. List your complete fee schedule in this section as well as any group or early-registration discounts. List your registration methods. Most seminars accept registration by telephone, mail, and fax. Your registration-at-the-door policy should also be stated.

Be sure to print a for-more-information telephone number in this section. (Note: It's a good idea to list this information number a few places in the brochure.)

□ *800 number.* An 800 number is a valuable tool to encourage inquiries and registrations.

$$$ **Saver.** Most phone services like Sprint offer inexpensive nonexclusive 800 numbers. This means your regular telephone line can be designated to receive 800 calls. You will pay a nominal monthly fee and for the incoming calls. Here are two services you can contact:

MCI Telecommunications   US Sprint
(800) 888-0800   (800) 877-4000

- *Tear-off registration.*   One section of the brochure can be used for a mail-in registration form. Perforate or print a dotted line.

- *What will be included?*   Are you giving out a workbook, reference material, audio or video tapes, samples, and so forth? Are you serving coffee, lunch, and/or dinner? Are you giving out certificates or diplomas? Will participants receive personal evaluations or personal consulting? Any feature that might contribute to your marketing success should be listed and perhaps highlighted in some way. You'd be surprised how important these freebies are to a lot of seminar participants.

- *Act-now motivation.*   How about a discount for early registration or a special gift like an audio tape for the first 25 people who register?

- *Guarantee.*   Many people feel more secure about taking a chance with a seminar or workshop if there is a money-back guarantee if they are not satisfied. Be sure to say that they must ask for your refund at a break or at some point *before* the seminar is over.

- *Refund policy.*   Your refund policy can act as an incentive. People are more likely to register early if you offer a refund policy. You will want to offer a full refund up until a certain date, and then a partial refund after that. A standard unwritten practice in the seminar business is to offer anyone who can't attend for whatever reason the opportunity to attend a later program. It is a goodwill gesture that will pay dividends at a later time.

- *Tax deductible.*   This is a reminder and can encourage additional registrations. "All expenses of continuing education (fees, travel, meals, and lodging) undertaken to maintain and improve professional skills are tax deductible. (Treas. Reg. 1-162-5, Coughlin vs. Commissioner, 203F 2d 307)."
  To be on the safe side, ask participants to consult their accountants. Provide a receipt so your seminar can be claimed as a tax deduction.

- *Market other products.*   Upsell. If you have supplementary material or related seminars, say so. Is your program available on audio or video tape? Do you have an in-house program you would like to mention in your mailing? In this way, you take full advantage of the marketing potential of your brochure.

Figure 8-3 illustrates many of the brochure design principles that have just been described.

Preliminary Evaluation

Your brochure should be proofread a few times for any errors in spelling, grammar, telephone numbers, names, dates, and so forth.

After you have completed your brochure, show it to people who might be prospects to attend your program or anyone familiar with the topic. Ask for feedback. Make changes accordingly.

How to Choose the Best Printer

When you are satisfied with your design and copy, you are ready to take your brochure layout and copy to the printer. The best printer is one who will do quality work, at an inexpensive price, and who is located conveniently. Your best source for leads for a good printer is referrals. If you have none, check the phone book yellow pages.

Comparison Shop

Make a series of appointments with three or four different printers. Printers rarely give price quotes without seeing the job. If possible, bring a sample of a similar brochure to give the printer some idea of how you want the finished job to look. Prices will often vary greatly among printers.

!!! Time Saver.   When you telephone a printer to make an appointment, briefly describe the brochure. Almost every printer specializes in specific types of printing. Make sure the printer offers the services you need and is equipped to produce the size, style, and quantity you require.

$$$ Saver.   If the printer is using computer typesetting and you have a computer software program that will interface with his, you can save money on typesetting by bringing in a computer disk with all of your copy on it.

Although price is important, your printer is someone who is a vital member of your marketing team. Therefore, it is important to choose someone you can get along with. Don't forget to take this human factor into consideration when you choose a printer.

SPEAK OUT WITH CLOUT

An action-packed one day communication seminar, with proven strategies and techniques to improve your power to:

- **Deliver Persuasive Presentations**
- **Project Confidence**
- **Gain Respect and Trust**
- **Conquer Nervousness**

Figure 8-3. Sample of a 4-page brochure illustrating many of the design principles.

***!!!* Resources for Brochure Development and Printing.**   The first brochure is always the most difficult. Just remember, it's not carved in stone. It's a creative process. Be prepared to modify it and make improvements. With experience, the process will become quicker, with lots less effort. With time, your printer will know what you like and will help you make creative and economical decisions based on your needs. The

The Single Most Important Activity of

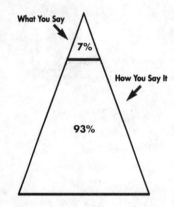

It's not only <u>what</u> you say, it's <u>how</u> you say it that counts.

What You Say

7%

How You Say It

93%

A research study by Stanford University Graduate School has shown that 93% of our communication effectiveness depends upon <u>HOW</u> we express ourselves.

Let's face it, your success often depends on your ability to influence, motivate and manage others.

Speaking confidently and persuasively can be your greatest asset.

"Speak Out With Clout" offers the practical, hands-on training necessary to your rapidly rising career.

In this program, you'll learn by doing. Our lively, experiential approach will take you step by step through a structured process with self-evaluations, practice sessions and instant video replay. You'll receive the coaching and individual personal attention you'll need to keep you confident in any situation...especially those times when you're not expecting to speak or when you face challenges, arguments or hostility.

SEMINAR CONTENT

Maximize Your Persuasiveness
- The 30 second first impression
- 4 secrets of body language
- Creating instant rapport
- Organizing your presentation
- 5 "hidden persuaders"
- Selling your ideas

Methods To Create Impact
- How to create your power image
- Thinking quickly on your feet
- 3 steps to build a "comfort zone"
- Diffusing anger and challenges
- Influencing with gestures
- Focusing strategies for impact
- Using "leading" and "pacing"

Master Voice Control
- 5 techniques for the "power voice"
- Controlling with pitch and volume
- Projecting energy and inflection
- Applying the "credibility component"
- Establishing your vocal style
- Winning intonation patterns

Expand Your Personal Style
- Projecting your natural self
- 3 methods for overcoming anxiety
- Establishing trust
- Building confidence with eye control
- Making the most of your strengths

✔ Do you want to enhance your professional image?

✔ Do you want to improve your ability to speak under pressure?

✔ Would you like to make the most of every important opportunity?

If you can answer YES to any of these quetions, then this seminar is for you!

SAVE MONEY...REGISTER EARLY... SEATING IS LIMITED.
Call (201)864-9149.

Figure 8-3. (*Continued*)

following books provide detailed information on how to design the brochure, how to find the right printer, and how to save both money and time getting your job done.

Designing Brochures For Results by Linda G. Leffel (Learning Resources Network, P.O. Box 1448, Manhattan, KS 66502)

Brochure Graphics by John Ziemann (Learning Resources Network)

Your Life Is Your Ability to Communicate.

HOW YOU'LL BENEFIT

- Create a powerful image
- Project confidence
- Win trust and support
- Take charge immediately
- Gain visibility
- Increase personal influence

ON-SITE TRAINING

Ask About Our **FREE** Intro Program

We can customize this seminar to fit your organization's needs.

It can be presented to your group at a time and location that's convenient. Also available:

- One on one coaching
- Consulting services
- Follow up support
- Special group rates

**For more information call:
(201) 864-9149**

SUPER SAVER REGISTRATION

The regular investment is $195 per participant.

Super Saver Registration: To reserve your seat for only $175, simply call and charge your registration to American Express, MasterCard, or Visa at least 10 days prior to the seminar.

Group Discounts Also Available

CALL: (201) 864-9149.

WHAT YOU'll RECEIVE

VIDEO TRAINING

See yourself the way others do. Thanks to instant video playback and individual coaching, you'll be able to measure your progress and have the opportunity to make immediate improvements in your speaking style.

SPECIALLY DESIGNED SEMINAR HANDBOOK

Every participant will receive a comprehensive handbook for use during the seminar and afterwards.

It contains all the major points covered during the course of the day, as well as specific action steps you will take to achieve your professional goals.

FREE TAKE-HOME BONUS

You will receive your own personal video of your presentations.

You will be able to review what you learned in the seminar and reinforce your achievements.

Your Personal Video

To ensure individual attention and maximum benefit, enrollment is strictly limited. **Reserve your seat now. Call: (201) 864-9149**.

YOUR SEMINAR LEADER

Paul Karasik is a professional speaker who has delivered speeches and conducted seminars for over 18 years.
His clients include Citibank, AT&T, Shell Oil, National Association of Accountants and National Council of Savings Institutions.

Paul has earned the reputation as the "Speaker's Speaker." He is founder and president of the American Seminar Leaders Association and an active member of the National Speakers Association and the American Society of Training and Development.

Better Brochures, Catalogs, and Mailing Pieces by Jane Maas (St. Martin's Press, 175 Fifth Ave., New York, NY 10010)

Words That Sell by Richard Bayan (Caddylak Publishing, 201 Montrose Rd., Westbury, NY 11590)

Getting It Printed: How to Work with Printers and Graphic Arts Services to Assure Quality, Stay on Schedule, and Control Costs by Mark Beach, Steve Shepro, and Ken Russo (Coast to Coast Books, Portland, OR)

HERE'S WHAT OTHERS ARE SAYING ABOUT "SPEAK OUT WITH CLOUT"

"Your program was by far the most important seminar I've attended in a long time. I can't thank you enough."

-George J. Wilson, District Manager, IBM

"Tremendous learning experience."

-Mary Ann DeCarlo, Training Director, AT&T

"A program whose time has come. Paul Karasik is riveting."

-Richard Zeif, Pres., The Negotiating Institute

"I found the program educational, as well as challenging and practical."

-Carol M. Evans, Criminal Attorney

"Stimulating, provocative, and informative presentation."

-Susan Goldstein, V.P., Citibank

"Paul, you helped me take my career to a new level of success."

-Walter J. Brown Jr., Bell Laboratories

SEMINAR GUARANTEE

If, after attending this seminar, you are not fully satisfied that we have delivered everything promised in this brochure, simply notify the seminar administrator by the lunch break and we will refund the entire registration fee.

TAX DEDUCTIBLE

All expenses of continuing education (fees, travel, meals, lodging) undertaken to maintain and improve professional skills are deductible (Treas. Reg. 1-162-5, Coughlin vs. Commissioner, 203F 2d 307)

CEUs AWARDED

Conforming to the guidelines of the National Task Force on the Continuing Education Unit,this one-day seminar is authorized for. 6 CEUs. If you would like to receive a CEU Certificate, please send your written request to the address below.

IT'S EASY TO REGISTER

Regular Tuition: $195 per participant

Super Saver Registration: $175 per participant, when you register 10 days or more in advance.

Group discounts are available.

ALL MAJOR CREDIT CARDS ACCEPTED.

VISA MasterCard AMERICAN EXPRESS

REGISTERING EARLY SAVES YOU MONEY.

REGISTRATION FORM

BY PHONE: Call us now at (201) 864-9149

BY MAIL: Mail registration form to:
Paul Karasik Associates
899 Boulevard East, Suite 6A
Weehawken, N.J. 07087
Make checks payable to:
Paul Karasik Associates

Paul Karasik Associates
899 Boulevard East, Suite 6A
Weehawken, N.J. 07087

PRESORT MAIL
FIRST CLASS MAIL
U.S. POSTAGE
PAID
FORT LEE NJ 07024
PERMIT NO. 239

Name _____
Title _____
Company _____
Address _____
City _____ State _____ Zip _____

❏ Visa   ❏ Master Card   ❏ American Express
My Acct. # _____ Exp. Date _____
Authorized Signature _____

If undeliverable as addressed, please forward to Training Director.

Figure 8-3. (*Continued*)

!!! Contacts. The American Seminar Leaders Association (ASLA) offers a service to help you design and produce an effective brochure. Call ASLA (800) 735-0511.

The Direct Marketing Association (DMA) has a variety of books and resources for creating your brochure. Call DMA (212) 768-7277.

9
Getting Results with Direct Mail

Three Keys to Success

It's no secret. The three keys for success with direct mail are the list, the list, and the list. Seriously, though there are a number of factors that will contribute to your success, the mailing list you use is by far the most important factor.

What Is the Best Mailing List?

The best list you can use is your own house mailing list. When you enter the seminar business, you won't have a list, but if you don't start assembling a list immediately, you never will. Your personal list will include names of qualified people who have expressed interest in or who have already attended a program similar to yours. The return rate from your personal list should be 5 percent or even more. The rate of return from your house list will typically be much higher than any purchased list.

When you do radio or TV interviews, be sure to give your address or an 800 number so that people who want more information can respond. Add the names and addresses of anyone who has either purchased or inquired about any products such as books or tapes. These names and addresses all become part of your house list.

Where to Find the Mailing List You Need

The encyclopedia of mailing lists is the *Direct Mail Lists Rates and Data*. It is published by:

Standard Rates and Data Service
3004 Glenview Rd.
Wilmette, IL 60091
(800) 323-4588

This is the list of lists. Standard Rates and Data Service can make available to you more than 20,000 mailing lists. Most public libraries have a copy of *Direct Mail Lists Rates and Data*.

Standard Rates and Data Service breaks down its lists with the following descriptions:

- Where you can obtain the list.

- The source of the list. Lists are assembled from a variety of sources, including magazines, associations, and companies.

- Rental rates. Rates are listed by cost per thousand. The price can vary from $25 to $100 per thousand names.

- Minimum number of names you must rent.

- How often the list is "cleaned." *Cleaned* means "updated."

- What labeling system is used. Usually labels are available in self-adhesive and chesire styles. Chesire labels cost less and must be applied with a machine. Most big mailing houses use Chesire labels.

- Miscellaneous information relevant to the list.

How to Work with List Brokers

List brokers are valuable consultants. They will assist you in choosing the best list for your seminar. List brokers act like travel agents. They make their commission from the original source of the list. The brokers are on *your* side. They want you to have a successful program and come back for more.

You will find names of list brokers in *Standard Rates and Data*. List brokers can also be found in the yellow pages of the telephone book under the heading "Mailing Lists."

!!! **Caution.** You are *renting* lists, not buying them. This means you can use the list on a one-time basis only. The control on the system is the inclusion of phony names. If you use the mailing list more than once, the source will know and you will be subject to legal action.

After someone on the rented mailing list responds to your mailing, he or she is eligible to be placed on your house list.

Test Before You Invest

Although you might feel confident you have a great mailing list, never initiate a major direct mail campaign without a test mailing first. Response to a direct mail campaign can vary tremendously. You can test using a minimum of 1000 names, but use more if possible. Testing different lists simultaneously will help you determine the best list.

The A/B Split

One variation of the direct mail test is called the A/B split. The computer is given the command to produce a list made up of every other name. In this way two different offers to the same list can be tested. By doing an A/B split, almost any feature of your offer can be tested to find out what will get the best response rate.

Important Factors to Test

You will be able to refine your direct mail campaign by testing these 10 factors:

1. Seminar fee
2. Brochure design and copy
3. Location
4. Day and time
5. Length of the seminar
6. Self-mailer vs. envelope
7. Bulk mail vs. first class
8. Mail permit number vs. postal meter vs. stamp
9. Multiple mailings
10. Telephone follow-up

Bulk Mail versus First Class

One obvious factor to consider in using bulk mail is its substantial savings. Bulk rates are generally about 45 percent lower than first-class rates. To be eligible for bulk rates, you must get a permit from your local post office. There is a one-time application fee of $75, and the permit is $75 per year. You are required to mail a minimum of 200 pieces each time you do a mailing.

When mailing in bulk, you must bundle according to zip codes, and, unless you state "Return postage guaranteed" somewhere on the mailing panel below the label, nondeliverable pieces will be discarded. Bulk mail is slow and unpredictable. First-class mail might take a few days for delivery; bulk mail might take a week or even weeks. Bulk mail is a low priority for the postal service, and it will be delivered when it is convenient for them.

Another important factor is perception. Bulk mail has the connotation of something's being of less importance. If image is vital to the success of your marketing effort, bulk mail might not be desirable.

The postal service offers a discount program to first-class-mail users if items are bundled according to zip code. This rate is worth considering if you want to enjoy the advantages of first-class mail at discount prices.

Results You Can Expect

The return rate from direct mail ranges from $1/10$ of 1 percent to 5 percent. Generally, 1 percent to $1\frac{1}{2}$ percent is accepted as a good return. The lower the registration fee, the greater the response. Remember that when charging higher fees, you don't need as high a response rate.

When to Use a Mailing House

Mailing houses can take care of the entire mailing procedure for you. They will label, insert, sort, and deliver your mailing to the post office. They will also maintain your house mailing list for you.

The cost for a mailing service is usually reasonable, and prices from one mailing house to the next are competitive. Naturally, the basic costs will be relative to the number of pieces you are mailing. As with any product or service, the quality varies. If you plan to deliver and/or pick up, location might also be a factor to consider.

!!! **Time and *$$$* Saver.**   You can save lots of time and money by employing the services of a mailing house. You can locate a mailing house by looking in the yellow pages of the telephone book under "Addressing and Mailing Services," "Direct Mail," or "Letter Shop Services."

Another way to save money on a direct mail campaign is to shop around for a printer who also offers the services of a mailing house.

When Is the Best Time to Mail Brochures?

Your mailing should arrive in the prospects' hands between three and four weeks before the event. If it arrives too early, it is likely to get lost or forgotten. If it arrives too late, the time may not be available to attend the event.

If you are mailing to an audience that will have to travel a considerable distance, your prospect should receive the mailing six to eight weeks before the event.

What Is the Total Cost of Direct Mail Promotion?

The variables in your direct mail promotion are:

- The cost of the list
- The cost to design and print the brochure
- The postage charge
- Any mailing services charges

The average cost of a direct mailing is between $25 and $45 per thousand.

A realistic cost for a 30,000-piece mailing of an 11- by 17-in four-page brochure would be in the neighborhood of $10,000. This would include all costs.

Once again, your rate of return is your measure of success in direct mail. As a rule of thumb, the return should total a minimum of twice your marketing costs.

!!! **Resources.** There are two primary resources for direct mail promotion. These two resources will provide you with a vast array of information and an expansive network of contacts in direct mail marketing.

Direct Marketing Association
6 East 43rd St.
New York, NY 10017-4646
(212) 768-7277

The Marketing Federation
109 58th Ave.
St. Petersburg, FL 33706
(813) 367-5629 (Ask for Anver Suleiman)

The Direct Marketing Association (DMA) has a huge library of information on the direct mail industry. It has more than 3500 company members. The DMA influences government legislation and regulations. It holds 2 major national conventions and 17 specialized conferences each year. Members receive eight publications and have free access to data resources unavailable anywhere else.

The Marketing Federation is dedicated to direct mail marketing of seminars, conferences, and meetings. Each year it holds a few major conferences and a number of meetings. The Marketing Federation can help anyone, from the beginner to the experienced, market programs more successfully. Call or write and ask to be put on the mailing list.

10

Promoting Your Seminar with Newspaper Ads and Media

Advertising versus Publicity

Whether you choose to go down the path of advertising or publicity, the end result is the same: media coverage. One important difference between the two is that advertising has to be bought. Excluding some incidental costs for phone calls and mailing, publicity is free, although you do have to invest your own time and creativity.

The other major difference is that when you pay to advertise, you have control of what is said or printed. Generally speaking, publicity is controlled by the media. They decide whether your seminar is appropriate to publicize in the print or broadcast media. Their decision is based upon what they think interests their audience.

Since publicity does not require a dollar investment but does generate registrations, it is cost-effective. See Chapter 11 to learn how to take advantage of all of the opportunities to get free publicity in the media.

!!! **Caution.** In theory, an ideal scenario for promoting a seminar would be to run an ad in the newspaper and thereby fill your seminar room with people. That would be wonderful if it could be counted on to work. Although advertising your seminar might generate a few registrations, more often than not it does not work. This chapter provides

the guidelines and resources you need to be aware of to advertise, but you should understand that this is a fairly risky marketing vehicle.

Prerequisites for Using Mass Media

There are a few specific instances when mass media can be utilized. Mass media advertising can be used effectively in five instances:

1. *You are unsure of your target audience.*   If you are unable to target your audience, and if locating a direct mail list is impossible, using mass media becomes a necessary alternative. By taking a detailed survey of the people who answer your advertisement, you should be able to locate the right mailing list for future marketing efforts. For example, if a large number of small-business owners answered your advertisement, in the future you would have the choice to substitute direct mail marketing, focusing on this target audience.

2. *Your topic is of broad, general interest.*   Topics like speed reading, reducing your taxes, investment opportunities, memory improvement, and personal growth appeal to a wide variety of people. Mass media can reach this wide audience.

3. *Your advertisement is being used to generate inquiries for your seminar.*   This advertisement is sometimes called the "tickler" ad. The intention here is not to sell the seminar but to create a prospect list from which you can market your seminar. You can follow up the "tickler" ad with a detailed brochure or even a telemarketing campaign. You can also use the names and addresses you collect to market books, tapes, and services on the same topic.

4. *You are advertising a celebrity speaker.*   There are a few seminar leaders who have reached celebrity status. They either have written a best-selling book, have hosted a radio or TV talk show, or have had some similar kind of media exposure already. Mass media advertising can work well to advertise this kind of seminar.

5. *Your advertisement is used to get people to a free introductory seminar.*   This is probably one of the best ways to take advantage of media advertising. The strategy is very simple. Advertise a free introductory seminar. At this seminar you provide people with the information that you promised, as well as the opportunity to register for a more extensive seminar that will be given a few days later. Of course, there is a charge for the follow-up seminar. This is referred to as the "rollover," because you roll people over from one seminar to another.

This technique is effective for promoting a variety of general-interest seminars, such as real estate investment, and a wide variety of personal-growth seminars. The Dale Carnegie seminars, for example, have been promoted this way for many years.

The free introductory seminar, or "two-step" technique, is discussed in greater detail in Chapter 12.

Mass Media Advertising Categories

There are two advertising categories in the broadcast media: radio and television. In the print media, you can choose between magazines and newspapers.

Radio and Television Advertising

Radio and television can work well for free introductory seminars and those featuring celebrity speakers. Aside from these two applications, radio and TV work better as vehicles for publicity. (As mentioned, see Chapter 11 for information on how to get radio and TV exposure.)

!!! **Contact.** Reference guides for radio and television advertising rates and information are available from:

Standard Rates and Data Service
3004 Glenview Rd.
Wilmette, IL 60091-9970
(800) 323-4588

In four volumes, Standard Rates and Data Service compiles all the information you need to know about buying radio and television advertising time. These volumes list the stations, who to contact, and the station format. They also give a complete market summary. The four volumes are "Network Rates and Data," "Spot Radio Rates and Data," "Spot Radio, Small Market Edition," and "Spot Television Rates and Data."

If you are considering using radio or TV, you will want to explore the advertising rates and broadcast media available in the various markets in which you will be promoting your seminar.

Magazine Advertising

The primary drawback of magazine advertising is the very long lead time necessary. You have to plan your advertisement months in advance. Another drawback is that, like all mass media advertising, magazine advertising is expensive. Test before you invest too much.

Of course, choosing the right magazine for your target audience also plays a major role in your success. One seminar promoter has found success using four small magazine ads in a weekly magazine to fill her monthly seminar on how to overcome the fear of public speaking. This technique works for her because of the multiday workshop format of her program and the expensive registration fee. She needs only 10 to 15 participants each month to make her seminar profitable.

Specialty magazines, such as trade journals, allow you to target your ad the most. For example, you might use a computer magazine to market a seminar on a computer topic. Although at first glance this would seem to be an effective form of advertising, a number of conditions must exist to make this kind of ad feasible:

- Circulation has to be considerable, since your results will be a small percentage of the total list.
- The audience has to be the type to attend seminars.
- The seminar promotion has to be further supported with other strategies, such as telemarketing.

!!! **Contact.**   Standard Rates and Data Service publishes two directories of magazine demographics and advertising rates.

Consumer Magazine and Farm Publication Rates and Data
Business Publication Rates and Data

Newspaper Advertising

Newspapers, by far, are the most effective means of filling seminar seats. Here are 13 guidelines for using newspaper ads efficiently.

1. Don't attempt to reach a pinpointed market. As was already mentioned about mass media as a whole, you will be reaching a broad audience. Your seminar should be geared to topics of general interest. How to make a million dollars and how to achieve peace of mind fall into this category.

2. Don't purchase more space than you actually need. In most cases, a small, well-placed ad will be as effective as a large one. Naturally, the newspaper will try to sell as large a space as they can. The best way to find out optimum size is through testing.

3. Don't be fooled by low rates; they may mean low circulation. Avoid newspapers with low circulation.

4. Design your ad with a catchy headline that is sure to attract atten-

tion and encourage the reader to continue reading. This is a cardinal rule for writing advertising copy. Your first goal is to "grab'em."

5. Focus your ad on communicating *benefits*. This marketing rule can not be repeated too many times. *Always focus your marketing efforts on the benefits the participant will receive.*

6. Allow your audience to register at the door. By not demanding advance registration, you are removing one more obstacle to the registration procedure.

7. Advertise in the Sunday edition when possible; it is more widely read. In general, avoid Friday and Saturday editions. They are the least effective.

8. Locate your ad on the right-hand side of the page near the top.

9. Place your ad in the front pages of a section rather than toward the back.

10. Use multiple exposures. This will substantially increase your registrations. However, this is an area where you should proceed cautiously to determine whether your advertising dollars are being spent wisely.

11. For a seminar geared to men, place your ad in the sports section; for affluent men or women, the business section; and for men or women in general, the main section.

12. Always test your advertisement program before making major investments. This applies to test size, multiple insertions, ad design and copy, placement, and newspaper choice.

13. Save money by using regional editions of national newspapers when possible. Newspapers like *The Wall Street Journal* have regional editions and rates.

!!! **Contact.**   Standard Rates and Data Service also publishes two important directories geared toward newspaper advertising.

Newspaper Rates and Data provides a list of newspapers in each market, the cost of advertising, and whom to contact.

Newspaper Circulation Analysis provides you with a complete demographic description of who reads the publication and the number of papers sold.

!!! **Resources.**   The following books are recommended if you want to develop and refine a mass media advertising campaign for your seminar.

Advertising and Marketing Checklists by Ron Kaatz (NTC Books, Lincolnwood, IL)

Advertising Made Easy by Susan Sewell (Price Stern Sloan, Los Angeles, CA)

Advertising Manager's Handbook edited by Richard Stansfield (Dartnell, Chicago, IL)

How to Make Advertising Twice as Effective at Half the Cost by Herschell Gordon Lewis (Nelson-Hall, Chicago, IL)

How to Write a Good Advertisement by Victor Schawab (Wilshire Books, North Hollywood, CA)

Tested Advertising Methods by John Caples (Prentice Hall, Englewood Cliffs, NJ)

The Copywriters Handbook by Robert W. Bly (Henry Holt and Company, New York, NY)

11

How to Exploit the Media for Free (or Low-Cost) Publicity

How to Profit from Publicity

The best kind of advertisement is free. The art and science of getting free media coverage is called publicity. Publicity can serve you in three specific ways that are similar to advertising; the big difference is you don't pay a lot for publicity.

First, it will help you fill seats at your seminar without increasing your overhead. Although you will incur minimal postage, copying, and telephone costs, overall they will be negligible. People will have the opportunity to learn about your seminar, and as a result, attend it.

Second, it will get you publicity. As the saying goes, "Any publicity is good publicity." This may not be absolutely true; but generally speaking, it will be to your advantage to have your name in front of the public or your target audience. Becoming a celebrity speaker should be one of your long-term goals if you want to become eligible for the really big money in the seminar business. Each time you get into the media, you move a little closer to that goal.

Third, it will give you a feeling of elation to see your name in print or to know that thousands or perhaps even hundreds of thousands of people are watching or listening to you. Don't underrate the boost in confidence that comes with publicity.

What Is a Press Kit?

You need a press kit. Your press kit is simply a package of all the material you believe will be of interest to the press. You give a press kit to any member of the press who might want to do a story on you or your seminar or to anyone you would like to attend one of your seminars.

You also send out your press kit to anyone who is considering hiring you to be a speaker or to conduct a seminar for their organization. Of course, the materials you include are only those relevant to the particular needs of the client. For example, if you are proposing an in-house seminar for the real estate industry, any materials you can generate related to the real estate industry, such as an article you wrote for a real estate trade magazine or an endorsement from a major real estate author, should certainly be included.

Components of a Press Kit

The contents of a press kit vary according to the situation and the event you are publicizing. However, it will always consist of one or more of the following 12 items:

1. Press release
2. Bio
3. Cover letter
4. Photograph
5. Public service/calendar announcement
6. List of previous appearances (or client list)
7. Copies of any previous publicity
8. Articles or books you have written
9. Your seminar or company brochure
10. Sample question list
11. Testimonials and endorsements
12. Video and audio demonstration tapes

Most of the material can be placed in a folder that has pockets on the inside. It is a good idea to add a little class to your package by buying a high quality folder. You should put a label on the front to identify the contents. A business card can also be stapled to one of the inner pockets.

Let's look at each element of the press kit in more detail.

The Press Release and How to Write It

Your press release should attract the attention of the media person who is reading it and then give this person a straightforward presentation about your program. The person to whom you have sent the release is usually under the constant pressure of deadlines and is bombarded with mail and incoming news possibilities. For this reason, if you are going to be given any consideration at all, you must provide your information in an easy-to-read format.

You should write a press release in a form that is ready to go to press. Think of the press release as if it were a final, actual printed story. Your goal is to make it as easy as possible for the news or feature editor to understand the importance of your seminar and to include a story about it in their publication or media.

Components of a Press Release.   Let's examine the five parts of a press release.

1. *Source information.*   This includes the name, address, and phone number of the person who should be contacted for more information. If it is written on your own letterhead, the name of the contact person and telephone number will be enough. Make sure to include your telephone number even if it is on the letterhead.

2. *Release date.*   Most press releases are labeled "FOR IMMEDIATE RELEASE." This indicates that the story can be used as soon as it is received. Only in special cases will you use a specific date. This would indicate to the press not to release the story until the date indicated.

3. *Headline.*   The headline should summarize the main content of the press release. It should tell what is happening and to whom. The headline should be written to appeal to the audience of the particular media. It should be typed in all capital letters.

4. *Dateline.*   This is nothing more than the city of origin of the press release. The dateline might be of importance if the newspaper or magazine covers many different regions.

5. *Body.*   The body of the press release should be written in the inverted pyramid style: The most important information up front and the information of lesser importance at the bottom. In this way, if the story needs to be reduced in length, it can be edited quickly without removing the more essential information.

Paragraph 1.   The first paragraph should include the who, what, when, where, why, and how. This will include the name of the featured event, speaker, and so forth.

Paragraph 2.   Repeat the name of the program and why the event is significant to the target audience. Reinforce the benefits or the importance of the seminar with a quote by the seminar leader or an authority on the topic. *This quote should be directed to the target audience of the program.*

Paragraph 3.   This paragraph gives additional information about the seminar and seminar leader. An additional quote can be used in this paragraph.

Paragraph 4.   More information that underscores the importance of the program or its benefits to the targeted population should be included. Another quotation can be added.

Paragraph 5.   Include registration information and whom to contact for more information.

Figure 11-1 shows the layout of a typical press release and Fig. 11-2 provides an example of a press release.

Contact: Name

       Company

       Address

       Phone Number

                           For Immediate Release

HEADLINE DESIGNED TO GRAB ATTENTION
(TYPED IN CAPS)

Dateline – Paragraph 1: Who, what, when, where, why, how

            Paragraph 2: Why program is important to audience

            Paragraph 3: Additional important information

            Paragraph 4: Good background information

            Paragraph 5: Registration or for more information

                     -End-

Figure 11-1. Sample of a layout for a typical press release.

THE BUSINESS INSTITUTE
53 Atwell Lane
Weehawken, NJ 07087

Contact: Lynne Lindahl
       (201) 794-8072

For Immediate Release

PERSUASION SKILLS GIVE BUSINESS PEOPLE
THE COMPETITIVE ADVANTAGE

Weehawken, NJ—"Speak Out with Clout" is the focus of a comprehensive one-day seminar for career-minded businesspeople. It will be held at the Hyatt Hotel in Bayonne, New Jersey, on Tuesday, March 7. This intensive program will begin at 8:30 a.m. and end at 4:30 p.m.

In order to be successful, businesspeople must present a powerful image, project self-confidence, win the trust of others, and "Speak Out with Clout." Dick Zeif, president, The Negotiating Institute, says, "This is a program whose time has come."

This program will provide proven communication strategies and techniques to achieve these objectives. Seminar leader for this program is Paul Karasik, author of the best-selling business book, *Sweet Persuasion*. He is a sales and management consultant to numerous Fortune 500 companies.

In today's marketplace, success often depends upon your ability to persuade, influence, and motivate others. According to a recent research study conducted by Stanford University, communication skills are responsible for up to 85 percent of the success of most people. "Speak Out with Clout" will provide participants with these specific skills.

For registration or information, contact Lynne Lindahl at (201) 794-8072.

-End-

Figure 11-2. Sample of a press release.

Tips for Writing a Winning Press Release

1. Keep your sentences short and to the point.

2. Avoid hype. Provide facts and information that can be substantiated, otherwise you eliminate the possibility of the media's providing an objective story.

3. Proofread it thoroughly. There should be *no* spelling, grammatical, or typing errors.

4. Keep it short. Keep your press release two pages or less in length. People who will be reading your press release are extremely busy. A short press release has a better chance of being read.

5. Always double-space your copy.

6. Use only one side of the paper for your press release.

7. Staple your press release together if it is more than one page.

8. Type the word *more* at the bottom of any page that leads on to a continuing page. The title and page number should appear on each page after the first ("TAX SEMINAR, Page _____").

9. Center the word *end* on the page after your last sentence.

10. Always send a good clean copy.

11. *Send your press release to a specific person.*

12. Make sure someone is always available to answer the telephone during business hours. There is a good chance the person will not call back if no one answers the first time.

Rules for Writing Your Bio

Your bio is an integral part of your brochure, press release, and other promotional materials. Here are the 10 guidelines for you to follow when writing a bio for the media.

1. Write your bio the way you would like to be seen by the media and the public.

2. Make your bio 250 to 400 words in length.

3. Provide interesting, unique, significant, and appealing background information about yourself.

4. Grab the reader's attention with the first paragraph. It should compel the reader to be interested in finding out more about you.

5. Provide the five Ws early in the bio. Your life, like a good story, can be partially described in terms of who, what, where, when, and why.

6. Use quotations freely throughout. They will add color and style.

7. Give the reader a sense of what you are really like personally.

8. Tell the reasons you are important or an expert in your field.

9. Give evidence and facts that clearly demonstrate your competence.

10. Provide interesting or humorous personal information.

Occasions When You Should Use a
Cover Letter and What to Say

It is not absolutely necessary to include a cover letter with a press release or a press kit, but it does add a nice personal touch. There are
three circumstances in which a cover letter or even a simple cover note
is particularly appropriate.

1. When you are sending material to a specific person, remind that
person of any previous conversation or of their request for the information.

2. Include a cover letter when you want to provide reasons why your
press release would be right for that specific medium. For example, if
your seminar is targeted toward women, a TV show aimed at women
might be perfect. Your cover letter should point out reasons such as this
to the program director or host of the show. In effect, your cover letter
becomes a marketing letter.

3. If you see an article or a program in which you believe you could
have been included, write a cover letter to explain why. Chances are
good the reporter will write a similar article in the future, and in this
way you will have a good shot at appearing in it.

Guidelines for Your Press Kit Photograph

You need to include a good photograph of yourself in your professional
press kit. Here are some guidelines to follow:

- Use a head shot.
- Use a black-and-white photograph.
- Use a portrait photographer.
- Smile, it is your best look.
- Get 100, 8- by 10-in copies. Copies are cheaper in lots of 100.
- Typeset your name on the bottom when you get your copies.
- Be honest. Have a new photograph made up every couple of years.

Public Service Announcement/Calendar
Announcement

Both broadcast and print media announce upcoming events such as
seminars. Making such announcements in the broadcast media is called
a public service announcement or PSA. In the print media they are
called calendar announcements.

Guidelines for a PSA or Calendar Announcement

1. Type and double-space the copy on a letterhead.

2. Give a release date for the announcement.

3. Include the name of the event sponsor, the contact name, and the telephone number.

4. List the who, what, where, when, and why.

5. Include the price for registration.

6. Make it short—50 words for a calendar announcement and a reading length of no more than 30 seconds for a PSA.

7. Send in your announcements at least three weeks in advance.

Figure 11-3 shows a sample PSA.

List of Previous Appearances

Have you ever heard the expression, money breeds money? The same can be said of publicity. The more publicity you get, the easier it becomes to get more publicity. Therefore, list all of the radio and TV shows you have been on. A client list is an acceptable substitute if you have no previous media appearances.

The Business Institute
53 Atwell Lane
Weehawken, NJ 07087

Contact: Lynne Lindahl
       (201) 794-8072

PSA for Use Through March 6

ANNOUNCER: Get the competitive advantage in business. Learn how to master the art of persuasion. You will be able to motivate and influence others after you attend the "Speak Out with Clout" seminar.

This one-day seminar will be held at the Hyatt Hotel in Bayonne, New Jersey, on Tuesday, March 7. Seminar tuition is $195. To register or for more information, call (201) 794-8072.

-End-

Figure 11-3. Sample of a public service announcement.

Copies of Any Print Publicity

The most persuasive previous publicity to include in a press kit is print media, since it can be seen and experienced by the person receiving it.

!!! **Caution.** Nothing looks worse than illegible photocopies of articles. When you succeed in getting written up in a newspaper or magazine, it is worth it to get good clean copies of the article printed on a high-quality paper stock.

Articles and Books You Have Written

If you have written any articles on the topic of your seminar, be sure to include them in your press kit. As with previous publicity, make sure you invest the extra time and money to get clean, attractive copies of your articles.

If you have a published book. it will be well worth the investment to mail a copy of it. Nothing adds to your credibility like being an author. It's no accident that the talk show circuit and media are filled with authors.

Your Seminar or Company Brochure

You would like to get some press coverage of your program. Hopefully you can get someone from the media to attend. Therefore, if you are promoting a specific event, you should include the brochure for this event in the press kit.

If you have a company that relates to the topic of your seminar, you will want to include your company brochure as well. For example, if you are giving a seminar on using hypnosis to lose weight, the press would probably like to see your company brochure for general background information.

Sample Question List

When you approach the broadcast media, you should include a list of questions your interviewer can ask you. Talk show producers and hosts are extremely busy. Part of your job is to make their job easier. Do the thinking for the hosts, and they will be more likely to book you on their show.

Here is what a sample question list might look like for a sales seminar:

1. Can everybody be sold?

2. Is there any can't-miss, closing technique?

3. How can you overcome an objection?

4. What can a salesperson do to avoid feeling bad about rejection?

5. What kind of person makes the most successful salesperson?

6. Why does the selling profession have a negative connotation?

7. How much money can a good salesperson earn?

Testimonials and Endorsements

Testimonials are statements from people who have attended one of your programs and want to testify to the effectiveness of it. Endorsements are testimonials by recognizable names or celebrities. Both testimonials and endorsements are useful for building credibility for you and your program.

In most cases, endorsements and testimonials will take the form of letters or excerpts from letters. There is a very simple, yet incredibly effective strategy for getting these letters. ASK!

If someone found your program to be exceptional, he or she will likely be more than willing to provide a letter saying so. If the person you are asking is very busy, you have two alternatives to ensure getting the endorsement or testimonial you ask for. First, you can ask for the statement from them orally, write down their words, and read them back. The second method is to ask them if you can write your own testimonial or endorsement. Then, mail or fax it to them for their approval or changes.

Video and Audio Demonstration Tapes

Although it is unlikely any of the media will watch or listen to a tape of your entire program, they will probably be willing to listen to or watch a 5- or 10-minute demo tape. Tapes can be especially helpful for the broadcast media.

Audio demo tapes are rapidly becoming a promotional device of the past. We live in the age of video. In almost all cases, a video demo is preferred to an audio demo.

A high-quality video demo is an important tool for getting media coverage as well as for promoting your in-house programs. It is the most expensive component of your promotional materials. It is also one of the most valuable for opening doors to opportunities. Your professional-quality video communicates the message that you are not a beginner in the business.

Here are seven guidelines you should follow for creating your demo tape. Although these suggestions are directed toward the production of a video demo, most of them can also be applied to the production of an audio demo.

1. *Make it short.* Because people are busy, they won't watch for more than 5 or 10 minutes. Your demo tape should *never* be more than 15 minutes long.

2. *Keep it fast paced.* Preferably, you should use "bites" with lots of edits. Think MTV.

3. *Start taping your talks and seminars now.* If you can get a few fantastic minutes from each taping session, you will be able to put together an incredible video demo tape.

4. *Use a professional quality format.* There are a number of video-tape formats. Home videotape formats are VHS and 8MM. The most common professional formats are Betacam, ¾ in, and 1 in. Other professional formats include a variety of digital formats. Professional video formats are referred to as broadcast quality.

Your video demo represents you. If the quality is poor, it will reflect poorly on you. It is important to work in a professional format so that the copies maintain their clarity. Copies made from home formats deteriorate very quickly.

The most cost-effective, yet high-quality formats are Betacam and ¾ in.

5. *Show some audience shots in your demo.* It is important to assure the viewer that the audience is reacting favorably to you. Let them see the audience listening attentively, laughing, or participating in your seminar.

6. *Include a few short studio interview clips.* If you have any footage from other TV shows you have done, review it to see if you can get a few good "bites." If you don't have any clips, you might want to record a few minutes in the studio. You can set it up as an interview type of format, answering any relevant questions about your program or topic.

7. *Be prepared to invest in your video demo.* Most video demos can be produced for a few thousand dollars. It will cost approximately $500 to have a professional-quality video recording made of your seminar or talk. If you personally take the time to review your tapes, you can save a lot of money in the editing studio. Editing time can cost from $50 to $200 an hour. Make sure you know exactly what you want to include in your finished product before begin to edit.

$$$ Saver. Two inexpensive resources for editing your demo are readily available. Most local cable TV companies and local colleges have video editing available. Although they don't advertise, most will make them available at a very low rate.

Get your seminar recorded for free. If you are doing an in-house seminar for an organization, ask if they would like to make your seminar available on videotape to those who could not attend. Many organizations have professional-quality video recording equipment on the premises. Let them record your seminar, and use the tape to get some clips for your demo. On some occasions the client might ask you if your presentation can be videotaped. If that happens, you can ask for a modest fee, such as $500, to allow the videotaping. You can grant permission with the stipulation that the tape be made available to you for your demo.

Steps for Getting Media Coverage

Your success in getting publicity will be largely determined by your ability to organize and implement your media campaign. Here are the steps you should take to achieve your publicity goals:

1. *Select the appropriate media to approach.* Identify the right media for you, your topic, and your seminar. Who is the target audience for your publicity? If your program is geared toward women, women's magazines such as *Working Woman* and *Woman's Day* might be perfect. If your program is financial, *The Wall Street Journal* or the Financial News Network would be good targets for your publicity efforts.

!!! **Resources.** The following directories will help you identify the appropriate media for you to approach for publicity.

All-in-One Directory	Bacon's Publicity Checker
Gebbie Press, Inc.	Bacon's Publishing Company
P.O. Box 1000	332 S. Michigan Ave.
New Paltz, NY 12561	Chicago, IL 60604
(914) 255-7560	(312) 922-2400

The *All-in-One Directory* includes more than 21,000 listings and basic information about daily newspapers, weekly newspapers, general consumer magazines, professional business publications, trade magazines, farm magazines, news syndicates, 7000 radio stations, and 900 TV stations.

Bacon's Publicity Checker, a two-volume directory, contains more than 17,000 listings and includes information on print media and the specific types of publicity used by general and trade magazines and by weekly and daily newspapers.

Bacon's publishes other directories that include radio and television listings and foreign media. It also provides media lists and mailing services for press releases.

Radio Contacts	Television Contacts
BPI Media Services	BPI Media Services
1515 Broadway	1515 Broadway
New York, NY 10036	New York, NY 10036
(212) 536-5351	(212) 536-5351

Radio Contacts and *Television Contacts* list more than 4000 radio stations and more than 1100 television stations that produce shows that use guests. Individual programs are listed as well as the name of who to contact.

BPI also has a number of other worthwhile directories and services available. They provide a phone-in service for daily updates with the purchase of any directory.

New York Publicity Outlets	Metro California Media
Public Relations Plus, Inc.	Public Relations Plus, Inc.
P.O. Box 1197	P.O. Box 1197
New Milford, CT 06776	New Milford, CT 06776
(800) 999-8448	(800) 999-8448

New York Publicity Outlets and *Metro California Media* have complete listings of all the media in the New York metropolitan area (within a 50-mile radius) and 23 metropolitan areas of California. Contact names for various departments at all of the newspapers, magazines, and radio and TV are listed. These directories are the most complete for these two geographical areas.

National Radio Publicity Outlets contains detailed information on more than 8000 radio stations. *National TV & Cable Publicity Outlets* contains similar information for more than 5000 TV and Cable stations. The third directory, *Feature News Publicity Outlets*, provides the same kind of information for 500 newspapers. All three are updated twice a year. They can be ordered from:

Morgan-Rand Publishing Company
2200 Sansom Street
Philadelphia, PA 19103
(800) 441-3893

2. *Send your material to the right person.*   Although the directories listed above are updated on a regular basis, personnel changes are frequent. Make sure you are sending your press material to the correct name.

3. *Prepare or select the proper material.*   If you are approaching a TV show, a demo tape would be great to send. On the other hand, if you are approaching the print media, don't bother to send tapes. They won't watch them.

!!! **Caution.**   Remember that the person who is reviewing your material is seeing it through the eyes of his or her audience. You should always be presenting your material with this fact in mind.

4. *Time your publicity efforts, if possible.*   For example, if you are doing a seminar for secretaries, a press release sent just before National

Secretaries Day stands a much better chance of getting used than if it were sent some other time.

Timing is also important in relation to your event. Daily newspapers, radio, and TV want your material approximately one week in advance. Weekly publications need to receive material two to three weeks in advance.

5. *Send out your press kit.*

6. *Follow up with a phone call.* After you wait an appropriate amount of time, it is good to phone to see if your material has been received. If it has, don't push. Just check. Respect their judgment. Offer some additional information, and develop some rapport. Keep the door open for future publicity efforts.

7. *Prepare thoroughly for the interview or show.* Interviewers will have questions you have provided and possibly some of their own. Rehearse your answers and offer a few specific points or tips that will interest your audience. Remember, you are the expert!

Short success stories also work well for media coverage. If your seminar is on office organization, tell a humorous story about someone you know and how they solved their problem using your organization methods.

There is no substitute for being totally prepared. The success of your interview or guest appearance on a show will be determined largely by your preparation.

8. *Be sure to say thank you.* You will have a good chance to get interviewed again if you leave a good impression. Send a thank-you note. Also, this is a small world. It is likely you will get to meet the same person somewhere else further down the road.

How to Get on National Radio and TV Talk Shows

There are three sources for getting on talk shows that you should become familiar with and use. Although it is difficult to coordinate the timing of your appearance with your seminar, if you manage it properly this can turn all publicity into dollars. The next section on how to exploit the media offers more detail.

1. *Radio-TV Interview Report.* This bimonthly magazine opens the door to lots of shows. It is distributed free to more than 4700 talk show producers and hosts. You pay for an ad, and there is an *excellent* chance someone from the talk shows will contact you. The magazine staff will help design the most effective ad.

Radio-TV Interview Report
Bradley Communications Corp.
135 East Plumstead Ave.
Landsdowne, PA 19050-1206
(215) 259-1070

2. *TalkOut.* This monthly magazine is distributed to practically every radio and television talk show producer and host in America who interviews guests over the telephone. In addition, *TalkOut* follows up with a comprehensive phone campaign each month to secure interviews and keep their lists up to date. This service offers two other attractive features. First, every person gets a full-page ad. Second, they offer a toll-free number through which a media representative contacts guests.

$$$ Saver. *TalkOut* gives a 10 percent discount to members of the American Seminar Leaders Association.

TalkOut
P.O. Box 201601
Austin, TX 78720-1620
(800) TalkOut

Both *Radio-TV Interview Report* and *TalkOut* give you your money's worth. Although they can't guarantee you results, if you follow their suggestions, your success is almost assured. *Most* people get on lots of shows.

3. *The Yearbook of Experts, Authorities, and Spokespersons.* This directory is sent out to 7000 of the top journalists in America. Listings in this 800-page publication cost $225. The fee includes a 50-word advertisement and multiple listings in the index. The problem is you have to be fairly prominent or famous to get results.

Mitchell Davis
Broadcast Interview Source
2500 Wisconsin Ave., NW, Suite 930
Washington, D.C. 20007-4570
(202) 333-4904

How to Exploit the Media and Fill Seminar Seats

It's fun and encouraging to appear on talk shows and see your name in print, but what is more important is turning these opportunities into money in your pocket. In order to fully exploit each of your media appearances, you must do the following:

1. *Provide real answers.*   In each interview or article, you must offer some valuable information that will position you as an expert and a resource.

2. *Exploit with permission.*   Arrange with the host or writer for your seminar, book, or tape to be mentioned. This is very simple, ask! Most media people will be glad to offer their audience an opportunity to get more information.

3. *Provide a response mechanism.*   Offer your audience an 800 number, a local number, or your mailing address to sign up for your seminar.

4. *Give your audience an incentive to respond.*   Offer an inexpensive gift or bonus for calling or writing you. This can consist of information such as a tip sheet or list of contacts and resources that you can mail out for the price of a stamp. You can also offer a special gift to those who call and register for your program. In either case, the incentive will guarantee valuable benefits to you each and every time you get media exposure.

Each time someone calls or writes, you will get invaluable, qualified names for your house mailing list. Remember, the most valuable mailing list you will ever own is your house mailing list that you develop. You will be able to market your books, tapes, and future programs to this list. You will also get registrations for your upcoming program using this proven strategy for exploiting the media.

!!! **Resources.**   These two books are excellent sources for the basics of the publicity game.

Professional's Guide to Publicity by Richard Weiner (Public Relations Publishing Co., Inc., 888 Seventh Ave. New York, NY 10106)

The Publicity Manual by Kate Kelly (Visibility Enterprises, 11 Rockwood Dr. Larchmont, NY 10538)

Write to Public Relations Publishing Co., Inc. for a complete list of their books. They produce a number of useful directories.

The Publicity Manual covers the basics of publicity in a complete step-by-step format.

!!! **Contact.**   The Public Relations Society of America is the major professional association of public relations practitioners in the United States. There are chapters nationwide.

Public Relations Society of America
33 Irving Pl.
New York, NY 10003
(212) 995-2230

12

Promoting Your Seminar for Less Than $100— The Two-Step Promotion

Would you like to create a profitable seminar business, but are you put off by the prospect of risking thousands of dollars and months of time and energy? Or perhaps you've got the spirit to get into the seminar business but lack the capital for promotion and advertising. In either case, it is important for you to learn and implement the following strategy carefully.

The two-step promotion is a method of marketing your seminar by first presenting a free or inexpensive introductory talk. At this short talk or miniseminar, your audience will have the chance to meet you, to learn more about your topic, and to decide whether they then want to attend a full-length program.

Your goal at the "intro" is to register people for your complete program. You want to sign them up on the spot or a short time later.

Many successful seminars are promoted using this simple technique. It works, but there are some rules to be followed if you want to be successful.

Four Golden Rules for the Two-Step Promotion

1. *Don't rip people off at the intro.* You must provide real information and give people real value at the intro. If you just give a sales pitch, it will turn people off and they will not trust you. Remember, at the intro your aim is to let people know how much valuable information you have for them.

2. *Don't give them too much.* Conversely, you don't want to spill your guts in the lobby. If you set up your intro with a limited time frame of an hour or less, you will by definition limit how much you can divulge. It's similar to going to an ice-cream store and tasting a spoonful. Chances are you would not have wandered into an ice-cream store unless you were seriously interested in ice cream. At this point you are working percentages. A certain percentage will like the taste you have given them and will be willing to buy the whole ice cream cone.

3. *Sell the sizzle, and they'll buy the steak.* You will want to create a motivational atmosphere at your intro event. Make it exciting and up-beat. Expose the benefits of your seminar. Point out how others have benefited from your seminar. Avoid the hard sell, though. Make people feel comfortable about you as their seminar leader. Be enthusiastic about your program without being phony. (See Chapter 17 on how to deliver a dynamic seminar.)

4. *Provide act-now motivation.* There are two simple act-now techniques that you should consider applying in order to get registrations at the intro event. The first is the discount. Emphasize the fact that registration on the day of the event will cost 20 to 30 percent more. Buy the ticket now and take advantage of the discount. You might also mention that the ticket is refundable if they change their mind.

The second act-now strategy is the gift. Offer the gift as an incentive for them to sign up at the intro. This gift should be relevant to the seminar itself. For example, if your seminar is on time management, a time organizer would be perfect. Books, audiotapes or videotapes, and nicely printed checklists also make excellent incentive gifts. You could even offer free personal consultations with you.

The idea here is to give your audience reasons to purchase their tickets right then at the intro.

The Two Types of Intro Events

The Public Intro

The public intro is basically promoted as if it were the seminar itself. You will need to rent a room, advertise the event, and prepare the room with a seminar setup.

Although you will be able to convert a good percentage of the audience to the full event, you will have to spend money on promoting the intro.

The big advantage to promoting your seminar with the two-step method is that you will be able to register many people for your seminar who would not otherwise have signed up for it.

The public intro works best for seminars that have mass appeal—topics such as stress control, weight loss, real estate, financial investment, or personal growth. The advantage of these seminars is that, in most cases, advertising in newspapers or radio works well to fill the intro event with people.

The most successful example of the public intro is the legendary Dale Carnegie seminars. The Dale Carnegie intro is free and offers to teach the audience a specific skill, such as memory training. Those who attend receive a rather entertaining program by a motivational speaker. At the intro, those present are invited to sign up for the longer, tuition-based programs on public speaking and the like.

The In-House Intro

The premise for the two-step promotion remains the same with an in-house intro, except the logistics for the intro are different. The intro is presented at an event that is sponsored by a specific group.

For example, let's say you are invited to speak at a meeting or conference of some kind. Although the event is not billed as an intro event for your seminar, at the end of your talk you can distribute flyers announcing an upcoming seminar. Basically, you will follow the same four golden rules described for the two-step promotion.

The mathematics for promoting a seminar with the in-house intro remain the same. That is, in order to sell X number of seminar seats, you have to speak to Y number of people at the intro.

The opportunities to speak at in-house events are endless and are described more fully in Chapter 13. Many trade and professional associations, nonprofit organizations, and church and civic groups are more than willing to let you promote your upcoming seminar in exchange for a free program to their group.

The one big advantage here is that the cost of promotion is negligible. A simple letter or phone call can often land you the speaking engagement for the intro. If you are hoping to attract 40 people to your full seminar, you should plan to speak to 200 or more people at the intro. The only additional expense, then, is the seminar flyer or brochure you will hand out at the intro. The following real-life case study illustrates how effectively this can work.

Case Study

Successful Seminar Promotion for Less Than $100 Using the In-House Intro

Goal: To sell out 20–25 seats to full seminar
Seminar topic: Selling skills
Target audience: Real estate salespeople
Place: Northern New Jersey

Procedure:

1. Telephone local real estate companies with 10 or more sales-people and speak with the sales manager.

2. Offer the sales manager a free mini sales training program for his or her sales staff. This program will be approximately 30 minutes in length and will be a part of their regularly scheduled weekly sales meetings.

3. Deliver a quality intro program and ask for sign-ups for your seminar at the end of each intro.

Total revenue (23 participants @ $99 each)		$2,277.00
Promotion expense (typesetting and printing)	$ 92.50	
Room rental expense	125.00	
Total expenses		217.50
Total profit		$2,059.50

As you can see from this actual case study, the profit margin on the two-step promotion using in-house intros is enormous. Promotion costs were kept to less than $100. The only additional expense is the room rental. This will vary according to your location and group size.

The two-step requires initiative, but if you follow the four golden rules of two-step promotion, it is practically impossible to lose. The two-step method is not theory; it is a promotional strategy that works.

$$$ Saver.   When you print the flyers that you will distribute at your intro, leave off the date, time, and place. Instead, leave a space where you can rubber-stamp or write in this information. Using this technique, you can extend your print run and save up to 50 percent in printing expenses.

The Rollover Principle

The success of the two-step promotion is dependent on your ability to roll people over from one program to another. If you are sincere and straightforward with your intentions, you will have no problem with the rollover principle. Let people know that you have information that will improve their lives, and they will be more than willing to roll over from the free program to the paid one.

13

How to Tap a Hidden Gold Mine— The In-House Market

Most newcomers seem to have a one-track mind when it comes to the seminar business. They immediately imagine the hotel meeting room filled to capacity with hundreds of participants who have paid a handsome fee to attend their program.

While it is true that there is lots of money to be made in the public seminar business, the same can be said of the in-house market. The big advantage of the in-house seminar market is that you do not have to sell the individual seats. You do have to market your program to the organizations that will utilize your program. But it is much simpler and requires much less investment and risk. The organization that sponsors your seminar will provide the people and take care of all of the detail work. This frees you to concentrate on delivering a great seminar.

If you don't like the sales and marketing game and the financial risk that accompanies it, you should seriously consider approaching the in-house market with your seminar. The sponsoring group offers a fixed fee for programs. The fees range usually from $500 to $5000 or more per day.

Let's look at the range of opportunities in the in-house market.

What Are the Three Major In-House Seminar Markets?

1. *Corporate.* The largest in-house seminar market is the corporate seminar market. It has been reported that corporations spend

more on education than the entire budget for all of the high schools and colleges in America combined. Corporations depend on a variety of outside sources for their programs. Although credibility helps, your success in marketing to corporations depends less on who you are than on how much you can deliver. Helping them to improve productivity and profitability is the name of the game. Seminar companies that specialize in delivering programs to corporations are known as training companies.

!!! Contacts.   In the Yellow Pages of this book, under the section titled "Corporate Training Companies," you will find a directory of more than 100 of the largest corporate training companies. In addition to the list of corporate training companies, there are thousands of individual consultants who deliver training programs to corporate America.

!!! Resource.   There are two excellent resources if you are interested in the corporate seminar market.

Training   Corporate Meeting Planners
50 S. Ninth St.   Macmillan Directory Division
Minneapolis, MN 55402   1140 Broadway
(612) 333-0471   New York, NY 10001
                                                (800) 223-1797

Training magazine is full of information on corporate training. It also sponsors a conference and trade show each year in the winter. The trade show offers an opportunity for you to meet representatives from many training companies. Many of the seminars offered there will help to tune you into the corporate training field as a whole. In both cases, your attending will help you get an overview of corporate training. Call or write and ask to be put on the mailing list.

If your program is appropriate for the corporate market, *Corporate Meeting Planners* is a directory listing 18,494 corporate meeting planners with information on how to locate them. What is particularly helpful is that the directory identifies which ones use professional speakers. They will customize a list for you. Lists are available on labels or computer disk. Call or write for more information.

2. *Trade and professional associations.*   America is association crazy. Practically everyone belongs to some kind of professional association. Taken together, associations hold many thousands of meetings each year in which seminar leaders and speakers are employed. They have meetings on the local, state, regional, and national levels, and they continually look for new speakers and seminar leaders to work at their various functions.

!!! Resources. There are three excellent references for organizations and contacts in the vast and lucrative association market.

National Trade and Professional
  Associations of America
Columbia Books, Inc.
1212 New York Ave., NW, Suite 330
Washington, D.C. 20005
(202) 898-0662

Association Meeting Planners and
  Conference/Convention Directors
Macmillan Directory Division
1140 Broadway
New York, NY 10001
(800) 223-1797

Encyclopedia of Associations
Gale Research Company
Book Tower
Detroit, MI 48226

National Trade and Professional Associations of America is a book that lists more than 6300 trade and professional associations. It also offers such other valuable information as when and where these associations hold their meetings and conventions.

The *Encyclopedia of Associations* is a three-volume reference source that lists associations and members as well as the names of individuals in charge of educational programs for their association.

The *Association Meeting Planners and Conference/Convention Directors* is one of the best directories for contacting 8000 national associations that hold conventions, meetings, and seminars. It notes which ones hire professional speakers. Customized lists are available on mailing labels and computer disk.

!!! Contact. The association business is a multimillion-dollar business. In fact, there is even a national association that consists of people who are the leaders of associations.

American Society of Association Executives
1575 Eye St., NW
Washington, D.C. 20005
(202) 626-ASAE

The American Society of Association Executives (ASAE) publishes an annual directory entitled *Who's Who in Association Management.* The directory lists the individual in charge of the educational programs for each association. ASAE holds three major conventions each year.

Breaking into the Association Market. ASAE has regional societies of association executives. Many of these local chapters hold monthly meetings and annual conferences for which they need the services of seminar leaders and speakers. You might want to attend some of their regional meetings or conferences and explore the possibility of speaking at one of them. You will be networking and speaking to the people who hire you or recommend you to speak at their association programs.

To learn more about ASAE and how it works, write to your regional chapter, listed below.

REGIONAL CHAPTERS OF AMERICAN SOCIETY OF ASSOCIATION EXECUTIVES

**National Headquarters:
American Society of
Association Executives
1575 Eye Street, NW
Washington, DC 20005
(202) 626-ASAE**

ARIZONA

Arizona Society of Association
 Executives
5301 North 7th St., Suite 301
Phoenix, AZ 85014
(602) 264-1956

CALIFORNIA

Sacramento Society of Association
 Executives
2580 Sierra Blvd., Suite E
Sacramento, CA 95825
(916) 481-5284

San Diego Society of Association
 Executives
P.O. Box 33089
San Diego, CA 92103
(619) 692-9182

COLORADO

Colorado Society of Association
 Executives
3545 South Tamarac Dr., Suite 310
Denver, CO 80237-1432
(303) 796-0124

CONNECTICUT

Connecticut Society of Association
 Executives
71 East Ave.
Norwalk, CT 06851
(203) 852-7168

DISTRICT OF COLUMBIA

Greater Washington Society of
 Association Executives
1426 21st St., NW, Suite 200
Washington, DC 20036-5901
(202) 429-9370

FLORIDA

Central Florida Society of
 Association Executives
P.O. Box 2156
Altamonte Springs, FL
 32715-2156
(303) 774-7880

Tallahassee Society of Association
 Executives
P.O. Box 10523
Tallahassee, FL 32302
(904) 222-7924

ILLINOIS

Chicago Society of Association
Executives
20 North Wacker Dr., Suite 1920
Chicago, IL 60606
(312) 236-2288

Illinois Society of Association
Executives
217 East Monroe, Suite 300
Springfield, IL 62701
(217) 522-0993

INDIANA

Indiana Society of Association
Executives
310 North Alabama, Suite A
Indianapolis, IN 46204
(317) 638-4402

MASSACHUSETTS

New England Society of
Association Executives
1357 Washington St.
West Newton, MA 02165
(617) 965-1229

MICHIGAN

Michigan Society of Association
Executives
116 West Ottawa St., Suite 600
Lansing, MI 48933-1602
(517) 485-9474

MISSOURI

St. Louis Society of Association
Executives
1221 Locust St., Suite 405
St. Louis, MO 63103
(314) 231-5582

NEW JERSEY

New Jersey Society of Association
Executives
P.O. Box 725
Belle Mead, NJ 08502
(201) 359-1194

NORTH CAROLINA

Carolina Society of Association
Executives
P.O. Drawer 40399
Raleigh, NC 27629
(919) 872-2224

OHIO

Ohio Society of Association
Executives
17 South High St., 12th Floor
Columbus, OH 43215
(614) 221-1900

OREGON

Oregon Society of Association
Executives
825 NE 20th St., Suite 120
Portland, OR 97232
(503) 236-9319

PENNSYLVANIA

Delaware Valley Society of
Association Executives
P.O. Box 579
Moorestown, NJ 08057
(609) 234-0330

Pennsylvania Society of
Association Executives
2941 North Front St.
Harrisburg, PA 17105
(717) 234-7544

TENNESSEE

Tennessee Society of Association
 Executives
430 Third Ave. North
Nashville, TN 37201
(615) 254-1986

WASHINGTON

Washington Society of Association
 Executives
P.O. Box 473
Edmonds, WA 98020
(206) 778-6162

TEXAS

Texas Society of Association
 Executives
2550 South IH-35, Suite 200
Austin, TX 78704-5795
(512) 444-1974

3. *Continuing education.*   There are more than 2000 colleges and
universities offering a variety of seminars or short multiday educational
programs. This is an extremely accessible market. It is an ideal market
in which to begin making money in the seminar business very quickly.
In fact, if you follow the simple seven-step plan described in Chapter
14, you may be able to jump start your career in the seminar business.

How to Market to Corporations and Associations

Whether you are marketing to corporations or associations, the steps
are very simple.

1. *Locate organizations that would profit from your seminar, and identify the decision maker.*   Some of the directories that have been mentioned in this chapter are a good place to start.

Direct mail companies might also be a source of lists of people who
could bring you in to speak to their group. For example, if you have a
seminar for salespeople, a list of corporate sales managers would be a
good list. List brokers can also provide you with the telephone numbers
of the people on their list.

2. *Contact your prospects.*   There are a few variations on this step.
You can use direct mail followed by a phone call, or you can phone first
to further qualify the prospect before mailing. The purpose of your direct mail campaign or phone calls is to generate inquiries for more detailed information about your program and to find out exactly what you
must do to get the job.

3. *Mail out detailed information to qualified prospects.*   They will
probably want a detailed outline of your program, background infor-

mation on you, and various items from your press kit. These items are described in more detail in Chapter 11.

4. *Follow up*. A follow-up call or letter is needed to make sure the information was received and to answer any questions the prospect might have.

5. *Don't give up*. They might not be immediately ready for your program, and they may ask you to call back at a later date. In most cases, they really do want you to call back. It is your responsibility to use a tickler file to give them a call or send a letter at a later date.

Corporations and associations take a considerable amount of time from contact to contract. You must be patient. Sometimes an association will be planning for a conference or meeting a year or more away. It is not unusual for it to take six months from contact to contract, but the wait is well worth it. If you do a good job, you have a very good chance of getting referral business within the same organization. Your time and investment marketing to the in-house market could easily result in tens of thousand of dollars of seminar programs.

$$$ Remember, as a general rule all expenses are billed back to the client. See Chapter 7 for a sample contract you can use when you have been accepted for an in-house program.

How to Use Speakers Bureaus to Get Booked for In-House Seminars

There are hundreds of speakers bureaus that focus their attention on the in-house market. These bureaus market speakers and seminar leaders to the corporate and association market. Although some of these organizations focus their efforts on celebrity speakers like Henry Kissinger or former President Gerald Ford, many book experts on a wide variety of topics.

Speakers bureaus will be willing to book you if you can provide information to the audiences of their clients. Of course, they will examine your experience and credentials closely.

There are a few basic steps you must take in order to get booked by speakers bureaus. First, you must contact them and find out what the bureau wants you to send them. Although it will vary slightly from bureau to bureau, initially they will want your press kit, and, in particular, most will want a video tape.

Speakers bureaus get a lot of inquiries, therefore you will need to niche market yourself. You can niche market by target industry or by topic. For example, you can say your focus is high-tech industries or your topic is humor in business.

In addition to niche marketing yourself, you must be persistent. Most bureaus need to get to know you to some degree. They will want to feel confident about you, your presentation, and your promotability. Some will want to come see you before they will book you. If you concentrate on developing rapport with the bureau, you will increase your chances of getting booked.

Financial arrangements vary from bureau to bureau, but you can count on paying a commission of somewhere between 20 percent and 30 percent. Most bureaus will also want a commission of spin-off engagements that result from the initial booking.

!!! **Contacts.**   The Yellow Pages of this book has a list of speakers bureaus you can contact.

If you decide you would like to start your own bureau, or if you want to get speaking engagements on a cruise ship, you should be aware of the following two contacts:

The International Group of
 Agents and Bureaus
18825 Hicrest Rd.
P.O. Box 1120
Glendora, CA 91740
(800) 438-1242

Lauretta Blake
The Working Vacation, Inc.
4277 Lake Santa Clara Dr.
Santa Clara, CA 95054
(408) 727-9665

The International Group of Agents and Bureaus is an association that is composed of speakers bureaus and agents who book speakers. They hold a conference each year and provide a variety of professional development programs.

The Working Vacation, Inc., is a unique speakers agency that focuses entirely on cruise ships. You will be able to combine speaking with the pleasure of a luxury cruise. They utilize speakers on a variety of topics.

14
How to Start Making Money Right Now

If you've got an idea for a seminar and want to get started right away, you can! The college and adult continuing education market is wide open and relatively simple to enter. Best of all, you'll make money while you're learning the ropes.

Besides making money and getting great experience, you can test your seminar and tune it up before rolling it out for a larger audience, possibly even on a national level.

Practically every college and university in America offers a variety of noncredit courses. In addition, most high schools and athletic clubs, such as your local YMCA and YWCA, offer adult education programs. Many parks and recreation facilities also offer similar programs. Check the bulletin board section of your local newspaper for groups or organizations that run adult education programs.

These groups are always looking for new programs and are open to trying new ideas. Program directors rely on outside suggestions to provide innovative programs. Because the fees paid are not exceedingly high, the requirements for getting the opportunity to present your program are not exceedingly high either.

Most of these adult continuing education programs are offered in the evening or on the weekend. The big advantage to you is that you can begin to make money in the seminar business while you maintain your regular job or profession.

All you have to do is adhere to the following seven-step system.

$$$ One seminar leader who followed this system booked 13 seminars within the first 30 days he applied this system.

Ways to Start Making Money Right Now

1. Identify your prospective local continuing education market. Investigate two-year and four-year colleges and universities. Most telephone books list educational facilities. If not, your local library will have a complete list in the *Educational Directory of Colleges and Universities.* Also, check with any Ys in your area, and ask if they offer adult education programs.

2. Call or write to them and ask for their continuing education catalog.

3. Study these catalogs to determine what kinds of programs they currently offer. Ideally, your seminar will not exist in their catalog. If it does, perhaps you can focus on a slightly different aspect of the topic. For example, if the school is offering a program on leadership, perhaps you could offer a program on leadership skills for women. Or if your specialty is writing and they already offer a program on creative writing, you could tailor a program on business writing.

4. Call the facility, and find out who the program director is. In order to prevent getting bounced around, it's best to ask specifically, "I'd like to speak to whoever is in charge of choosing your programs." When you speak to that person, simply ask, "What do I have to do to be considered for your next seminar catalog listing."

5. Mail out whatever the program planner requests from you. More than likely you will be asked for one or more of the following: a description of your program; your bio, including credentials *and the experience that makes you an expert on the topic*; and endorsements or reference letters.

It is also helpful to the program director to include reasons why you think your seminar would be popular and timely.

6. Follow up with another phone call about 10 days later. Find out what else is needed in order to make a decision. Set up another contact date if no decision has been made.

7. Follow up. Be persistent without being a pest. Don't be upset if you don't get into the catalog the first time. There is a good chance you will get into a later one if you stay in touch.

The two best times of the year to pursue seminar opportunities at colleges and universities are September for programs beginning in February, and March for programs beginning in September. The other adult education programs are not as predictable when it comes to accepting proposals for new programs.

Additional Techniques for Getting Booked Quickly

There are two additional techniques for increasing your chances of getting booked quickly. First, offer to assist the program director in marketing your program. Perhaps you have friends or associates who would be interested in attending your program and could be used to prime the pump. Or maybe you can pull strings to get some publicity in the newspaper or on local radio talk shows.

Second, you might try a direct mail marketing program to all of the potential continuing education programs throughout the country. Although the costs of the mailing can run into the hundreds of dollars, you would only need to book one or two programs to recover your investment and break even. Anything beyond that is profit.

The fees paid for these programs usually vary from about $50 an hour to a couple of hundred dollars a day. Some programs pay you according to the number of participants.

$$$ You can match, double, or triple your profits by offering additional services or products such as books and tapes. Remember, you don't need to have your own books and tapes. You can make substantial profits by selling products you get at wholesale prices. See Chapter 16 for more strategies and techniques you can use to produce substantial income.

!!! **Contacts.**   There are three excellent organizations you will probably want to contact if you are going to deliver your seminars to the continuing education market.

Learning Resources Network
 (LERN)
1554 Hayes Dr.
Manhattan, KS 66502
(913) 539-5376

American Association for Adult
 and Continuing Education
 (AAACE)
1112 16th St., NW, Suite 420
Washington, D.C. 20036
(202) 463-6333

National University Continuing
 Education Association
One Dupont Plaza Circle
Suite 420
Washington, D.C. 20036
(202) 659-3130

15

How to Get a Job with a Seminar Company

Help Wanted: Seminar Leader

You may never have seen an ad for a seminar leader in the want ad section of your local paper. Nevertheless, there are hundreds of companies that hire seminar leaders to deliver the company's seminar program. These seminar leaders travel all around the country making really good money, and so can you.

Getting a job as a seminar leader is much like a job search in any particular industry. The biggest problem is finding the industry. Who do you call? Where are they located? Which are the best seminar companies for you to apply to?

Do You Fit the Job Description? Fill Out This Questionnaire

	Yes	No
1. Are you highly motivated?	☐	☐
2. Are you able to travel?	☐	☐
3. Do you love to be in front of an audience?	☐	☐
4. Do you enjoy helping others?	☐	☐
5. Do you like to teach?	☐	☐
6. Do you love to learn?	☐	☐

If you can't answer yes to *all* the above questions, you probably aren't suited to pursue a career working for a seminar company. You might succeed in promoting your own seminars, but it's not likely you would enjoy working with a seminar company.

Unlike many other professions, there is no career development track in the seminar business. You can't major at the university in seminar leading.

Expertise and experience as they relate to the seminar topic are always helpful. But in most cases, if you are teachable and highly motivated, you'll be seriously considered and have a reasonable chance of getting hired.

Advantages and Disadvantages of Working for a Seminar Company

Advantages:

- No investment necessary
- Excellent financial rewards
- Great experience
- No seminar marketing necessary
- No need to develop your own seminar

Disadvantages:

- Limited control of seminar content
- Less autonomy (You're not your own boss.)
- Definite ceiling on earnings

In brief, if you are ready to make money presenting seminars but lack marketing expertise and money, working for a seminar company might be perfect for you. In addition, the professional experience you will get is invaluable. Many of the most famous speakers and seminar leaders in America started by delivering seminars for national companies.

Who Hires Seminar Leaders?

Organizations that hire seminar leaders come in three varieties: public seminar companies, training companies, and corporations that have in-house training departments. They all rely on talented leaders to present programs.

How Much Do Seminar Leaders Get Paid?

In order to understand how much seminar leaders get paid, you must first understand how seminar leaders get paid.

Per Diem

Per diem means literally "by the day." Public seminar companies and corporate training companies pay their speakers a daily rate. This does not include expenses. Rates vary considerably—from $300 to $1500 per day. Per diem rates will vary according to your expertise, experience, type of seminar, company, and length of time with the company. Your pay scale can also be affected by the amount of product (books and tapes) or consulting services sold as a result of the seminar.

The number of days you work on a per diem basis will vary according to the needs of the company with which you are affiliated. As a contract or per diem employee, you will be on call. On many occasions these companies are very busy and utilize the services of many seminar leaders. Likewise, when the company's business is slow, you are affected too.

Hiring seminar leaders on a per diem basis is standard for the seminar business. It is the most economical and efficient hiring system for public seminar companies and training companies to use. By hiring you as an outside consultant, they have the freedom to use you on an as-needed basis.

Standard Weekly Salary

Many established corporate training companies and public seminar companies offer full-time staff positions for seminar leaders. Because of their steady number of programs, both of these types of companies find it economical to hire full-time speakers. The Yellow Pages of this book will help you identify, target, and pursue these prospective employers.

In the Yellow Pages you will find a section titled, "Corporate Training Companies." All of these companies provide high-quality business seminars on a wide variety of topics. To get an idea of the variety of topics offered by these companies, refer back to Fig. 1-2, the professional development topic list.

Also in the Yellow Pages of this book, you will find a list titled "Public Seminar Companies." This list notes which public seminar companies utilize staff seminar leaders, which ones utilize outside consultants who work on a per diem basis, and which ones use both. All depend on qualified seminar leaders to deliver their programs. As in any business, there is turnover and openings occur on a regular basis.

The third opportunity for anyone seeking a full-time salaried position as a seminar leader is to work as a trainer within a corporation or a large nonprofit organization. Because of the constant need to train employees, all large organizations, and even most medium-sized ones, have a training department. Many of these training departments consist of 10 to 20 full-time seminar leaders. Along with the opportunity to deliver programs on a regular basis, you get the job security and benefits that come with a salaried position of this kind.

!!! **Contact.** If you are seeking a full-time salaried position within a training department, the best place to start networking is with members of the American Society for Training and Development (ASTD). ASTD has more than 50,000 members nationally. This organization provides job postings for in-house trainers. To find out about meetings in your local area, contact the national office:

American Society for Training and Development
1630 Duke St., P.O. Box 1443
Alexandria, VA 22313
(703) 683-8100

How to Conduct a Job Search

The strategies for finding a position as a seminar leader are similar to the ones you would use for any position. The big difference is that, except for a position as an in-house trainer, there are very few help-wanted listings.

!!! **Contact.** As any career counselor will tell you, networking is one of the most effective techniques you can use. Check the Yellow Pages of this book under "Professional Organizations for Networking and Education." By speaking with other seminar leaders, speakers, and trainers, you will learn about topics and about the seminar companies themselves. You will also get some idea of salaries and benefits.

Besides networking, you can phone and write specific seminar companies to get more information. You might want to start with some located nearby if possible. Find out what kinds of programs they specialize in and where they market their programs.

After you have targeted some companies that you feel are compatible with your interests, area of expertise, and experience, you should make inquiries to learn what steps you must take to apply for a position as a program leader.

The application procedure will vary according to the company. Some companies will ask for a videotape of you in action. Others will ask you to come in and deliver a few minutes of a program in their office.

Sometimes you will be accepted for a position, but there will not be a job opening. In that situation, your challenge is to remind the company subtly that you are ready to begin as soon as an opening arises. In other cases, the company will only interview when it needs seminar leaders. If you are accepted, you will start immediately.

Once you have been accepted as a program leader, the company will teach you how to deliver its seminar. There is usually some form of payment for this learning period. In the final step, you are evaluated as you deliver the program. If the quality of your work is satisfactory, you will be offered either a staff or per diem position.

Many companies allow some leeway in how you present the material. This offers you some creative input into the seminar itself and allows you to control the program to some degree.

Getting a job as a seminar leader can be an important first step for anyone seriously considering a career in the seminar business. Don't eliminate this possibility as a strategic step in your professional growth. Many giants in the business started this way.

16

Double Your Profits with Back-of-the-Room Sales

It's no secret that book and tape sales at seminars result in millions of dollars in additional revenues for the seminar business as a whole. In many cases, the profits derived from the sale of products and services far outweigh those produced by the seminar tuition. Let's first examine the various products and services that lend themselves to back-of-the-room, or BOR, sales, and then the best strategies and techniques to market them.

The Three Most Profitable Products

Printed Materials

Although not everybody is a writer, it is safe to say that anyone who is in the seminar business is capable of producing some form of printed material that can generate extra income.

The Resource Guide.   The most simple and quickly printed document you can produce is the resource guide. A resource guide can be as short as 5 pages or as long as 50. The essential component is the value of the information contained within it. For example, if your seminar is on investing in real estate, you might want to include sample contracts, letters of agreement, and lists of various banks and mortgage companies. Similarly, if your seminar is on some aspect of personal growth, a complete list of all books and tapes that relate to your topic would be worthwhile.

Names, addresses, and phone numbers that provide important contacts make excellent information for a resource guide. The type of information found in the Yellow Pages of this book is a good example of resource information you can make available for sale.

There is no limit to the types of information you can include in a resource guide. Checklists, tips, dos and don'ts, sample forms, and so forth, are the kinds of resources for which people are willing to pay good money to take home with them.

The price you will be able to charge for your resource guide depends upon its size and value. A minimum price for a resource guide is probably about $10. In most cases, it should be a minimum length of 10 to 20 pages.

The beauty of the resource guide is that it is assembled rather than written. This means you don't need highly refined writing skills to make this idea work. Anyone who has a grasp of his or her topic can quickly assemble a valuable resource guide.

$$$ Remember, hard-to-find information is the most valuable kind. Your profit margin on a resource guide should be a minimum of 100 percent and can easily exceed 200 percent.

The Monograph.   The monograph, or minireport, is a short booklet that summarizes or expands the material discussed at the seminar. It is a short treatise on your topic, *written by you.* Ideally, a monograph should focus on a specific area. In general, it should be a minimum of 10 to 20 pages. By definition, your monograph graduates to the status of a book when it exceeds about 50 pages.

Besides the obvious advantage of being an additional source of income, a monograph or a series of monographs has another important benefit. It provides you with an added level of credibility as an authority. There is no doubt our society places tremendous importance on the printed word. You further your image, enhance your reputation, and ultimately increase your value in the marketplace as a result of producing these short written expositions.

$$$ It's also easy to see how a series of monographs could become chapters for a subsequent book. Keep this possibility in mind as you develop your monographs.

How to Self-Publish Resource Guides and Monographs.   It is important to mention here how *easy* and *inexpensive* it is to produce printed products once they are written. You don't need to find a literary agent or a publisher. Your local copy center will do. After you have written your resource guide or monograph, print it out on a word processor (or a typewriter, if any still exist). Then simply copy it for a few cents a page, and staple it together.

If you are more exacting or ambitious, there are a number of ways you can jazz up your resource guide or monograph.

- Typeset your material using desktop publishing technology, and have it printed on a laser printer.
- Typeset your front cover.
- Use a colored card stock for the front and back covers.
- Instead of using one staple in the corner, use two or three staples along the left edge to give it more of the appearance of a book.
- Insert your resource guide or monograph into fancy colored folders with a clear-plastic cover.
- If your resource guide or monograph is 25 pages or more, use a plastic spiral binding.

The creative possibilities are endless. All of the above features can be provided by any good quick-copy shop or by your local stationery store.

!!! Caution.   The costs of all of these improvements add up quickly and can reduce your profits substantially. Your material has the potential of being a gold mine of revenue for you, but you must keep your production costs to a minimum.

After you have completed your prototype product, bring the actual product with you and shop around for prices.

The Book.   The ultimate in printed products is, of course, the book. The book has immense financial value as a product. It is also your passport to big money in the seminar business. A book establishes you as an expert. Your value as a speaker and seminar leader increases significantly when you're the person who literally wrote the book.

View it as a building process. You may not feel capable of sitting down and writing a book right now, but you can begin to write down and organize your thoughts, ideas, and words of wisdom.

Slowly but surely you will begin to assemble a collection of writings. Your monographs, articles, resource material, seminar workbooks, and notes will take shape as a longer treatise. You can also get lots of great material for your book from the people who attend your seminars.

Also, as you continue to speak at your seminars and market them, your knowledge of the needs of your audience will increase and you will develop a better idea of the direction your book should take.

Two Paths to Profit from a Book

1. *Sell it to a publisher.* This is a long-term process. First you must write a proposal, then submit it to publishing companies that might handle your type of book. An alternative to speaking directly to the publisher is to find an agent who will send it out to the appropriate prospective publishers.

!!! **Resources.** One of the best all-around sources for information on becoming a published author is *Writer's Digest* magazine. It is a cornucopia of information on all aspects of the book business. The monthly issues of this magazine have great in-depth how-to articles on both the creative process and the marketing of your book idea. *Writer's Digest* is also one of the best sources for books on how to succeed as a writer. Books advertised in the magazine include such topics as how to get published, how to write a nonfiction book, how to write a proposal, and how to find a literary agent. Write or call for a complete book catalog.

Writer's Digest
P.O. Box 2123
Harlan, IA 51593
(800) 333-0133

If you want more information on the services literary agents provide and how they work, the following resource is recommended.

Independent Literary Agents Association, Inc.
Ellen Levine Literary Agency
432 Park Ave. South, Suite 1205
New York, NY 10016

Another good source for information on literary agents is:

Literary Agents: A Writer's Guide by Debbie Mayer (Poets and Writers, Inc., 201 West 54 St., New York, NY 10019, 212-757-1766)

All agents require a query letter before submission of a manuscript. Not all agents will handle your type of book, nor will they necessarily be willing to take on new clients. Remember the cardinal rule in any form of promotion and marketing: Persistence is the key to success.

2. *Self-publish your book.* Although prestige is a primary factor in selling your book to a mainstream publisher, your profits are greater if you self-publish your book.

You can self-publish in two different ways. The first is the low-budget route. Put your book into a word processor, and print it out on regular

8½- by 11-in paper, quick copy at your local copy center, and have it spiral bound. You can spruce it up with some of the same suggestions made above regarding resource guides and monographs.

The second way to self-publish is with a perfect binding. Perfect binding makes the book look "real." There are countless choices to make when you choose to publish your book with a perfect binding; hard cover or soft cover, size of the book, type of paper, and number of copies to print are just a few of the most obvious ones.

Although self-publishing might seem like a tall order, it is a relatively simple thing to do. In addition, the financial reward is outstanding. The average royalty on a book published by a mainstream publisher usually isn't more than 10 percent of the selling price. The same book self-published will return an average of 40 percent of the selling price.

Naturally the biggest advantage of selling your book to a publisher is that the publisher has a distribution network in place. As a self-publisher, you have to design your own avenues of distribution.

!!! **Resources.**   If you choose to investigate the self-publishing route, there are several excellent resources available.

The Editorial Free-Lancers
 Association
P.O. Box 2050
Madison Square Station
New York, NY 10159
(212) 677-3357

Dan Poynter
Para Publishing
P.O. Box 4232-P
Santa Barbara, CA 93140-4232
(805) 968-7277

John Kremer
Ad-Lib Publications
P.O. Box 1102
Fairfield, IA 52556-1102
(800) 669-0773

Marilyn and Tom Ross
Communication Creativity
425 Cedar Street, P.O. Box 909
Buena Vista, CO 81211
(719) 395-8659

Publishers Marketing Association
2401 Pacific Coast Highway
Suite 102
Hermosa Beach, CA 90254
(213) 372-2732

The foremost authority and one-stop resource on the subject of self-publishing is Para Publishing. For a complete list of the products and services offered, write or call for their complete catalog. Ad-Lib Publications and Communication Creativity are good sources as well. The Editorial Free-Lancers Association is a good contact if you are interested in hiring a free-lance editor to review your manuscript before self-publishing.

Publishers Marketing Association provides a wide variety of educational resources as well as actual marketing services to help you market your book successfully. This association is a must for any self-publisher.

Audiocassettes

Audiocassettes are another product you can produce yourself, and they are extremely profitable. Audiocassettes cost $1 to $2 to produce and have a retail value of about $10. Of course, packaging adds to your expenses. Your recording and set-up charges will be amortized in accordance with how many tapes you sell. As in the printing business, duplication costs per unit decrease as your quantity increases.

$$$ The profit margin for an audiocassette program is at least 100 percent with all of your expenses included. This is based upon a run of at least 100 units. Profits quickly soar to 200 percent or more in succeeding runs.

Figure 16-1 represents an expense and profit sheet for a six-audiocassette package. These prices are based on producing an initial run of 100 units. In the case of the covers, the cost to produce 500 covers is almost the same as it is for 100, so the printing price given is based upon a quantity of 500.

A Quick Way to Estimate the Cost of Producing an Audiocassette Album.
The basic rule of thumb for producing an audiocassette album is:

Number of cassettes in album × $2 + cost of printing album cover

+ cost of recording and editing master = total cost

Should You Record Your Tapes Live or in the Studio? Recording your cassette album will be one of your one-time overhead costs and probably the first consideration you will face once you have decided to produce an audio product. There are three methods of recording an audio-cassette album. Let's look at each method so that you can make the best decision for your product.

Method 1. Recording Your Seminar Live
    Advantages:

- Live conversational feeling
- Interaction with the audience
- No need to write a script

    Disadvantages:

- Audience distraction
- Logistical problems of microphones and equipment
- More expensive editing

Gross receipts (for 100 albums at $59.95)			$5,995
Expenses			
One-time expenses			
Set-up			
Remastering of 6 cassettes	$120		
Label typeset @ $20 × 12	240		
Label mats @ $20 × 12	240		
Cover design	300	$900	
Recording			
6 hours for studio recording			
(@ $25 an hour)	150		
6 hours for editing (@ $25 an hour)	150		
Tape costs	150	450	
Cover printing (two-color — front, back,			
and spine — 500 copies)		450	
Total one-time expenses			1,800
Packages and duplicating expenses			
Cassettes		510	
Cassettes albums		500	
Label imprints		60	
Cassette assembly		25	
Total packaging and duplicating expenses			1,095
Total expenses for first 100 albums			$2,895
Total profit for first 100 albums			$3,100
To figure the total profit on the next 100 albums, add $1800 in one-time costs to the total profit. Therefore:			
Total profit for the next 100 albums			$4,900

Figure 16-1. Example of an expense and profit sheet for a six-audiocassette package.

Athough you can invest in the equipment to record your seminar, unless you intend to produce lots of audio programs, it is a lot simpler and probably cheaper to hire a professional to set up a high-quality microphone and recorder. The ideal setup is two ¼-in reel-to-reel tape recorders so that there will be no downtime while fresh reels of tape are being mounted.

With someone else recording you, you can focus your attention on speaking and not on changing reels of tape. A professional recording company oversees the myriad details that must be attended to in order to create a quality product.

The easiest way to find a professional recording company is to check the yellow pages of your local telephone book. Look under the heading "Recording Service." More than likely, you will find a number of companies to choose from, although not all of them will have the capability of remote recording.

The charge for a professional recording company to record your seminar live will generally run a couple of hundred dollars for a full-day seminar.

Method 2. Recording Your Seminar in the Studio
    Advantages:

- High-quality recording
- No distractions
- Opportunity to retake when necessary
- Less editing time

    Disadvantages:

- No live spontaneous feeling
- Time required to write a script
- No audience interaction

Again, the easiest way to find a studio is the yellow pages of your telephone book. Shop around. Prices for voice recording in the studio can vary from $20 to $50 an hour. Check your local radio station. In many cases radio stations offer excellent recording and editing services to outside clients.

Method 3. Combine Live Segments with Studio Segments
    Advantages:

- Audio variety
- Best of both worlds, live and studio

    Disadvantages:

- Planning time
- Extensive editing

Even though this method requires even more planning and design, many popular cassette programs are now being produced this way.

!!! **Contacts.**   Here are two of the best audiocassette duplication companies. Both companies specialize in producing audiocassettes for speakers and seminar leaders. Call or write for more information.

Ms. Janita Cooper
Master Cassette and Duplicating
2002 N. 25th Dr.
Phoenix, AZ 85009
(800) 228-8919

Johnny Berguson
Kingdom Tapes and Electronics
U.S. Route 6, P.O. Box 506
Mansfield, PA 16933
(800) 334-1456

Add Value to Your Audio Album to Increase Sales. Perceived value will always increase sales. The best way to add value is to include a workbook or booklet with your audiocassette album. The written material should reinforce the material on the cassettes.

Videotapes

The age of the videotape is upon us, now! Educational videotape sales have begun to rival audiocassettes and are a multimillion-dollar business.

Almost any information can be transferred to the video medium. Many people prefer the videotape to the audiocassette. You should consider producing a video product, especially if your information lends itself to a training film or if it will be viewed by groups.

Guidelines for Producing and Marketing a Video Product

1. *Increase the value of your video using TADA.* Generic videos tend to sell for much less than targeted products. The difference between the titles "Stress Management" and "Stress Management for Nurses" could mean a 100 percent increase in profits for you.

2. *Keep your video less than an hour in length.* In general, videotape programs are less than an hour long. Many programs are just 20 to 30 minutes. There are two good reasons for this. First, many people have limited viewing time. Second, people are already mentally conditioned to viewing half-hour and hour TV shows (including commercial breaks).

3. *Script your program, and record in the studio.* Videotaping live is much more complicated than audio taping. Lighting, room design, and the presence of an audience create a multitude of technical problems. Unless you absolutely require a live audience, avoid taping live. Live recordings are necessary, however, when you are creating a videotape to promote your program to the in-house market.

4. *Do not record on VHS or other home-video formats.* The quality of home-video formats is not suitable for professional use. Tape formats that are acceptable are 3/4 inch, Betacam, and 1 inch.

5. *Plan to add video effects when you edit your tape.* The eyes of the TV generation are very sophisticated. A cheap production will get you poor reviews and, in some cases, returned tapes. Some added cost for video effects is worth it.

6. *Do your marketing homework.*   Check your trade and professional associations. See what the market for your tape is like. Determine whether you can produce a tape that is not currently available or is unique in some way.

7. *Price your tape competitively.*   The selling price of videotapes varies widely, from $50 to $500. Some go even higher, especially if the information is hard to find.

!!! **Contact.**   Producing a videotape is much more complicated than producing an audiotape album. Before you proceed, discuss your project with the Videotape Wizard, Bob Chesney. He specializes in videos for seminar leaders and speakers. He will save you money and help you produce the most economical and profitable videotape product. Discounts are offered to members of the American Seminar Leaders Association. Call or write:

Mr. Bob Chesney
Chesney Communications
2302 Martin St., Suite 125
Irvine, CA 92715
(714) 756-1905

Secrets for Selling Your Consulting Services

Books, audiocassettes, and videotapes are not the only source of additional income your seminar can produce for you. Chances are, if you present a quality seminar, your participants will want to tap you for more information. You are in a perfect position to sell your services as a consultant. Consultants, like doctors and lawyers, usually sell their services by the hour. And, like doctors and lawyers, you have the opportunity to earn big money. Here are some tips for marketing consulting services:

1. Avoid the hard sell. The hard sell gives people the wrong message. You will appear hungry, and that impression will turn off your audience.

2. Make yourself accessible. Let participants know they can call you. Follow up with a letter reminding them of your availability. Freely answer any quick question they have, but politely suggest that for more detailed discussions your time is billable.

3. Be sure to refer to your consulting service in your materials.

4. Indirectly refer to your consulting services in case studies.

5. Don't forget to put *everyone* on your mailing list.

6. Do a fantastic job! If you do, you will be the first person people call when they need more help. Everyone should be totally convinced you are a gold mine of information in your field of expertise.

!!! **Contacts.** Here are three excellent contacts for information on how to develop and market consulting services:

Consultants National Resource
 Center
27-A Big Spring Rd.
P.O. Box 430
Clear Spring, MD 21722
(301) 791-9322

American Consultants League
2030 Clarendon Blvd., Suite 206
Arlington, VA 22201
(703) 528-4493

Institute of Management
 Consultants
19 West 44th St., Suite 208
New York, NY 10036
(212) 921-2885

Secrets for Closing the Back-of-the-Room Sale

Your success selling products and services from the back of the room will depend largely on following a few simple strategies and techniques. Follow these guidelines, and your products and services will practically sell themselves.

1. Display your products near the door where people will see them when they arrive.

2. Sell products in the morning.

3. Sell products just before the break.

4. Bring enough products to sell to at least 10 percent of your audience. If your products truly fill the needs of your audience, you can sell up to 40 percent.

5. Avoid the hard sell. It is appropriate to refer to your products during appropriate times, in reference to additional information.

6. Increase your sales by 10 to 20 percent by accepting credit cards. (See Chapter 7 for information on how to open up a merchant's account.)

7. Increase sales by creating product packages or combining your products. For example, attendees who buy the video, get the audiotape for free.

8. Increase sales by offering discounts for purchasing on the spot.

Take advantage of the fact that people are most motivated the day of the program.

9. Always have a drawing for one or more of your products. The best time to do this is just before the break. You will create goodwill as well as the perfect opportunity to introduce your products and describe some of the benefits.

10. Hire temporary help to facilitate fast sales transactions.

11. Include information on how to order other products in your handouts, workbooks, or other take-home materials.

12. Always remember, if you are providing people with valuable information, they will *want* to buy. This means you don't have to sell; you simply have to make your products and services available.

PART 3

How to Hold Your Audience in the Palm of Your Hand

17

How to Deliver
a Dynamic Seminar

The Building Blocks of a
Dynamic Delivery

Like a great broadway show, a hit song, or an Academy Award-winning
film, all top-rated seminars have a few consistent elements. Here are the
four cornerstones of a dynamic seminar.

Content

It goes without saying that to enjoy success as a seminar leader, you
have to do your homework. That means identifying the needs of the
participants and researching your topic thoroughly. There are three
primary sources of information. First, your own experience and expertise provide the best credibility. Second, you should speak with experts
on the topic to get other first-hand perspectives. Third, you can supplement experience and interview-based material by doing research in
books, articles, and reports.

Tactics to Make Your Content More Solid and More Interesting. In
order to make your content substantial and mentally stimulating, utilize
the following devices:

1. *Figures and statistics.*   These help quantify statements and demonstrate preciseness. Many audiences, such as engineers, accountants, and
doctors, not only appreciate but also demand exactness of information.

2. *Research reports.*   These give your content credibility.

3. *Facts.*   Facts provide pivotal support material. They can also be

fascinating. The popularity of publications such as the *World Almanac* and the *Guinness Book of World Records* underscore the universal interest almost everybody has with concise tidbits of information.

4. *Definitions.*   Definitions help to clarify meaning. Definitions can be used to open a seminar or a module of a seminar and thereby help to focus the content more effectively.

5. *Anecdotes.*   These provide you with the opportunity to make your content engaging. Everybody loves a good story. Be on the lookout for stories related to your topic.

6. *Examples.*   Examples serve as models that your participants can refer to as they apply the content of your seminar to their own situation.

7. *Case studies.*   Case studies combine the personal touch of the anecdote with the specificity of the example. They make the transference of information to your participants own story easier.

8. *Authoritative sources.*   These work best when they are named. (Don't just say, "An expert told....") Authoritative sources allow you to reinforce the credibility of your information. Remember to choose your sources with care to make sure they really are perceived as a higher authority.

Participation

Adults need to be involved in order to have a motivational learning environment. More important, research has proven that adults also retain more when they are actively involved. The wisdom of Confucius is still true today.

> What I hear, I forget;
> What I see, I remember;
> What I do, I understand.

Techniques for Generating Audience Participation.   The only limit to making your seminar participatory is your own imagination. Each one of these twelve techniques is a door to an infinite number of effective, exciting, and fun ways to keep your seminar lively. For example, under the first technique, tests and quizzes, you could include riddles or even brainteasers that open a door to further discussion. Or under the 14th technique, right before a break you could ask your participants to join in on a funny chorus to a song.

1. *Tests and quizzes.*   These are especially effective when they allow the participants to evaluate their knowledge or skill level in a specific area related to the seminar topic.

2. *Group questions.*   Posing open-ended questions provides the participants an opportunity to respond with their opinions and personal experiences. This works best with groups of fewer than 30 people, but can work with virtually any size group.

One of the most simple yet highly effective questioning techniques to use is asking for a show of hands. You can say something like, "How many people...?" or "Can I see a show of hands of anyone who...?"

3. *Brainstorming.*   Ask participants to contribute quickly and spontaneously to an issue or problem. Record all responses on a flipchart or chalkboard. Then lead the group through a discussion and evaluation of each item on the list.

4. *Pairs.*   Break your group into pairs, and give them an activity to do. This is good for breaking the ice and for a large group.

5. *Triads.*   Break up your audience into groups of three. Triads are excellent when two members are engaged in a role-playing activity and the third is providing feedback.

6. *Small groups.*   Breaking up into small groups of four or more people is very effective when you have broken down a problem or an issue into smaller topics and you want each group to work on a specific area and report back to the whole group.

7. *Role playing.*   Two or more of your participants can act out a real or hypothetical situation. The advantage of this technique is that it allows your audience to examine a situation from another perspective. This technique can be further enhanced with videotape replay, if you can arrange the technology.

8. *Show and do.*   This technique requires the seminar leader to demonstrate a particular skill. The participants are then asked to perform the skill.

9. *Games.*   There are a lot of games that can be created to allow full participation while teaching a lesson. Awarding simple, inexpensive prizes, such as T-shirts or coffee mugs adds excitement and interest.

!!! **Resource.**   There is a series of books with an assortment of great games for seminars. The games included in these three books are proven winners.

Games Trainers Play, More Games Trainers Play, and *Still More Games Trainers Play* by Edward E. Scannell and John W. Newstrom (McGraw-Hill, Inc., 1221 Avenue of the Americas, New York, NY 10020)

10. *Props.*   Giving your participants something they can touch helps keep them involved. Props like Playdoh, peanuts, potatoes, and paper hats can add fun to your presentation and be used to make important points.

11. *Staging of a debate.*   If you set up a debate on an emotionally charged issue, your audience will automatically become involved. The challenge here is to channel the participation in a constructive direction.

12. *Questions and answers (Q&A sessions).*   When possible, it is best to allow questions throughout your seminar. If this is not possible, at least allow time for questions at appropriate intervals within each module you are presenting.

13. *Food.*   Eating always helps to get your participants involved. Even if your group is fairly large, you can easily distribute inexpensive, yet welcome snacks, such as peanuts or a candy. Use the food to reinforce a point. For example, you can say, "You're bound to go nuts if you don't manage your time effectively." Then hand out nuts to everybody.

14. *Music.*   Another technique for getting the participants involved is to have them listen to a musical "bite" or song that makes a point.

15. *Movement.*   Getting participants involved in any kind of movement works well to create interaction and participation. For example, it's extremely easy to get a group to take a one-minute stretch or make movement a component of a game or role-playing exercise.

Visual Aids

Hotels and conference centers can usually provide or rent you any visual aid you might need. Traveling with your own equipment is more of an inconvenience than it is worth. Nevertheless, always check with your facility beforehand to make sure it has everything you need.

There are seven reasons why you *must* use visuals in your seminar.

1. To increase retention of material

2. To teach more in less time

3. To keep and maintain the attention of your audience

4. To provide a picture of something you have described in words

5. To minimize misunderstanding or to clarify your information

6. To add some drama and variety by creating a multimedia effect

7. To add a level of professionalism to your presentation

Among the visuals available to you are:

1. *Flipcharts.*   The flipchart is one of the most inexpensive, easy to use, and versatile teaching aids available. It is usually a 24- by 36-in pad of fairly heavy-weight paper mounted on an easel. The advantage of the flipchart is that you can write quickly using colored markers. You

can write spontaneously or prepare your pad beforehand. The flipchart is most effective with groups of fewer than 30 people, since it becomes difficult for larger groups to read flipcharts from a distance.

2. *Chalkboards and marker boards.*   Remember elementary school? Well, the chalkboard is still an effective teaching aid, although the more modern marker board has largely replaced it. The marker board uses colored markers and is erasable. The biggest drawback to both of these is that it requires time to erase. As with the flipcharts, these are most useful with groups of fewer than 30 people.

3. *Overhead projector.*   The overhead projector is the most versatile and easy to use visual aid device for groups of more than 30 people. Overhead transparencies can be drawn spontaneously or can be prepared beforehand and placed on the projector as needed. Any material on a printed page can be transferred to the transparency at a copy shop. The cost is usually less than a dollar per transparency. If you find a cartoon, graph, drawing, or illustration you like, you can have it transferred to a transparency with minimal time and effort for inclusion in your presentation.

4. *Slide projector.*   If you are speaking to large groups or have wonderful color slides that will enhance your presentation, nothing is better than a carousel projector. The average cost to have slides designed for your seminar is between $5 and $20 per slide. Cost depends upon the complexity. Most word and graphic slides are computer generated, and the only limit on the creativity of your slides is your budget.

There are three disadvantages of slides, however. First, they are inflexible. If your slide tray is set up in a certain order, it becomes very inconvenient to change it at the last minute. Second, slides require that the room be dark, which makes it difficult for people to take notes. Some people will even fall asleep. Third, the chances for technical problems increase. Inevitably, slides are put in upside down or jam in the tray, or the bulb blows in the middle of your presentation. Be prepared—do a rehearsal run-through, and triple check.

5. *Videotapes.*   Showing a videotape at some point in your seminar can be a wonderful addition. Videos are most effective when they are used to emphasize a point, to serve as an icebreaker, or to open the group to discussion.

The disadvantage of the video is that it requires a video projector or multiple monitors if the group numbers more than 15. This can add expense and inconvenience to your seminar.

!!! **Caution.**   Showing a video is not the same as presenting a seminar. Use it as a tool, not as a crutch. The best use of video is in small doses. Try to keep videos less than 10 minutes in length.

!!! **Resources.**   There are quite a few good sources for training videos on a full range of topics. They can be previewed and either rented or purchased. If you are interested in using videos, call or write for a catalog. Here are some of the most notable sources:

Bureau of Business Practice
Prentice Hall
24 Rope Ferry Rd.
Waterford, CT 06386
(800) 243-0876

Monad Trainer's Aid
163-60 22nd Ave.
Whitestone, NY 11357
(718) 352-2314

The Bureau of Business Practice offers a wide variety of videos, as well as other multimedia material aimed at improving performance in the workplace.

Monad is a master distributor of all of the major producers. It is a great one-stop video connection. The personnel will help you choose the best video for your seminar.

6. *Objects.*   Using tangible objects — similar to the grade school show-and-tell — is still an effective teaching technique. Objects are wonderful to use in games and puzzles. Adults, like children, enjoy the fun of touching and holding things. Seminar leaders can use everything from rubber bands and paper clips to potatoes and paper planes to add dimension to their seminars. The possibilities are endless.

!!! **Resource and $$$.**   Two excellent resources for more detailed descriptions on how to design effective visuals are:

Creative Training Techniques
 Handbook
Lakewood Books
50 S. Ninth St.
Minneapolis, MN 55402
(612) 333-0471

ICIA
3150 Spring St.
Fairfax, VA 22031
(703) 273-7200

Lakewood Publications also produces a monthly newsletter called *Creative Training Techniques*.

The International Communications Industries Association (ICIA) offers a wide variety of *free* material. Ask for their tip sheets. ICIA will also help you locate companies and distributors for presentation equipment and materials.

Presentation Skills

Your appeal as a seminar leader is largely determined by your personal delivery style and the presentation techniques you use during the seminar.

Components of Your Personal Style

1. *Clothing and accessories.* It is important to dress appropriately for your audience. If you have a formal business audience, dress formally. If your seminar is at a resort and people are dressed in a more informal manner, you should dress informally also.

2. *Grooming.* This goes without saying. Your own image aside, good grooming shows your audience you think they are important.

3. *Facial expression.* Your face should communicate your message. Of course, one of the best facial expressions is the smile. Use it liberally throughout your seminar as you see performers do on TV. This is, after all, a form of show biz.

4. *Gestures.* Using your arms and hands tends to keep people's interest. It is rare that anyone uses gestures too much.

5. *Body movement.* Get out from behind the lectern. Your participants will react positively to movement. Move around the room freely. You will be able to focus your audience's attention. Be careful though that you don't pace. Pacing is usually an expression of nervous energy and can be distracting to your audience. Try not to be too predictable in your body movement.

6. *Posture.* Stand tall but avoid appearing stiff or nervous.

7. *Enthusiasm.* You can use both your voice and your body to express enthusiasm.

8. *Tone of voice.* How you say your words is important. Your tone of voice should be expressive, not a monotone.

9. *Clarity.* Speak clearly. Make sure your pronunciation is correct and that you enunciate your words well, but without exaggeration or affectation.

10. *Rate of delivery.* As a general rule, it is better to speak at as quick a pace as possible without forfeiting clarity. This works best to keep the attention of your audience, and you can cover more ground. But since variety is the spice of a seminar delivery, slowing down and speeding up at different times makes any presentation more dynamic.

11. *Eye contact.* Always maintain good eye contact with your audience—all of them, not just the closest, best looking, or most attentive.

12. *Audience contact.* Greet the people at the beginning, roam the aisles, and chat at breaks. Props are great, but physical obstructions between you and your audience should be removed.

13. *Personal information.* Your audience will respond better to you if you reveal something about yourself. They will see you more as a person and become more engaged in the seminar.

14. *Simple language.* Don't speak above an audience's level of understanding. Don't use unfamiliar words.

15. *Listening.* Listen when your participants share. By doing so, you are telling them that they are important.

!!! **Resources and Contact.** There are numerous sources of information on public speaking. Two books and one organization are particularly worthy of your attention.

> *Presentations Plus* by David Peoples (John Wiley & Sons, 605 Third Ave., New York, NY 10158-0012)
>
> *The Presentation Kit* by Claudyne Wilder (John Wiley & Sons)

Both books deal with various aspects of public speaking and presentation.

Toastmasters International
P.O. Box 9052
Mission Viejo, CA 92690
(714) 858-8255

Toastmasters International will help you develop your public speaking skills. The organization holds literally thousands of meetings each month nationwide. Everyone gets a chance to speak in a supportive environment, which is great for learning how to overcome nervousness and get public speaking experience. Contact them to find out about meetings near you.

How to Hold an Audience in the Palm of Your Hand

In order to get excellent evaluations, every seminar leader should master the basics of the craft of leading seminars: substantive and interesting content, audience participation, proper use of audiovisuals, and personal presentations skills. At the top of the profession are presenters who incorporate the following additional techniques that allow them to rise above the rest.

1. *Tell stories.* People love to hear stories. Your stories should have relevance to your topic or to a specific point you are making. The best source for stories is your own personal experience. Review your own experiences, and identify good stories that are relevant to your topic. Be on the lookout for new ones. The other good source for stories is the

people who attend your seminar. Many people will share with you personal experiences that make great "war stories" for future seminars.

!!! Resource. The best resource for wonderful stories is the journal that you keep. You can begin immediately by writing down personal experiences you've had that make good stories. Keep your eyes and ears open for new ones, and write them down.

2. *Use humor.* You can tell jokes and use prepared one-liners. You don't have to be funny to get laughs. Find cartoons and use them to make transparencies or slides. Always make sure your humor does not put any one down, except possibly yourself.

!!! Resources. The following three publications are great sources for books, tapes, newsletters, magazines, materials, seminars, conferences, and associations that focus on humor.

The Whole Mirth Catalog
1034 Page St.
San Francisco, CA 94117
(415) 431-1913

The Laugh Connection Newsletter
3643 Corral Canyon Rd.
Bonita, CA 91902
(619) 479-3331

The Humor Project
110 Spring St.
Saratoga Springs, NY 12866
(518) 587-8770

3. *Use quotes.* Quotes are a wonderful way to state a truth, motivate, or elicit a response. When you hear or read an excellent quote that you might want to use, put it in your journal, in a file labeled "quotes," or on your computer.

!!! Resources. Many excellent quotes, as well as anecdotes and ideas, can be found in the following sources:

The Executive Speechwriter
 Newsletter
Emerson Falls
St. Johnsbury, VT 05819
(802) 748-4472

Quotemaster Plus
PennComp Software Development
4031 Villanova St.
Houston, TX 77005
(800) 326-6145

Call or write the newsletter for a free sample.
Quotemaster Plus is a computer program that has more than 5000 quotes on disk. Write for more information.

4. *Recite a poem.* A poem is a wonderful tool for creating an emotional response to your presentation. As with stories and quotes, begin

to collect special poems that you can use in a moment when you want to inspire your audience.

5. *Motivate with benefits.*   Since most seminars are designed to solve problems, you must continuously relate what you are talking about to the benefits your audience will receive.

As you begin each new module, open with a reminder of the benefits they can expect to receive. For example, use statements such as, "Next we're going to be talking about.... This is very important because it will...." Reminding your audience of benefits will keep their attention on you and on what you are saying.

Be sure to amend that old speaker's adage, "Tell'em what you're gonna tell'em, then tell'em, then tell'em what you told'em," with the *benefits* of what you're tellin'em.

!!! **Contacts and Resources.**   Without a doubt, the best source for tips, exercises, methodology, and content is networking with your peers. If you want to learn how to climb the mountain, speak to someone who has done it is especially true for your development as a professional seminar leader. See the Yellow Pages of this book under "Professional Associations for Networking and Education" for the addresses and phone numbers of organizations that will provide this opportunity.

18

How to Create Valuable Handout Material

Generally, any material which is included in the price of the seminar is referred to as a handout. The handout material is free to the participants.

Why You Need Handouts

Remember you are an "information entrepreneur." Although people are attending your seminar to hear you speak, the printed word is a critical element to the success of your seminar.

1. *Handouts add value.* You are more likely to get good evaluations and referral business if you give out good handouts that supplement your spoken presentation.

2. *People expect handouts.* Most participants probably have already attended one or more seminars at which they received handouts. If you don't give them anything, they will be disappointed. Really.

3. *Handouts create flexibility.* If your handouts are somewhat comprehensive and cover your major points, you will be able to refer your participants to them if you run short on time or if you want to skip a particular module of your seminar.

4. *Handouts provide take-home information.* You will provide your audience with the opportunity to continue learning after the seminar is over.

5. *Handouts are good, inexpensive advertising.* Your name, address, and phone number should be on all your handouts. People usually save them, and you will very likely get inquiries at a later date.

Types of Handout Material You Can Use

There is a variety of material you can include as handouts. The best handouts often include combinations from the following list:

1. *Outline.* The outline summarizes the major points of your presentation. It usually follows the flow of the seminar. It is best to leave space on the outline sheet or sheets for note taking.

2. *Fill-in-the-Blank.* The fill-in-the-blank handout creates instant audience participation. It also gives the audience a certain kind of satisfaction. In most cases, participants will try to guess the correct words in advance, so this format becomes a kind of game.

3. *Quizzes, tests, and self-evaluations.* This type of handout also creates participation and gives the participant nonthreatening feedback.

4. *Resource lists.* You can include names, addresses, phone numbers, local contacts, organizations, and anything else that will give your participants sources they can draw upon later.

5. *Reprints.* Articles you have written that are relevant to your seminar make good handout material. Also, articles others have written are good for handouts. Always be sure to get copyright permission.

6. *Roster of participants.* In most seminars that last a half a day or longer, people network and get to know each other. They may also want to contact each other at a later date. Your participants will appreciate having a complete list of participants, including company affiliations, addresses, and phone numbers, when they leave.

7. *Bibliography.* If you have been successful as a seminar leader, your audience will be motivated to reinforce what they have learned by consulting other books and articles. A complete bibliography on the topic presented at the seminar is always welcome.

8. *Books.* Many types of high-priced seminars will include one or more books in the handout materials. Ideally, these books are written by you. If not, you can distribute a book you consider to be the best on the given topic. You may be able to get books at a discount by simply calling the publisher and telling him or her what you are doing. These books are distinguished from the ones you sell at the back of the room because the handout books are free of charge.

9. *Extra paper.*   If you give your participants exercises and lots of information that they will want to write down, you might want to include blank unlined or lined sheets of paper with the handouts.

Handout Formats from Which to Choose

In most cases, the length and price of your seminar are the most critical elements affecting the number of handouts you distribute and the format. Naturally the three-day seminar will probably require more handouts and a more elaborate format than the one-day seminar.

Bound

You can assemble your material to correspond with the order in which you will be presenting it in the seminar and bind it together. The simplest and least expensive way to bind it is to staple the sheets together. Binding with staples works best when your handout materials have fewer than 20 pages.

Another way to bind your pages is with a spiral plastic-comb binding. This usually costs between $3 and $5 per workbook. Most quick-copy printers offer a comb binding service.

The third method you can use to bind your workbook is with a perfect binding. This is a soft-cover book style, and it gives your workbook a more professional appearance. If you are printing more than a couple of hundred copies, a perfect binding can become cost-effective. It costs around $2 to $5 dollars a copy in large quantities, depending on paper stock, cover, and number of pages.

!!! **Contacts.**   A complete list of printing companies who print short runs (100 or more) of perfect-bound workbooks can be found in Dan Poynter's book, *The Self-Publishing Manual.* See Chapter 16, in a list of contacts for self-publishing, for the information on where to write or call to get this book.

Loose-leaf

Using a three-ring loose-leaf binder allows a lot of flexibility.

Double-number your pages according to the module. For example, pages in the first module would be numbered 1-1, 1-2, 1-3, 1-4, and so forth. Pages in the second module would be numbered 2-1, 2-2, 2-3, 2-4, and so forth. In this way you can revise, add, or delete material easily and inexpensively.

You can purchase three-ring loose-leaf binders at local office supply stores. In quantity they are usually available for $2 to $3.

$$$ and Contacts. Use the binders that have a clear overlay on the front cover. By printing a page with the title of your seminar on a colored paper stock and inserting it beneath the clear overlay, you can create an extremely inexpensive and yet totally professional-looking workbook.

Here are two good sources for binders of all kinds. Their prices are excellent. Call and ask for their catalogs.

Quill Corporation   Viking Office Products
(708) 634-4800   (800) 421-1222

Loose Pages

If you deliver a variety of shorter programs, it is convenient to have handouts that consist of loose pages. If you develop a library of one- and two-page handouts, you can instantly pull together effective hand-out material in various configurations. Then just clip them together with a paper clip.

Another big advantage of loose pages is that you can control the flow of the seminar and the attention of the participants by handing out a page at a time. They will not be able to read ahead or get distracted by the handout material.

One problem with loose pages is that you will have to organize the flow and distribution of the material carefully to make sure the correct material is handed out at the proper time.

In addition, there is the logistical challenge of getting the various loose pages handed out quickly and efficiently. You can usually solve this problem in two ways. The first way involves precounting your handouts and putting them into piles according to the number of peo-ple at each table, the number of people in each row, and so forth. Then, before you begin, ask your assistants or a few participants if they would help you pass out the materials. With this technique you will be able to pass out hundreds of loose pages in a minute or two. The second way you can distribute a set of loose pages quickly is to preassemble them in folders. The folders give your material a professional look and still al-low for a lot of flexibility.

The Most Important Handout: The Seminar Evaluation Form

The evaluation is the last handout you will be giving your audience. Be-cause it needs to be returned to you, it *must be* a loose page. The completed evaluation forms can give you the exact information you need to make improvements on your seminar. Look for patterns in the comments.

For example, if you consistently receive comments on the readability of your handouts or your overhead transparencies, you know this is an area in which you should make adjustments.

Besides giving you valuable feedback, the evaluation allows participants to share any strong feelings they might have. It serves as a release for both positive and negative emotions.

It is helpful to get the name of the participant on the completed evaluation because comments make more sense if you know who made them. For example, if the evaluation is very negative and if the individual was very negative even before the seminar began, you will be able to evaluate the comments in the proper light. So, ask for signed evaluations, but don't demand them. Participants are usually less forthright if they are signing the form.

Remember, your seminar participants will be asked to fill out the evaluation at the end of the seminar. Since many of them will be rushing off to something else, it is best to keep it simple and brief. Schedule a few minutes at the very end for completing evaluations. This will maximize your response rate.

Figure 18-1 shows a sample of a basic evaluation that works.

$$$ The completed evaluation forms can be a source of valuable endorsements. With initialed approvals, you can use any positive comments on future promotional material.

The completed evaluations can also be a source of valuable referrals for future programs. If your participants filled out the last question, you have valuable leads for your mailing list and prospects for future programs.

Additional Evaluation Questions

If you want more refined feedback, the questions in Figure 18-2 can be added. Respondents should be instructed to award each question a numerical rating on a scale of 1 to 5, with 1 being the lowest and 5 being the highest.

Name _____

Date _____

Location _____

Please circle the appropriate number.

1. How valuable were the ideas, concepts, and program content?

10   9   8   7   6   5   4   3   2   1
Highly   Mostly   Fairly   Slightly

2. How effective was the presentation of the material?

10   9   8   7   6   5   4   3   2   1
Highly   Mostly   Fairly   Slightly

3. How do you rate the program overall?

Excellent   Good   OK   Fair   Poor

4. What did you like most about this seminar?

_____

_____

5. What did you like least about this seminar?

_____

_____

6. May we use your comments for our promotional material?
   If yes, please initial for your approval.   Yes   No

7. Who do you know that might be interested in attending this type
   of program?

Name _____

Title _____

Company _____

Address _____

City _____   State _____

Zip _____

Telephone _____

Figure 18-1. Sample of an effective evaluation form.

Seminar Leader

    1. How extensive was the presenter's
knowledge of the subject matter?   1 2 3 4 5

    2. How effective was the presenter's style?   1 2 3 4 5

    3. Was the presenter successful in achieving
group participation?   1 2 3 4 5

    4. Did the presenter maintain control?   1 2 3 4 5

    5. What was the quality of the visual aids?   1 2 3 4 5

Seminar Content

    6. How well was the content organized?   1 2 3 4 5

    7. How was the quality of the workbook
or handout material?   1 2 3 4 5

    8. Do you think you will be able to apply
the content?   1 2 3 4 5

    9. Did you find the exercises beneficial?   1 2 3 4 5

Program Overall

    10. Did the program address your particular
needs?   1 2 3 4 5

    11. Did you feel challenged by the program?   1 2 3 4 5

    12. How would you rate the facility where
the seminar was held?   1 2 3 4 5

Figure 18-2. Additional evaluation questions that can be added to the evaluation form for more refined feedback.

19

How to Set Up
Your Seminar Room

Factors You Must Consider
When You Set Up Your Room

The setup of your seminar room is critical to the success of your seminar. Although the five factors discussed here may seem to be simple and you might take them for granted, the comfort of your audience is at stake. Part of your job is to create as ideal a learning environment as possible.

1. *Temperature.* The ideal temperature of your room should be between 66 and 72°F. If it is warmer, your participants will get drowsy. If it is cooler, they will turn blue. It is always preferable, however, to err on the cooler side.

No matter what the temperature is when you begin, there always seems to be some difficulty with the temperature of the room at some point during the seminar. The best way to deal with a temperature problem is to make plans for handling it when you first arrive. Find out who is in charge of controlling the temperature of your room. Contact this individual and, if possible, arrange in advance for someone to make adjustments as necessary during the presentation.

2. *Smoking or nonsmoking.* Although you can allow smoking in your seminar room, it can be distracting and annoying to nonsmokers. Smoke in the room diminishes the learning environment for smokers and nonsmokers alike.

The best answer to the question of smoking is to remove all ashtrays from the room and disallow it. Announce the no-smoking policy in a nonjudgmental way, and make it clear that smokers can leave the room during breaks to smoke.

3. *Lighting.*   Become acquainted with the lighting controls. Set up the room with enough lights to facilitate note taking and alertness. Make sure, however, that your lights do not interfere with any projectors you might be using. If necessary, you can unscrew a few bulbs if they are shining directly on your screens.

4. *Logistics.*   The ideal setup for your registration area is to the right and left of the door to the seminar room. Set up enough tables to allow for a quick signing in or registration process. If you set up your registration tables outside the seminar room, latecomers will not disturb the people who arrived on time. If you cannot set up registration tables outside the room, set them up just inside the door.

An additional table should be set up at the back of the room for books and tapes and any materials you want to put out for sale or display. Food and refreshments should also be put on a table in the back.

Always make a detailed diagram of your particular setup. Send this to the banquet department of the hotel or facility before you arrive. Include the table locations, where you want the refreshments, seating layout, and any other details you would like to have attended to.

Figure 19-1 illustrates a sample layout.

5. *Seating.*   There are a number of ways to set up the seating in your seminar room. In many cases you will have little control over how your seating is arranged. For example, if your seminar is part of a luncheon program, it might already be set up banquet style. Similarly, if you are using a conference center facility and have a large group, you might be in an auditorium with theater style seating.

Figures 19-2 through 19-7 suggest various seating arrangements from which you can choose. There are advantages and disadvantages to each arrangement, as listed below each drawing presented on pages 149 to 153.

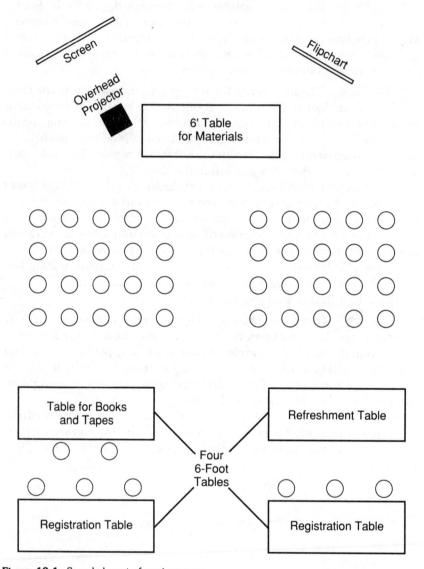

Figure 19-1. Sample layout of seminar room.

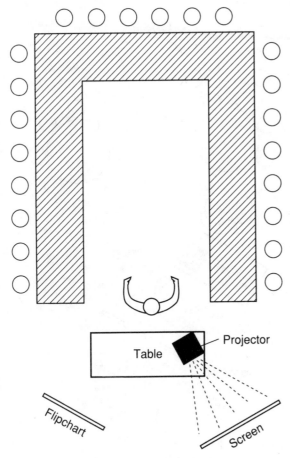

Figure 19-2. U-shaped seating arrangement.

Advantages:

- Interaction and participation encouraged
- Good available writing surfaces

Disadvantage:

- Limited space (10–25 participants)

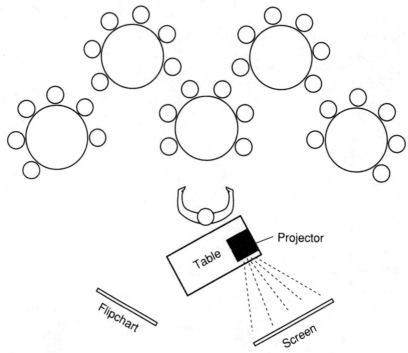

Figure 19-3. Banquet-style seating arrangement.

Advantages:
- Space for group exercises
- Convivial atmosphere encouraged

Disadvantages:
- Poor viewing
- Distractions from food and drink service
- Considerable floor space required

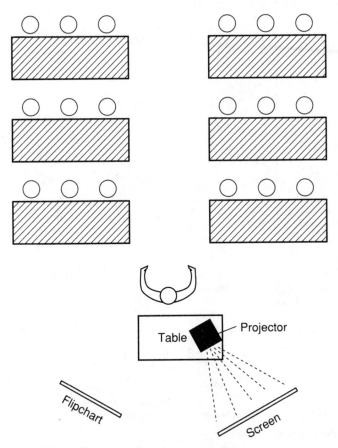

Figure 19-4. Classroom-style seating arrangement.

Advantages:

- Easy setup
- Good available writing surfaces
- Good format for lectures

Disadvantages:

- Bad for interactive exercises
- Considerable floor space required

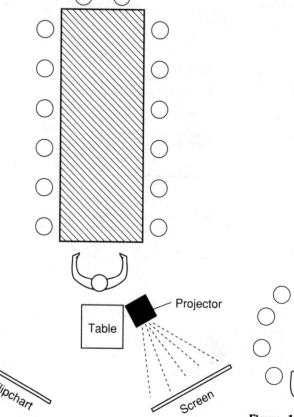

Figure 19-5. Conference table seating arrangement.

Conference Table Arrangement

Advantages:

- Good available writing surfaces
- Interaction encouraged

Disadvantage:

- Limited space (10–15 participants)

Figure 19-6. Circle seating arrangement.

Circle Arrangement

Advantage:

- Interaction and participation encouraged

Disadvantages:

- Difficult use of visual aids
- Limited space (10–20 participants)

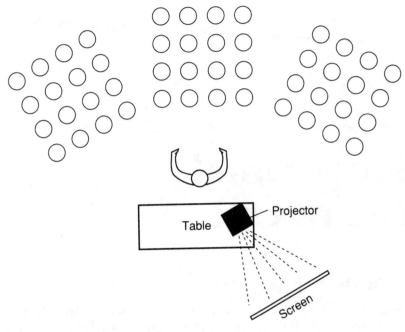

Figure 19-7. Theater-style seating arrangement.

Advantages:

- Large audiences accommodated
- Good viewing

Disadvantages:

- No writing surfaces
- Interactive exercises discouraged

20

Show Time! You're On!

What to Do the Night Before

If possible, it is best to arrive at the site of the seminar the day before so you can check it out. If there are any problems, you still have an opportunity to correct them. By arriving the night before, you also have a chance to relax a bit and get a good night's rest. This is especially important if you have traveled across a few time zones.

Why You Must Arrive at the Seminar Room Early

Arriving early means getting into the room a minimum of one hour before your program is scheduled to begin. Whenever possible, you should arrive closer to two hours in advance. The reasons for this are:

1. To make sure the signs in the lobby are properly displayed and are correct
2. To test all the audiovisual equipment
3. To locate the rest rooms, telephones, and other points of interest to which you will want to orient your participants
4. To correct the temperature so that your audience will be neither too hot nor too cold
5. To arrange the furniture appropriately
6. To help set up the registration or sign-in table
7. To place the handouts on the chairs

8. To meet with support staff and review the agenda

9. To make sure coffee or food will be delivered on time

10. To set up your products table at the back of the room

11. To allow time for you to relax before anyone arrives

12. To make sure you arrive before your first participant

The Seminar Leader's Tool Kit

Although every seminar leader has specific unique tools of the trade, the following items are the most common. In the beginning, it is a good idea to include them all. After a while, you can personalize your checklist.

Name tags	List of participants
Felt-tipped pens	Handout materials
Chalk	Leaders guide and notes
Masking tape	Props
Sign-in sheets	Overhead transparencies
Clock or watch	Tape recorder
Change for your product sales	Blank and recorded tapes
Cash receipt book	Video training tapes
Credit card machine	List of contact names and telephone
Stapler and staples	numbers
Scissors	Books and tapes for sale
Blank pads of paper	Brochures of future programs
Pushpins and thumbtacks	Your introduction

See Fig. 20-1 for a last-minute checklist of important items to review before you begin the seminar.

What to Do as People Start to Arrive

1. Check people in and give them their name tags and any materials they will need for the seminar.

2. Play some soft, easy-listening music (classical is good) to create a pleasant, relaxed atmosphere. Baroque chamber music works very well.

3. Introduce yourself to people who arrive early. Find out why they signed up for the program and what their specific needs are. Show them that you care. Speaking with the participants at this point will help both you and your participants to relax.

4. Introduce people to other people. Many people are too shy to introduce themselves to others but will speak freely if you introduce them

---

☐ Personal grooming and clothes

☐ Microphone (if needed)

☐ Projectors or audiovisual equipment (including spare bulbs)

☐ Overhead transparencies or slides (slides checked)

☐ Spare pens for flipcharts

☐ Water pitcher and glass at front

☐ Handouts or workbooks ready for distribution

☐ Props (for activities)

☐ Room temperature

☐ Stopwatch or clock

☐ Introduction (if needed)

☐ Extra pencils, pens, and paper

☐ Your leader's guide

☐ Prearranged meal and breaks

☐ A few deep breaths to relax before stepping up to speak

Figure 20-1. Last-minute checklist.

to each other. Identify some nonthreatening areas for them to discuss, such as where they come from or their business affiliations.

5. Encourage your participants to have coffee and whatever refreshments you have available.

Rules for Beginning Your Presentation

1. *Begin on time.*   Don't penalize the people who arrive on time by waiting for latecomers. You will antagonize the punctual ones, and the others will fail to appreciate your kindness. Sometimes there are legitimate excuses for lateness, such as traffic problems. If you want to buy a few minutes, you could say, "We're going to start on time with a short networking opportunity. Please introduce yourself to someone you do not know and find out a little about each other."

This technique turns a negative into a positive. People need to feel comfortable and relaxed. This little technique will help you create the most favorable climate for the success to your seminar, and it buys four or five minutes for latecomers.

2. *Start out with lots of energy.* Show a lot of enthusiasm for your audience in your delivery style. Your opening remarks and attitudes in general will set the tone for the whole day.

3. *Thoroughly prepare your opening.* In order for you to gain the confidence of your participants, you should know exactly what you are going to say and do when you begin.

A Winning Agenda for Your Seminar

Using the modular design approach to the actual content of your seminar, here is a proven agenda that works. You can amend this format to meet the specific needs of your seminar length and content.

1. *Introduction.* Whether you are introduced by someone else or you introduce yourself, make your introduction brief. But make sure you provide information that lets the audience know you are qualified to speak on the topic at hand.

2. *Opening remarks.* Once again, keep it brief. Also, keep it light. A joke or humorous remark works wonderfully here. You might want to refer to the city or locale the seminar is in or remark on some of the comments you have heard from the participants. This helps connect you to the audience.

There are three points you will want to communicate to your audience in some way:

- Let them know you're glad to be there.
- Let them know you're happy *they* are there.
- Let them know that you care. Your audience will always respond favorably to you when they know you really care about them.

3. *Introductions.* If the group numbers fewer than 25, each person can introduce himself or herself to the whole group. If the group is larger, you can break up into groups of four or five.

!!! **Remember.** The sweetest sound to anyone's ear is his or her own name. Name tags or name cards are one of the most valuable tools a seminar leader has for creating a relaxed atmosphere that is conducive for adults to learn. Call people by their names as much as possible throughout the program, but be sensitive to sounding phony.

4. *Needs and concerns.*   By asking the audience about their needs and concerns, you are accomplishing two very important objectives. First, you are letting the audience know that you care about them. Second, you will be able to modify your presentation to address the needs of that specific audience.

There are two ways to elicit the audience's needs and concerns. If the group is small, ask participants to voice their needs and concerns when they introduce themselves. Make sure you list each concern on a flipchart. If people mention areas they want to cover but you know you will not cover them, stop and tell that to them.

If the group is large, the second way to do this exercise is first to have the members of the group write down their personal needs and concerns. Then break them up into groups of four or five and have them come to a group decision about what they specifically want discussed. Ask each group what they have decided, and list the information on a flipchart.

If you have done your homework or have had even minimal experience delivering the seminar, you will have a very good idea in advance of what they want to know.

5. *Details.*   Most people are concerned about the flow of the day and logistics. Although they are important, it is best to delay discussing these mundane details until you've broken the ice. You can deal with the details anytime before you begin discussing specific subject matter.

Details include the location of bathrooms, rules about smoking, location of telephones, break times, lunch information, and any other logistical information that you need to announce.

6. *Lecture.*   The very word *lecture* makes many people uncomfortable. Most people identify it with a negative experience from childhood. Nevertheless, you will have to spend a portion of each seminar providing specific information to the participants.

The best way to keep the energy alive and everyone awake and engaged is to encourage questions to be asked throughout. Just be careful about getting sidetracked with questions. If necessary, say, "I can talk to you more about that at the break," or, when appropriate, "I think we'll be addressing that problem a little later."

7. *Participatory exercises.*   You can choose from any of the exercises discussed in Chapter 17. Your audience will come alive each time you give them the opportunity to get actively involved in the learning process. Be sure to use a variety of participatory exercises throughout the seminar.

8. *Breaks.*   You should schedule breaks every hour to hour and a half. You can ask everyone to join in a stretch with you.

When you take a break, it is important to announce exactly how many minutes the break will be. Say, "We will begin again in exactly 14 minutes. Keep your word. Regardless of how many people have made it back, start speaking to whoever is present. If you do not keep your word, you will quickly find that the members of your audience will not keep theirs. Likewise, if they find out you mean what you say, they will be seated and ready to go when you are.

A valuable tool for timing breaks, seminar exercises, and maintaining your schedule in general, is a digital stopwatch. A digital wristwatch that has this feature works well and is convenient as you move around the room.

Sample Agenda for a Seminar on Stress Management

Here is a script for a half-day seminar on stress management.

8:30 a.m.–8:40 a.m.	Introduction of seminar leader and goals of the program
8:40 a.m.–8:50 a.m	Introductions — participants' names, company affiliations, and job functions
8:50 a.m.–9:00 a.m.	Sources of stress for participants
9:00 a.m.–9:15 a.m.	Needs and concerns
9:15 a.m.–9:20 a.m.	Details
9:20 a.m.–9:45 a.m.	Stress theory lecture
9:45 a.m.–10:00 a.m.	Break
10:00 a.m.–10:30 a.m.	Self-scoring self-evaluation stress test
10:30 a.m.–11:00 a.m.	Overview of stress-management techniques
11:00 a.m.–11:10 a.m.	Break
11:10 a.m.–11:30 a.m.	Relaxation exercise
11:30 a.m.–12:00 noon	Personal stress management goal setting
12:00 noon–12:20 p.m.	Open question-and-answer period
12:20 p.m.–12:30 p.m.	Closing remarks and participants' evaluations

Rules for Ending Your Seminar

1. *Summarize your key points.* Tell'um what you told'em is an old adage. Review the most important things you covered.

2. *Acknowledge sponsors or assistants.* If your program was sponsored by an organization, thank them. If anyone helped you with administration, express your gratitude.

3. *Thank your participants for coming.*   Without an audience there is no seminar. Let them know they are important to you. Every audience appreciates hearing this.

4. *Call for action.*   Provide your participants with a challenge to apply the information they received at your seminar, to continue their research, or to take any step that might be appropriate.

5. *Close with a motivational flair.*   You want to leave everyone feeling positive about the seminar experience, the material they learned, and you. You can use humor, wit, quotes, a success story about a former seminar participant, music, or anything else that will make everyone feel good. See Chapter 17 for some creative ideas.

Leave them with the feeling they have what it takes to put the information or skills they learned to work.

6. *Plan and rehearse your closing.*   Your closing should be well thought out and specially designed. Don't try to wing it. Very often what stands out in people's minds is the last feeling they had. A big finish is the best policy.

7. *End on time.*   A professional seminar leader starts on time and ends on time. Your participants have arranged their schedules according to the announced completion time. Finishing late is discourteous and breaks a cardinal rule—avoid breaking late at all costs.

When possible, you can offer to stay around for a short while after the completion of the program. This will show good will, help anyone who still has a few quick questions, and allow anyone who wants to talk to you about further professional assistance to make arrangements.

Don't Forget! Leading Seminars Is a Calling and an Art

At the end of your seminar you will experience an incredible feeling of deep satisfaction. You have made a positive contribution to the lives of others. Winston Churchill said, "We make a living by what we get, but we make a life by what we give."

Besides providing you with the opportunity to make both a living and a life, the seminar business is an incredible vehicle for your own creativity. No matter how successful you become, you will find new inspiration and information to share with your audience. From the creative point of view, your possibilities are endless.

Like any artist you will continually want to experiment, modify, and improve your skills. And like any artist you will enjoy the immense rewards that result from continually investing your energy in maximizing your professional skills.

PART 4

The Seminar Business Yellow Pages

National Seminar Sites

Here is a list of seminar sites that are equipped to provide seminar services. These sites are located in areas where a majority of seminars are presented, including convenient airport locations.

ARIZONA

Phoenix

Arizona Biltmore
24th St. & Missouri, 85016
(602) 954-2523,

Crescent Hotel of Phoenix
2620 W. Dunlap Ave., 85021
(602) 943-8200, (800) 423-4126

Embassy Suites Biltmore
2630 E. Camelback Rd., 85016
(602) 955-3992, (800) 362-2779

Fountains Suite Hotel
2577 W. Greenway Rd., 85023
(602) 375-1777, (800) 338-1338

Holiday Inn & Holidome
Phoenix Corporate Center
2532 W. Peoria Ave., 85029
(602) 943-2341, (800) 843-3663

Hyatt Regency
122 N. 2nd St., 85004
(602) 252-1234, (800) 228-9000

Pointe at South Mountain
7777 S. Pointe Pkwy., 85044
(602) 438-9000

Ritz-Carlton Phoenix
2401 E. Camelback Rd., 85016
(602) 468-0793

Rodeway Inn Metro Center
10402 N. Black Canyon, 85051
(602) 943-2371, (800) 228-2000

Sheraton Phoenix
111 N. Central Ave., 85004
(602) 257-1525, (800) 274-6364

Westcourt Hotel
10220 N. Metro Pkwy. E., 85051
(602) 997-5900, (800) 858-1033

CALIFORNIA

Anaheim

Anaheim Plaza Resort Hotel
1700 S. Harbor Blvd., 92802
(714) 772-5900, (800) 228-1357

Disneyland Hotel
1150 Cerritos Ave., 92802
(714) 778-6600

Grand Hotel
One Hotel Way, 92802
(714) 772-7777, (800) 421-6662

Quality Hotel
616 Convention Way, 92802
(714) 750-3131, (800) 777-1455

Los Angeles Area
Bel Air

Radisson Bel Air Summit Hotel
11461 Sunset Blvd., 90049-2099
(213) 475-6571, (800) 333-3333

Beverly Hills

Beverly Hills Hotel
9641 Sunset Blvd., 90210
(213) 276-2251, (800) 283-8885

Four Seasons Hotel
300 S. Doheny Dr., 90048
(213) 273-2222, (800) 268-6282

Hilton Beverly
9876 Wilshire Blvd., 90210
(213) 274-7777, (800) 445-8667

Sofitel Ma Maison
8555 Beverly Blvd., 90048
(714) 278-5444, (800) 221-4542

Century City

Century Plaza
2025 Ave. of the Stars,
 90067-9986
(213) 277-2000, (800) 228-3000

J. W. Marriott Hotel at Century
 City
2151 Ave. of the Stars, 90067
(213) 277-2777, (800) 228-9290

City of Commerce

Radisson Hotel City of Commerce
6300 E. Telegraph Rd., 90040
(213) 722-7200, (800) 333-3333

City of Industry

Sheraton Resort Industry Hills
One Industry Hills Pkwy., 91744
(818) 965-0861, (800) 325-3535

Hollywood

Hyatt on Sunset
8401 Sunset Blvd., 90069
(213) 656-4101, (800) 228-9000

Roosevelt Hotel Hollywood
7000 Hollywood Blvd., 90028
(213) 466-7000, (800) 950-7667

L.A. Int'l. Airport Area
Culver City

Pacifica Hotel & Conference
 Center
6161 Centinela Ave., 90231-3200
(213) 649-1776, (800) 854-2608

El Segundo

Embassy Suites Los Angeles
 Airport
1440 E. Imperial Ave., 90245
(213) 640-3600, (800) 362-2779

Inglewood

Airport Marina Hotel
 International Airport
8601 Lincoln Blvd., 90045
(213) 760-8111, (800) 225-8126

Hilton & Tower Los Angeles
 International Airport
5711 W. Century Blvd., 90045
(213) 410-4000, (800) 445-8667

Holiday Inn Los Angeles
 International Airport
9901 S. La Cienaga Blvd., 90045
(213) 649-5151, (800) 465-4329

Hyatt at Los Angeles Airport
6225 W. Century Blvd., 90045
(213) 670-9000

Marriott Los Angeles Airport
5855 W. Century Blvd., 90045
(213) 641-5700, (800) 228-9290

Sheraton Plaza La Reina Hotel
6101 W. Century Blvd., 90045
(213) 642-1111, (800) 325-3535

Stouffer Concourse Hotel
5400 W. Century Blvd., 90045
(213) 216-5858

Vicount Hotel
9750 Airport Blvd., 90045
(213) 645-4600, (800) 255-3050

Manhattan Beach

Radisson Plaza Hotel
1400 Parkview Ave., 90266
(213) 546-7511, (800) 333-3333

Los Angeles

Biltmore Hotel
506 S. Grand Ave., 90071
(213) 624-1011, (800) 421-0156

Hilton & Towers Los Angeles
930 Wilshire Blvd., 90017
(213) 629-4321, (800) 465-8667

Holiday Inn Los Angeles Downtown
750 Garland Ave., 90017
(213) 628-5242, (800) 465-4329

Hyatt Regency Los Angeles
711 S. Hope St., 90017
(213) 683-1234, (800) 228-9000

New Otani Hotel & Garden
120 S. Los Angeles St., 90012
(213) 629-1200, (800) 421-8795

Sheraton Grande Hotel
333 S. Figueroa St., 90071
(213) 617-1133, (800) 325-3535

UCLA Conference Services
310 DeNeve Dr., 90024
(213) 825-5305

Westin Bonaventure
404 S. Figueroa St., 90071
(213) 624-3000, (800) 228-3000

San Diego

Bahia Resort Hotel
998 W. Mission Bay Dr., 92109
(619) 488-0551, (800) 288-0770

Catamaran Resort Hotel
3999 Mission Blvd., 92109
(619) 488-1081, (800) 288-0770

Hanalei Hotel
2270 Hotel Cir. N., 92108
(619) 297-1101, (800) 854-2608

Hilton Beach & Tennis Resort
San Diego
1775 E. Mission Bay Dr., 92109
(619) 276-4010

Holiday Inn Montgomery Field
8110 Aero Dr., 92123
(619) 277-8888, (800) 992-1441

Hyatt Islandia
1441 Quivira Rd., 92109
(619) 224-1234, (800) 233-1234

Marriott Hotel & Marina San
Diego
333 W. Harbor Dr., 92101-7700
(619) 234-1500

Mission Valley Inn
875 Hotel Circles, 92108
(619) 298-8281, (800) 854-2608

Omnia San Diego Hotel
910 Broadway Cir., 92101
(619) 239-2200, (800) THE-OMNI

Radisson Hotel San Diego
1433 Camino del Rio, 92108
(619) 260-0111, (800) 333-3333

Ramada Hotel Bayview
660 K St., 92101
(619) 696-0234, (800) 766-0234

Rancho Bernardo Inn
17550 Bernardo Oaks Dr., 92128
(619) 487-1611, (800) 854-1065

San Diego Hotel
339 W. Broadway, 92101
(619) 234-0221, (800) 621-5380

San Diego Princess
1404 W. Vacation Rd., 92109
(619) 274-4630, (800) 542-6275

Town & Country Hotel
500 Hotel Cir. N., 92108
(619) 297-6006, (800) 854-2608

U. S. Grant
326 Broadway, 92101
(619) 232-3121, (800) 854-2608

Westgate Hotel
1055 2nd Ave., 92101
(619) 238-1818, (800) 221-3802

San Francisco

Campton Place
340 Stockton St., 94108
(415) 781-5555, (800) 647-4007

Cathedral Hill Hotel
Van Ness & Geary Sts., 94109
(415) 776-8200, (800) 227-4730

Donatello
501 Post St., 94102
(415) 441-7100, (800) 227-3184

Fairmont Hotel & Tower
Nob Hill, 94106
(415) 772-5000, (800) 527-4727

Four Seasons Clift Hotel
495 Geary St., 94102
(415) 775-4700, (800) 332-3442

Handlery Union Square Hotel
351 Geary St., 94102
(415) 781-7800, (800) 223-0888

Hilton San Francisco on Hilton
Square
333 O'Farrell St., 94102
(415) 771-1400, (800) 445-8667

Holiday Inn Civic Center
50 8th St., 94103
(415) 626-6103, (800) 465-4329

Hyatt Park
333 Battery St., 94111
(415) 392-1234, (800) 233-1234

Mark Hopkins Inter-Continental
Hotel
One Nob Hill, 94108
(415) 392-3434, (800) 327-0200

Lone Mountain Conference Center
USF
2800 Turk St., 94117
(415) 666-6166

Marriott San Francisco
55 4th St., 94103
(415) 896-1600

Meriden Hotel
50 3rd St., 94103
(415) 974-6400, (800) 223-9918

Mikayo Hotel
1625 Post St., 94115
(415) 922-3200, (800) 533-4567

Parc Fifty Five Hotel
55 Cyril Magnin St., 94102-2865
(415) 392-8000, (800) 338-1338

Queen Anne Hotel
1590 Sutter St., 94109
(415) 441-2828, (800) 227-3970

Sir Francis Drake
450 Powell St., 94102
(415) 392-7755, (800) 227-5480

Stouffer Stanford Court Hotel
905 California St., 94108
(415) 989-3500, (800) 227-4736

Westin Saint Francis
335 Powell St., 94102
(415) 397-7000, (800) 228-3000

San Francisco Int'l. Airport Area

Burlingame

AMFAC Hotel
1380 Old Bayshore Hwy., 94010
(415) 347-5444, (800) 227-1117

Embassy Suites Burlingame
150 Anza Blvd., 94010
(415) 342-4600, (800) 362-2779

Holiday Inn Crowne Plaza
600 Airport Blvd., 94010
(415) 340-8500, (800) 827-0800

Marriott San Francisco Airport
1800 Old Bayshore Hwy., 94010
(415) 692-9100, (800) 228-9290

Millbrae

Best Western El Rancho Inn
1100 El Camino Real, 94030
(415) 588-2912, (800) 826-5500

Clarion Hotel San Francisco Airport
401 E. Millbrae Ave., 94030
(415) 692-6363, (800) 252-7466

Westin Hotel San Francisco Airport
One Old Bayshore Hwy., 94030
(415) 692-3500, (800) 228-3000

Redwood City

Sofitel Hotel San Francisco Bay
223 Twin Dolphin Dr., 94065-1514
(415) 598-9000

San Mateo

Dunfey San Mateo Hotel
1770 S. Amphlett Blvd., 94402
(415) 573-7661, (800) 228-2121

Villa Hotel
4000 S. Camino Real, 94403
(415) 341-0966, (800) 341-2345

South San Francisco

Best Western Grosvenor
 Airport Inn
380 S. Airport Blvd., 94080
(415) 873-3200, (800) 528-1234

Holiday Inn San Francisco
 International Airport
245 S. Airport Blvd., 94080
(415) 589-7200, (800) 452-3456

COLORADO

Denver

Brown Palace Hotel
321 17th St., 80202
(303) 297-3111, (800) 321-2599

Comfort Inn
401 17th St., 80202
(303) 296-0400, (800) 631-2090

Embassy Suites Hotel Denver
 Southeast
7525 E. Hampden Ave., 80237
(303) 696-6644, (800) 525-3585

Executive Tower Inn
1405 Curtis St., 80202
(303) 571-0300, (800) 525-6651

Holiday Inn Denver North
4849 Bannock St., 80216
(303) 292-9500, (800) 465-4329

Hyatt Regency Tech Center
7800 E. Tufts Ave., 80237
(303) 779-1234, (800) 233-1234

Marriott Hotel City Center
1701 California St., 80202
(303) 297-1300, (800) 228-9290

Oxford Alexis Hotel
1600 17th St., 80202
(303) 628-5400, (800) 228-5838

Radisson Hotel Denver
1550 Court Pl., 80202-5199
(303) 893-3333

Regency Hotel
3900 Elati St., 80216
(303) 458-5555, (800) 525-8748

Warwick Hotel
1776 Grand St., 80203
(303) 861-2000, (800) 525-2888

Writer's Manor
1730 S. Colorado Blvd., 80222
(303) 756-8877, (800) 525-8072

Stapleton Int'l. Airport Area

Denver

Embassy Suites Denver Airport
4444 N. Havana St., 80239
(303) 375-0400, (800) 345-0087

Hilton Inn Denver Airport
4411 Peoria St., 80239
(303) 373-5730

Holiday Inn Denver I-70 Hotel,
  Conv. & Trade Center
15500 E. 40th Ave., 80239
(303) 371-9494, (800) 465-4329

Registry Denver
3203 Quebec St., 80207
(303) 321-3333, (800) 325-6064

Sheraton Denver Airport Hotel
3535 Quebec St., 80207
(303) 333-7711, (800) 325-3535

Stapleton Plaza Hotel & Fitness
  Center
3333 Quebec St., 80439
(303) 321-3500, (800) 950-6070

CONNECTICUT

Greenwich

Hyatt Regency Greenwich
1800 E. Putnam Ave., 06870
(203) 637-1234, (800) 233-1234

Hartford

Hilton Parkview
One Hilton Plaza, 06103
(203) 249-5611

Holiday Inn Downtown
50 Morgan St., 06120-2994
(203) 549-2400, (800) 465-4329

Sheraton Hartford Hotel
315 Trumbull St., 06103
(203) 728-5151, (800) 325-3535

Bradley Int'l. Airport Area

Windsor Locks

Holiday Inn Bradley International
  Airport
16 Ella Grasso Tpke., 06096
(203) 627-5171 (800) 465-4329

Howard Johnson Hotel
383 S. Center St., 06096
(203) 623-9811 (800) 654-2000

Ramada Inn Bradley International
  Airport
5 Ella Grasso Tpke., 06096
(203) 623-9494, (800) 272-6232

Sheraton Hotel at Bradley
  International Airport
Bradley Int'l Airport, 06096
(203) 627-5311

Stamford

Holiday Inn Crowne Plaza
700 Main St., 06901
(203) 358-8400, (800) 562-9110

Marriott Hotel Stamford
2 Stamford Forum, 06901
(203) 357-9555, (800) 228-9290

Sheraton Stamford Hotel
One 1st Stamford Plaza 06902
(203) 967-2222, (800) 325-3535

Westin Hotel Stamford
2701 Summer St., 06905
(203) 359-1300, (800) 228-3000

Trumbull

Marriott Trumbull
Merritt Parkway
180 Hawley Ln., 06611
(203) 378-1400, (800) 221-9855

DISTRICT OF COLUMBIA

Dupont Plaza Hotel
1500 New Hampshire Ave., NW,
  20036
(202) 483-6000, (800) 421-6662

Embassy Row Hotel
2015 Massachusetts Ave., NW,
20036
(202) 265-1600, (800) 424-2400

Four Seasons Hotel
2800 Pennsylvania Ave., NW, 20007
(202) 342-0444, (800) 268-6282

Georgetown University
Conference Center
37th & O Sts., NW, 20016
(202) 625-4763

Grand Hotel of Washington D.C.
2350 M St., NW, 20037
(202) 429-0100, (800) 848-0016

Grand Hyatt Washington
1000 H St., NW, 20001
(202) 582-1234, (800) 223-1234

Hilton & Towers Washington
1919 Connecticut Ave., NW, 20009
(202) 483-3000, (800) 445-8667

Holiday Inn Capitol
550 C St., NW, 20024
(202) 479-4000, (800) 465-4329

Park Hyatt Hotel
24th & M Sts., NW, 20037
(202) 789-1234, (800) 922-7275

Madison Hotel
15th & M Sts., NW, 20005
(202) 862-1600, (800) 424-8577

J. W. Marriott at National Place
1331 Pennsylvania Ave., NW,
20004
(202) 393-2000, (800) 228-9290

Omni Shoreham
2500 Calvert St., NW, 20008
(202) 234-0700, (800) 843-6664

Quality Inn Capitol Hill Hotel
415 New Jersey Ave., NW, 20001
(202) 638-1616, (800) 228-5151

Radisson Park Terrace
1515 Rhode Is. Ave., NW, 20005
(202) 232-7000, (800) 333-3333

Ramada Renaissance Techworld
999 Ninth St., NW, 20001
(202) 898-9000, (800) 228-9898

Ritz-Carlton Hotel
2100 Massachusetts, NW, 20008
(202) 293-2100, (800) 241-3333

Sheraton Washington Hotel
2660 Woodley Rd., NW, 20008
(203) 328-2000, (800) 325-3535

Stouffer Mayflower Hotel
1127 Connecticut Ave., NW, 20036
(202) 347-3000, (800) 468-3571

Vista International Hotel
1400 M St., NW, 20005
(202) 429-1700, (800) 847-8232

Washington Plaza Hotel
Massachusetts & Vermont Aves.,
NW, 20005
(202) 842-1300, (800) 424-1140

Washington Nat'l. Airport Area
Alexandria, VA

Old Colony Inn
625 1st St., 22314
(703) 548-6300

Hyatt Regency Crystal City
2799 Jefferson Davis Hwy., 22202
(703) 486-1234, (800) 228-9000

Marriott Suites Alexandria
801 N. Saint Asaph St., 22314
(703) 836-4700, (800) 228-9290

Radisson Plaza Hotel at Mark Center
5000 Seminary Rd., 22311
(703) 845-1010, (800) 228-9822

Ramada Hotel Old Town
901 N. Fairfax St., 22314
(703) 683-6000, (800) 272-6232

Arlington, VA

Holiday Inn Crowne Plaza at
National Airport
300 Army Navy Dr., 22202
(703) 892-4100, (800) 848-7000

Hyatt Arlington at Washington
 Key Bridge
1325 Wilson Blvd., 22209
(703) 525-1234, (800) 233-1234

Marriott Crystal City
1999 Jefferson Davis Hwy., 22202
(703) 521-5500, (800) 228-9290

Quality Hotel Arlington
1200 N. Courthouse Rd., 22201
(703) 524-4000, (800) 638-2657

Sheraton Crystal City Hotel
1800 Jefferson Davis Hwy., 22202
(703) 486-1111, (800) 325-3535

Stouffer Concourse Hotel
2399 Jefferson Davis Hwy., 22202
(703) 418-6800, (800) 468-3571

FLORIDA

Miami

Doral Resort & Country Club
4400 NW 87th Ave., 33178-2192
(305) 592-2000, (800) 327-6334

Du Pont Plaza Hotel
300 Biscayne Blvd. Way, 33131
(305) 358-2541, (800) 327-3480

Howard Johnson Golden Glades
16500 NW 2nd Ave., 33169
(305) 945-2621, (800) 654-2000

Hyatt Regency Miami
400 SE 2nd Ave., 33131
(305) 358-1234, (800) 228-9000

Inter-Continental Hotel Miami
100 Chopin Plaza 31331
(305) 577-1000, (800) 327-3005

Marriott Biscayne Bay Hotel &
 Marina
1633 N. Biscayne Dr., 33132
(305) 374-3900, (800) 228-9290

Omni International Hotel Miami
1601 Biscayne Blvd., 33132
(305) 374-0000, (800) 228-2121

Palm Bay Hotel & Club
780 NE 69th St., 33138
(305) 757-3500, (800) 854-5636

Radisson Center
777 NW 72nd Ave., 33126
(305) 261-2900

Sheraton Brickell Point Miami
495 Brickell Ave., 33131
(305) 373-6000, (800) 325-3535

Miami Beach

Dilido Beach Resort Hotel
155 Lincoln Rd., 33139
(305) 538-0811, (800) 327-1641

Eden Roc Resort Hotel
4525 Collins Ave., 33140
(305) 531-0000, (800) 327-8337

Miami Int'l. Airport Area
Coral Gables

Biltmore Hotel
1200 Anastasia Ave., 33134
(305) 445-1926, (800) 445-2586

Hyatt Regency Coral Gables
50 Alhambra Plaza, 33134
(305) 441-1234, (800) 228-9000

Miami

Best Western Miami Airport Inn
1550 NW LeJeune Rd., 33126
(305) 871-2345, (800) 327-6087

Hilton & Marina Miami Airport
5101 Blue Lagoon Dr., 33126
(305) 262-1000, (800) 445-8667

Holiday Inn LeJeune Center
950 NW LeJeune Rd., 33126
(305) 446-9000, (800) 465-4329

Marriott Miami Airport
1201 NW LeJeune Rd., 33126
(305) 649-5000, (800) 228-9290

Mia Hotel
P.O. Box 592077, 33159-2077
(305) 871-4100, (800) 327-1276

Radisson Mart Plaza Hotel
711 NW 72nd Ave., 33126
(305) 361-3800, (800) 333-3333

Ramada Hotel Miami
 International Airport
3941 NW 22nd St., 33142
(305) 871-1700, (800) 272-6232

Regency Airport Hotel
1000 NW 42nd Ave., 33126
(305) 441-1600, (800) 367-1039

Sheraton River House
3900 NW 21 St., 33142
(305) 871-3800, (800) 325-3535

Sofitel Hotel Miami
5800 Blue Lagoon Dr., 33126
(305) 264-4888

GEORGIA

Atlanta

Colony Square Hotel
Peachtree & 14th St., 30361
(404) 892-6000, (800) 422-7895

Doubletree Hotel at Concourse
7 Concourse Pkwy., 30328
(404) 395-3900, (800) 528-0444

Embassy Suites Galleria
2815 Akers Mill Rd., 30339
(404) 984-9300, (800) 362-2779

Hilton & Towers Atlanta
255 Courtland St., NE, 30303
(404) 659-2000, (800) 445-8667

Holiday Inn Buckhead
3340 Peachtree Rd., NE, 30026
(404) 231-1234, (800) 241-7078

Hyatt Regency at Atlanta
265 Peachtree St., NE, 30303
(404) 577-1234, (800) 223-1234

Marriott Marquis Atlanta
265 Peachtree Ctr. Ave., NE,
 30303
(404) 521-0000, (800) 228-9290

Omni Hotel at CNN Center
100 CNN Ctr., 30335
(404) 659-0000, (800) 843-8664

Penta Hotel Atlanta
590 W. Peachtree St., NW, 30308
(404) 881-6000, (800) 633-0000

Radisson Hotel Atlanta
165 Courtland St., 30303
(404) 659-6500, (800) 333-3333

Ritz-Carlton Atlanta
181 Peachtree St., NE, 30303
(404) 659-0400, (800) 241-3333

Sheraton Century Center Hotel
2000 Century Blvd., NE,
 30345-3377
(404) 325-0000, (800) 325-3535

Stouffer Waverly Hotel
2450 Galleria Pkwy., 30339
(404) 953-4500, (800) 468-3571

Swiss Hotel Atlanta
3391 Peachtree Rd., NE, 30326
(404) 365-0065

Travelodge Hotel Atlanta
2061 N. Druid Hills Rd., NE,
 30329
(404) 321-4174, (800) 255-3050

Westin Lenox
3300 Lenox Rd., NE, 30326
(404) 262-3344, (800) 228-3000

Wyndham Hotel Midtown Atlanta
Peachtree & 10th Sts., NE, 30309
(404) 873-4800, (800) 822-4200

Hartsfield Int'l. Airport Area

College Park

Hyatt Atlanta Airport
1900 Sullivan Rd., 30337
(404) 991-1234, (800) 233-1234

Marriott Atlanta Airport
4711 Best Rd., 30337
(404) 766-7900, (800) 228-9290

Ramada Renaissance Hotel
4736 Best Rd., 30337
(404) 762-7676, (800) 228-9898

Sheraton Airport Hotel Atlanta
1325 Virginia Ave., 30344
(404) 768-6660, (800) 325-3535

Hapeville

Hilton Hotel Atlanta Airport
1031 Virginia Ave., 30354
(404) 767-9000, (800) 455-8667

HAWAII

Honolulu

Ala Moana Hotel
410 Atkinson Dr., 96814
(808) 955-4811, (800) 367-6025

Halekulani Hotel
2199 Kalia Rd., 96815
(808) 923-2311, (800) 367-2343

Hawaiian Regent
2552 Kalakaua Ave., 96815
(808) 922-6611, (800) 367-5121

Hilton Hawaiian Village
2005 Kalia Rd., 96815
(808) 949-4321, (800) 445-8667

Hyatt Regency Waikiki
2424 Kalakaua Ave., 96815
(808) 923-1234, (800) 923-1234

Ilikai
1777 Ala Moana Blvd., 96815
(808) 949-3811, (800) 255-3811

Outrigger Prince Kuhio Hotel
2500 Kuhio Ave., 96815
(808) 922-0811, (800) 733-7777

Outrigger Waikiki
2335 Kalakaua Ave., 96815
(808) 923-0711, (800) 367-5170

Pacific Beach Hotel
2490 Kalakaua Ave., 96815
(808) 922-1233, (800) 367-6060

Pagoda Hotel
1525 Rycroft St., 96814
(808) 941-6611, (800) 367-6060

Sheraton Princess Kaiulani
120 Kaiulani Ave., 96815
(808) 922-5811

Waikiki Beachcomber Hotel
2300 Kalakaua Ave., 96815
(808) 922-4646, (800) 622-4646

Waikiki Parc Hotel
2233 Helumoa Rd., 96815
(808) 921-7272, (800) 422-0450

ILLINOIS

Chicago

Allerton Hotel
701 N. Michigan Ave., 60611
(312) 440-1500, (800) 621-8311

Radisson Plaza Ambassador West
1300 N. State Pkwy., 60610
(312) 787-7900, (800) 333-3333

Barclay Chicago Hotel
166 E. Superior, 60611
(312) 787-6000, (800) 621-8004

Best Western Inn of Chicago
162 E. Ohio St., 60611
(312) 787-3100, (800) 848-2031

Bismarck Hotel
171 W. Randolph St., 60601
(312) 236-0123, (800) 643-1500

Blackstone Hotel
636 S. Michigan Blvd., 60605
(312) 427-4300, (800) 622-6330

Chicago Lake Shore Hotel
600 N. Lake Shore Dr., 60611
(312) 787-4700, (800) 343-8908

Congress Hotel of Chicago
520 S. Michigan Ave., 60605
(312) 427-3800

Days Inn Lake Shore Drive
644 N. Lake Shore Dr., 60611
(312) 943-9200, (800) 325-2525

Drake Hotel Chicago
140 E. Walton St., 60611
(312) 787-2200, (800) 445-8667

Essex Inn
800 S. Michigan Ave., 60605
(312) 939-2800, (800) 621-6909

Executive House Hotel
71 E. Wacker Dr., 60601
(312) 346-7100, (800) 621-4005

Fairmont Hotel
200 N. Columbus Dr., 60601
(312) 565-8000, (800) 527-4727

Four Seasons Chicago
120 E. Delaware Pl., 60611
(312) 280-8800, (800) 332-3442

Hilton & Towers Chicago
720 S. Michigan Ave., 60605
(312) 922-4400, (800) 445-8667

Holiday Inn Mart Plaza
350 N. Orleans St., 60654
(312) 836-5000, (800) 238-8000

Hyatt Park Chicago
800 N. Michigan Ave., 60611
(312) 280-2222, (800) 223-1234

Inter-Continental Hotel
505 N. Michigan Ave., 60611
(312) 944-4100, (800) 628-2468

Knickerbocker Chicago
163 Walton Pl., 60611
(312) 751-8100, (800) 621-8140

Lenox House
616 N. Rush St., 60611
(312) 337-1000, (800) 445-3669

Marriott Chicago Downtown
540 N. Michigan Ave., 60611
(312) 836-0100, (800) 228-9290

Mayfair Regent
181 E. Lake Shore Dr., 60611
(312) 787-8500, (800) 545-4000

McCormick Center Hotel
Lake Shore Dr., & 23rd St., 60616
(312) 791-1900, (800) 621-6909

Midland Hotel
172 W. Adams St., 60603
(312) 332-1200, (800) 621-2360

Morton Hotel
500 S. Dearborn St., 60605
(312) 663-3200, (800) 843-6678

Oxford House
225 N. Wabash Ave., 60601
(312) 346-6585, (800) 344-4111

Quality Inn Downtown Chicago
One Mid City Plaza, 60606
(312) 829-5000

Ritz-Carlton
160 E. Pearson St., 60611
(312) 266-1000, (800) 268-6282

Sheraton Plaza
160 E. Huron St., 60611
(312) 787-2900, (800) 325-3535

Westin Hotel Chicago
909 N. Michigan Ave., 60611
(312) 943-7200, (800) 228-3000

Whitehall Hotel
105 E. Delaware, 60611
(312) 944-6300, (800) 621-8295

O'Hare Int'l. Airport Area

Des Plaines

Holiday Inn Chicago Des Plaines
1450 E. Touhy, 60018
(708) 296-8866, (800) 465-4329

Elmhurst

Holiday Inn Elmhurst
624 N. York Rd., 60126
(708) 279-1100, (800) 465-4329

Itasca

Nordic Hills Resort & Conference
Center
Nordic Rd., 60143
(708) 773-2750, (800) 334-3417

Stouffer Hamilton Hotel
400 Park Blvd., 60143
(708) 773-4000, (800) 468-3571

Rosemont

Embassy Suites Chicago O'Hare
6501 N. Mannheim, 60018
(708) 699-6300, (800) 548-4193

Hilton O'Hare
P.O. Box 66414, 60666
(708) 686-8000, (800) 445-8667

Holiday Inn O'Hare Airport
5440 N. River Rd., 60018
(708) 671-6350, (800) 465-4329

Hyatt Regency O'Hare
9300 W. Bryn Mawr Ave., 60018
(708) 696-1234, (800) 233-1234

Marriott O'Hare
8535 W. Higgins Rd., 60631
(312) 693-4444, (800) 228-9290

Plaza Hotel O'Hare
5615 N. Cumberland Ave., 60631
(312) 693-5800

Radisson Suite Hotel
5500 N. River Rd., 60018
(708) 678-4000, (800) 333-3333

Ramada Hotel O'Hare
6600 N. Manheim Rd., 60018
(708) 827-5131, (800) 228-2828

Sheraton Int'l. at O'Hare
6810 N. Manheim Rd., 60018
(708) 297-1234, (800) 325-3535

Westin Hotel O'Hare
6100 River Rd., 60018
(708) 698-6000, (800) 228-3000

Schaumburg

Best Western
1725 E. Algonquin Rd., 60173
(708) 397-1500, (800) 631-1510

Embassy Suites Hotel
1939 N. Meacham, 60173
(708) 397-1313, (800) 654-8089

Hyatt Regency Woodfield
1800 E. Golf Rd., 60173
(708) 605-1234, (800) 228-9000

Marriott Hotel Schaumburg
50 N. Martingate Rd., 60173
(708) 240-0100, (800) 228-9290

Schiller Park

Howard Johnson O'Hare Int'l.
 Hotel & Conference Center
10249 W. Irving Rd., 60176
(708) 671-6000, (800) 323-1239

INDIANA

Indianapolis

Adam's Mark Hotel
2544 Executive Dr., 46241
(317) 248-2481, (800) 444-2326

Embassy Suites Hotel North
3912 Vincennes Rd., 46268
(317) 872-7700, (800) 362-2779

Hilton at the Airport
2500 S. High School Rd., 46241
(317) 244-3361, (800) 445-8667

Holiday Inn Airport
2501 S. High School Rd., 46241
(317) 244-6861, (800) 465-4329

Hyatt Regency Indianapolis
One S. Capitol Ave., 46204
(317) 632-1234, (800) 228-9000

Marriott Hotel Indianapolis
7202 E. 21st St., 46219
(317) 352-1231, (800) 228-9290

University Place Executive
 Conference Center & Hotel
850 W. Michigan Ave., 46202
(317) 269-9000, (800) 627-2700

LOUISIANA
New Orleans Int'l. Airport Area

Kenner

Hilton New Orleans Airport
901 Airline Hwy., 70063
(504) 469-5000, (800) 445-8667

Holiday Inn New Orleans Airport
2929 Williams Blvd., 70062
(504) 467-5611, (800) 465-4329

Sheraton Hotel New Orleans
 International Airport
2150 Veterans Blvd., 70062
(504) 467-3111, (800) 325-3535

Metairie

Landmark Motor Hotel & Towers
2601 Severn Ave., 70002
(504) 888-9500, (800) 277-7575

Sheraton New Orleans North
3838 N. Causeway Blvd., 70002
(504) 836-5253

New Orleans

Bourbon Orleans Hotel
717 Orleans St., 70116
(504) 523-2222, (800) 521-5338

Clarion Hotel New Orleans
1500 Canal St., 70112
(504) 522-4500, (800) 824-3359

Doubletree Hotel
300 Canal St., 70130
(504) 581-1300, (800) 528-0444

Fairmont Hotel
University Pl., 70140
(504) 529-7111, (800) 527-4727

Hilton & Towers Riverside
 New Orleans
Poydras at Mississippi River, 70140
(504) 561-0500, (800) 445-8667

Holiday Inn Crowne Plaza
333 Poydras St., 70130
(504) 525-9444, (800) 522-6963

Holiday Inn Downtown Superdome
330 Loyola Ave., 70112
(504) 581-1600, (800) 654-2000

Hyatt Regency New Orleans
500 Poydras Plaza, 70140-1012
(504) 561-1234, (800) 223-1234

Inter-Continental Hotel
444 Saint Charles Ave., 70130
(504) 525-5566

Le Pavillion
800 Poydras St., 70140
(504) 581-3111, (800) 535-9095

Marriott New Orleans Hotel
555 Canal St., 70140
(504) 581-1000, (800) 228-9290

Meridien New Orleans
614 Canal St., 70130
(504) 525-6500, (800) 543-4300

Monteleone Hotel
214 Royal St., 70140
(504) 523-3341, (800) 535-9595

Omni Royal Orleans Hotel
621 St. Louis St., 70140
(504) 529-5333, (800) 843-6664

Pontchartrain Hotel
2031 Saint Charles Ave., 70140
(504) 524-0581, (800) 777-6193

Radisson Suite Hotel New Orleans
315 Julia St., 70130
(504) 525-1993, (800) 333-3333

Sheraton New Orleans Hotel
500 Canal St., 70130
(504) 525-2500, (800) 325-3535

Sonesta Royal Hotel
300 Bourbon St., 70140
(504) 586-0300, (800) 343-7170

Westin Canal Place Hotel
100 Iberville St., 70130
(504) 566-7006

Windsor Court Hotel
300 Gravier St., 70130
(504) 523-6000, (800) 262-2662

MARYLAND

Baltimore

Days Inn Inner Harbor
100 Hopkins Pl., 21201
(301) 576-1000, (800) 325-2525

Holiday Inn Inner Harbor
301 W. Lombard St., 21201
(301) 685-3500, (800) 465-4329

Hyatt Regency Baltimore on the
 Inner Harbor
300 Light St., 21202
(301) 528-1234, (800) 228-9000

Marriott Baltimore Inner Harbor
Pratt & Eulaw Sts., 21201
(301) 962-0202, (800) 228-9290

Omni Inner Harbor Hotel
101 W. Fayette St., 21201
(301) 752-1100, (800) 228-2121

Radisson Plaza Lord Baltimore
 Hotel
20 W. Baltimore St., 21201
(301) 539-8400, (800) 333-3333

Sheraton Inner Harbor Hotel
300 S. Charles, 21201
(301) 962-8300, (800) 325-3535

Stouffer Harborplace Hotel
202 E. Pratt St., 21202
(301) 547-1200, (800) 468-3571

Tremont Plaza Hotel
222 St. Paul Pl., 21202
(301) 727-2222, (800) 638-6266

MASSACHUSETTS

Boston

Boston Harbor Hotel at Rowes
 Wharf
70 Rowes Wharf, 02110
(617) 439-7000, (800) 752-7077

Boston Park Plaza Hotel & Towers
50 Park Plaza, 02117
(617) 426-3323

Colonnade Hotel
120 Huntington Ave., 02116
(617) 424-7000

Copley Plaza Hotel
138 St. James Ave., 02116
(617) 267-5300

Fifty Seven Park Plaza Hotel
 Howard Johnson
200 Stuart St., 02116
(617) 482-1800, (800) 654-2000

Four Seasons Hotel Boston
200 Boylston St., 02116
(617) 338-4400

Guest Quarters Suites Hotel
400 Soldiers Field Rd., 02134
(617) 783-0090, (800) 424-2900

Hilton Back Bay
40 Dalton St., 02115
(617) 236-1100, (800) 874-0663

Holiday Inn Government Center
5 Blossom St., 02114
(617) 742-7630, (800) 465-4329

Lafayette Swissotel Boston
One Ave. de Lafayette, 02111
(617) 452-2600, (800) 621-9200

Lenox Hotel
710 Boylston St., 02116
(617) 536-5300, (800) 225-7676

Marriott Copley Place
110 Huntington Ave., 02116
(617) 236-5800, (800) 228-9290

Meridien Hotel Boston
250 Franklin St., 02110
(617) 451-1900, (800) 543-4300

Omni Parker House
60 School St., 02108-4198
(617) 227-6600, (800) 843-6664

Quality Inn Downtown Boston
275 Tremont St., 02116-5694
(617) 426-1400, (800) 228-5151

Ritz-Carlton Hotel
15 Arlington St., 02117
(617) 536-5700, (800) 241-3333

Sheraton Hotel & Towers Boston
39 Dalton St., 02199
(617) 236-2000, (800) 325-3535

Westin Hotel Copley Place
10 Huntington Ave., 02116
(617) 262-9600, (800) 228-3000

Cambridge

Charles Hotel at Harvard Square
One Bennett at Eliot St., 02138
(617) 864-1200, (800) 882-1818

Hyatt Regency Cambridge
575 Memorial Dr., 02139
(617) 492-1234, (800) 233-1234

Marriott Boston Cambridge Hotel
2 Cambridge Ctr., 02142
(617) 494-6600, (800) 228-9290

Sheraton Commander Hotel
16 Garden St., 02138
(617) 547-4800, (800) 325-3535

Sonesta Royal Hotel
5 Cambridge Pkwy., 02142
(617) 491-3600, (800) 343-7170

Logan Int'l. Airport

East Boston

Hilton Logan Airport
75 Service Rd., 02128
(617) 569-9300, (800) 445-8667

Ramada Hotel Logan Airport
225 McClellan Hwy., 02128
(617) 569-5250

MICHIGAN

Detroit

Omni International Hotel Detroit
333 E. Jefferson Ave., 48226
(313) 222-7700, (800) 843-6664

Radisson Pontchartrain Hotel
2 Washington Blvd., 48226
(313) 965-0200, (800) 333-3333

Westin Hotel
Renaissance Ctr., 48243
(313) 568-8000, (800) 228-3000

Detroit Int'l. Airport Area

Detroit

Hilton Airport Inn
31500 Wick Rd., 48174
(313) 292-3400

Ramada Inn Detroit Metro
 Airport
8270 Wickham Rd., 48174
(313) 729-6300, (800) 228-2828

MINNESOTA

Minneapolis Int'l. Airport Area

Bloomington

Days Inn Minneapolis-Saint Paul
 Airport
8401 Cedar Ave., S, 55425
(612) 854-8400, (800) 654-2000

Embassy Suites Airport
7901 34th Ave., 55425
(612) 854-1000, (800) 362-2779

Embassy Suites Bloomington
2800 W. 80th St., 55431
(612) 884-4811, (800) 362-2779

Hilton Minneapolis-Saint Paul
 Airport
3800 E. 80th St., 55425
(612) 854-2100, (800) 637-7453

Holiday Inn International Airport
3 Appletree Sq., 55425
(612) 854-9000, (800) 465-4329

Marriott Bloomington
2020 E. 79th St., 55425
(612) 854-7441, (800) 228-9290

Radisson Hotel South & Plaza
 Tower
7800 Normandale Blvd., 55435
(612) 835-7800, (800) 333-3333

Registry Hotel
7901 24th Ave., 55425-0099
(612) 854-2244, (800) 247-9810

Sheraton Airport Hotel
2525 E. 78th St., 55425
(612) 854-1771, (800) 325-3535

Sofitel Hotel
5601 W. 78th St., 55439
(612) 835-1900, (800) 328-6303

Minneapolis

Embassy Suites Hotel
425 S. 7th St., 55415
(612) 333-3111, (800) 362-2779

Hilton Inn Minneapolis
1330 Industrial Blvd., 55413
(612) 331-1900, (800) 445-8667

Holiday Inn Minneapolis
 Downtown
1313 Nicollet Mall, 55403
(612) 332-0371

Hyatt Regency Minneapolis
1300 Nicollet Mall, 55403
(612) 370-1234, (800) 228-9000

Luxeford Suites Hotel
1101 La Salle Ave., 55403
(612) 332-6800, (800) 662-3232

Marquette
710 Marquette Ave., 55402
(612) 332-2351, (800) 328-4782

Marriott City Center Minneapolis
30 S. 7th St., 55402
(612) 349-4000, (800) 228-9290

Normandy Inn Minneapolis
405 S. 8th St., 55404
(612) 370-1400, (800) 372-3131

Radisson Hotel Metrodome
615 Washington Ave., 55414
(612) 379-8888, (800) 333-3333

Regency Plaza Hotel
41 N. 10th St., 55403
(612) 339-9311, (800) 523-4200

NEW JERSEY
Newark Int'l. Airport Area

East Rutherford

Sheraton Meadowlands Hotel
Sheraton Plaza Dr.
2 Meadowland Plaza, 07073
(201) 896-0500, (800) 325-3535

Elizabeth

Holiday Inn Jetport
1000 Spring St., 07201
(201) 355-1700, (800) 44PRIME

Sheraton Newark Airport
901 Spring St., 07201
(908) 527-1600, (800) 325-3535

Vista International at Newark
 Airport
Newark Airport, 07201-2114
(201) 351-3900, (800) 678-4782

Newark

Holiday Inn North
160 Holiday Plaza, 07114
(201) 589-1000, (800) 238-8000

Marriott Newark Airport
Newark Int'l. Airport, 07114
(201) 623-0006, (800) 228-9290

Hasbrouck Heights

Sheraton Hasbrouck Heights
 Hotel & Towers
650 Terrace Ave., 07604
(201) 288-6100, (800) 832-6663

Morristown

Headquarters Plaza Hotel
3 Headquarters Plaza, 07960
(201) 898-9100, (800) 225-1942

Royce Hotel Governor Morris
2 Whippany Rd., 07960
(201) 539-7300, (800) 221-0241

Parsippany

Hilton Parsippany
One Hilton Ct., 07054
(201) 267-7373, (800) 445-8667

Sheraton Tara Hotel
199 Smith Rd., 07054
(201) 515-2000, (800) 525-3535

Princeton

Scanticon Princeton Conference
  Center & Hotel
100 College Rd. E., 08540
(609) 452-7800, (800) 222-1131

NEW YORK
JFK Int'l. Airport Area
Queens

Hilton JFK Airport
138-10 135 Ave., 11436
(718) 322-8700

Holiday Inn JFK Airport
144-02 135th Ave., 11436
(718) 659-0200

La Guardia Airport Area
Queens

Days Hotel La Guardia
100-15 Ditmars Blvd., 11369
(718) 898-1225

Marriott Hotel La Guardia
102-05 Ditmars Blvd., 11369
(718) 565-8900, (800) 229-9290

Royce Hotel La Guardia Airport
90-10 Grand Central Pkwy., 11396
(718) 446-4800, (800) 237-6923

New York City

Beekman Tower Hotel
3 Mitchell Pl., 10017
(212) 335-7300, (800) 637-8483

Days Inn New York
440 W. 57th St., 10019
(212) 581-8100

Doral Inn
541 Lexington Ave., 10022
(212) 755-1200, (800) 223-5823

Doral Park Avenue Hotel
70 Park Ave., 10016
(212) 687-7050, (800) 847-4135

Drake Swissotel
440 Park Ave., 10022
(212) 421-0900, (800) 372-5369

Essex House
160 Central Park S., 10019
(212) 247-0300, (800) 228-9290

Golden Tulip Barbizon Hotel
140 E. 63rd St., 10021
(212) 838-5700, (800) 223-1020

Grand Bay Hotel at Equitable
  Center
152 W. 51st St., 10019
(212) 765-1900, (800) 237-0990

Grand Hyatt New York
Park Ave. at Grand Central, 10017
(212) 883-1234, (800) 233-1234

Halloran House Hotel
525 Lexington Ave., 10017
(212) 755-4000, (800) 223-0939

Helmsley Hotel New York
212 E. 42nd St., 10017
(212) 490-8900, (800) 221-4982

Hilton & Towers New York at
  Rockefeller Center
1335 Ave. of the Americas, 10019
(212) 586-7000, (800) 445-8667

Inter-Continental New York
111 E. 48th St., 10017-1297
(212) 755-5900, (800) 332-4262

Loew's Summit Hotel
569 Lexington Ave., 10022
(212) 752-7000, (800) 223-0888

Macklowe Hotel & Conference Ctr.
141 W. 44th St., 10036
(212) 869-5800, (800) 622-5569

Marriott Marquis New York
1535 Broadway, 10036-4017
(212) 398-1900, (800) 228-9290

Mayfair Regent
610 Park Ave., 10021-7086
(212) 288-0800, (800) 223-0542

Meridien Parker Hotel
118 W. 57th St., 10019
(212) 245-5000, (800) 543-4300

Milford Plaza Hotel
270 W. 45th St., 10036
(212) 869-3600, (800) 221-2690

Novotel New York
225 W. 52nd St., 10019-5804
(212) 315-0100, (800) 221-3185

Omni Berkshire Place
21 E. 52nd St., 10022
(212) 753-5800, (800) 843-6664

Peninsula New York
700 5th Ave., 10019
(212) 247-2200

Penta Hotel New York
7th Ave. & 33rd St., 10001
(212) 736-5000, (800) 223-8585

Pierre Hotel
2 E. 61st St., 10021-8402
(212) 838-8000, (800) 268-6282

Plaza
5th Ave. & 59th St., 10019
(212) 759-3000, (800) 228-3000

Regency Hotel
540 Park Ave., 10021
(212) 759-4100, (800) 223-0888

Rihga Royal Concordia
151 W. 54th St., 10019
(212) 307-5000, (800) 432-7272

Ritz-Carlton Hotel
112 Central Park S., 10019
(212) 757-1900, (800) 241-3333

Roosevelt Hotel
45th St. & Madison Ave., 10017
(212) 661-9600, (800) 223-1870

St. Moritz on Central Park
50 Central Pk. S., 10019
(212) 755-5800, (800) 221-4774

Sheraton St. Regis Hotel
2 E. 55th St., 10022
(212) 753-4500

Sheraton Center Hotel & Towers
811 7th Ave., 10019
(212) 581-1000, (800) 223-6550

Sheraton City Squire
790 7th Ave., 10019
(212) 581-3300, (800) 325-3535

United Nations Plaza Hotel
One United Nations Plaza, 10017
(212) 355-3400

Vista International Hotel
3 World Trade Ctr., 10048
(212) 938-9100, (800) 258-2505

Waldorf Astoria
301 Park Ave., 10022
(212) 355-3000, (800) 445-8667

Warwick Hotel
65 W. 54th St., 10019
(212) 247-2700, (800) 223-4099

Westbury Hotel
15 E. 69th St., 10021
(212) 535-2000, (800) 321-1569

OHIO

Cincinnati

Carrousel Inn
8001 Reading Rd., 45237
(513) 821-5110, (800) 543-4970

Clarion Hotel Cincinnati
141 W. 6th St., 45202
(513) 352-2100, (800) 352-2100

Harley Hotel of Cincinnati
8020 Montgomery Rd., 45236
(513) 793-4300, (800) 321-2323

Hilton Terrace
15 W. 6th St., 45202
(513) 381-4000, (800) 445-8667

Holiday Inn Queensgate
800 W. 8th St., 45203
(513) 241-8660, (800) 465-4339

Howard Johnson Plaza Suite
11440 Chester Rd., 45246
(513) 771-3400, (800) 654-2000

Hyatt Regency Cincinnati
151 W. 5th St., 45202
(513) 579-1234, (800) 233-1234

Marriott Cincinnati
11320 Chester Rd., 45246
(513) 772-1720, (800) 228-9290

Omni Netherland Plaza
35 W. 5th St., 45202
(513) 421-9100, (800) 843-6664

Ramada Hotel Northeast
5901 Pfeiffer Rd., 45242
(513) 793-4500, (800) 228-2828

Westin Cincinnati
Fountain Sq., 45202
(513) 621-7700, (800) 228-3000

Columbus

Embassy Suites Hotel
2700 Corporate Exchange Dr.,
 43231
(614) 840-8600, (800) 362-2779

Hilton East
4560 Hilton Corp. Dr., 43232
(614) 863-1380

Holiday Inn City Center
175 E. Town St., 43215
(614) 221-3281, (800) 465-4329

Radisson Hotel Columbus North
4900 Sinclair Rd., 43229
(614) 863-0300, (800) 333-3333

Ramada Inn North
1213 E. Granville Rd., 43229
(614) 885-4084, (800) 272-6232

Ramada University Hotel &
 Conference Center
3110 Olentangy River Rd., 43202
(614) 267-7461, (800) 282-3626

Sheraton Inn Columbus
2124 S. Hamilton Rd., 43232
(614) 861-7220, (800) 866-9067

OREGON

Portland

Benson Hotel
SW Broadway at Oak, 97205
(503) 228-2000, (800) 426-0670

Heathman Hotel
SW Broadway at Salmon, 97205
(503) 241-4100, (800) 551-0011

Hilton Portland
921 SW 6th Ave., 97204
(503) 226-1611

Holiday Inn Portland Airport
 Hotel & Trade Center
8439 NE Columbia Blvd., 97220
(503) 256-5000, (800) 465-4329

Marriott Hotel Portland
1401 SW Front Ave., 97201
(503) 226-7600, (800) 228-9290

Red Lion Inn Jantzen Beach
909 N. Hayden Island Dr., 97217
(503) 283-4466, (800) 547-8010

Sheraton Portland Airport Hotel
8235 NE Airport Way, 97220
(503) 281-2500, (800) 325-3535

Travelodge Hotel Portland
1441 NE 2nd Ave., 97232
(503) 233-2401, (800) 255-3050

PENNSYLVANIA

Philadelphia

Adam's Mark Hotel Philadelphia
City Ave. & Monument Rd.,
 19131
(215) 581-5000, (800) 444-2326

Barclay Hotel
237 S. 18th St., 19103
(215) 545-0300, (800) 421-6662

Four Seasons Hotel
One Logan Sq., 19103
(215) 963-1500

Hershey Philadelphia Hotel
Broad & Locust Sts., 19107
(215) 893-1600

Holiday Inn Center City
1800 Market St., 19103
(215) 561-7500, (800) 465-4329

Latham Hotel
135 S. 17th St., 19103
(215) 563-7474, (800) 528-4261

Penn Tower Hotel
34th St. & Civic Center Blvd.,
  19104-4385
(215) 387-8333

Radisson Suite Hotel
18th St. & the Pkwy., 19103
(215) 963-2222, (800) 223-5672

Sheraton Society Hill
One Dock St., 19106
(215) 238-2000, (800) 325-3535

Sheraton University City
36th & Chestnut Sts., 19104
(215) 387-8000, (800) 325-3535

Temple University Conference
  Center Sugarloaf
9230 Germantown Ave., 19118
(215) 242-9100

Wyndham Franklin Plaza
2 Franklin Plaza, 19103
(215) 448-2000, (800) 822-4200

Philadelphia Int'l. Airport Area

Philadelphia

Guest Quarters Suite Hotel at
  Philadelphia Int'l. Airport
4101 Island Ave., 19153
(215) 365-6600, (800) 424-2900

Hilton Inn Philadelphia Airport
10th St. & Packer Ave., 19148
(215) 755-9500, (800) 445-8667

Marriott Philadelphia Airport
4509 Island Ave., 19153
(215) 356-4150, (800) 228-9290

TENNESSEE
Nashville

Doubletree Hotel
2 Commerce Pl. 37219
(615) 244-8200, (800) 528-0444

Executive Plaza Inn
823 Murfreesboro Rd., 37217
(615) 367-1234, (800) 251-5964

Hermitage Hotel
231 6th Ave., N, 37219
(615) 244-3121, (800) 251-1908

Holiday Inn Briley Parkway
2200 Elm Hill Pike, 37214
(615) 883-9770, (800) 465-4329

Howard Johnson North
2401 Brick Church Pike, 37207
(615) 226-4600, (800) 654-2000

Hyatt Regency
7th & Union Sts., 37219
(615) 259-1234, (800) 228-9000

Loew's Vanderbilt Plaza Hotel
2100 W. End Ave., 37203
(615) 320-1700

Marriott Nashville Hotel
One Marriott Dr., 37210
(615) 889-9300

Maxwell House Hotel
2025 Metrocenter Blvd., 37228
(615) 259-4343, (800) 252-7466

Opryland Hotel
2800 Opryland Dr., 37214
(615) 889-1000

Park Suites Hotel
10 Century Blvd., 37214
(615) 871-0033, (800) 432-7272

Sheraton Music City
777 McGavock Pike, 37214
(615) 885-2200, (800) 325-3535

Stouffer Nashville Hotel
611 Commerce St., 37203-3707
(615) 255-8400, (800) 468-3571

TEXAS

Dallas

Adolphus Hotel
1321 Commerce, 75202
(241) 742-8200, (800) 331-4812

Bristol Suites
7800 Alpha Rd., 75240
(214) 233-7600, (800) 922-9222

Crescent Court Hotel
400 Crescent Ct., 75201
(214) 871-3200, (800) 654-6541

Doubletree Hotel
5410 LBJ Frwy., 75240
(214) 934-8400, (800) 528-0444

Fairmont Hotel
1717 N. Akard St., 75201
(214) 720-2020, (800) 527-4727

Harvey Hotel Dallas
7815 LBJ Frwy., 75240
(214) 960-7000, (800) 922-9222

Hilton Dallas Parkway
4801 LBJ Frwy., 75244
(214) 661-3600, (800) 356-3924

Holiday Inn Crowne Plaza
4099 Valley View Ln., 75244
(214) 385-9000, (800) 465-4329

Hyatt
300 Reunion Blvd., 75207
(214) 651-1234, (800) 228-9000

Loews Anatole Hotel
2201 Stemmons Frwy., 75207
(214) 748-1200

Mansion on Turtle Creek
2821 Turtle Creek Blvd., 75219
(214) 559-2100, (800) 527-5432

Marriott Hotel Dallas Quorum
14901 Dallas Pkwy., 75240
(214) 661-2800, (800) 228-9290

Plaza of the Americas Hotel
650 N. Pearl Blvd., 75201
(214) 979-9000, (800) 225-5843

Sheraton Park Central Hotel
12720 Merit Dr., 75251
(214) 385-3000, (800) 325-3535

Stouffer Hotel Dallas Market Ctr.
2222 Stemmons Frwy., 75207
(214) 631-2222, (800) 468-3571

Summit Hotel
2645 LBJ Frwy., 75234
(214) 243-3363

Westin Hotel Galleria
13340 Dallas Pkwy., 75240
(214) 934-9494, (800) 228-3000

Dallas/Fort Worth Int'l. Airport Area

Arlington

Hilton Arlington
2401 E. Lamar Blvd., 76006
(817) 640-3322, (800) 445-8667

Radisson Suite Hotel
700 Ave. H E., 76011
(817) 640-0440, (800) 333-3332

Sheraton Centerpark Hotel
 Arlington
1500 Stadium Dr. E., 76011
(817) 261-8200, (800) 442-7275

Grapevine

Hilton DFW International
 Executive Conference Center
1800 Highway 26, 76051
(817) 481-8444, (800) 645-1018

Hyatt Regency DFW Airport
P.O. Box 619014, Int'l. Pkwy.,
 75261
(214) 453-1234, (800) 223-1234

Irving

Airport Inn DFW
120 W. Airport Frwy., 75062
(214) 579-8911, (800) 255-3571

Crown Sterling Suites
4650 W. Airport Frwy., 75062
(214) 790-0093

Four Seasons Hotel & Resort
4150 N. MacArthur Blvd., 75038
(214) 717-0700, (800) 332-3442

Harvey Hotel DFW Airport
4545 W. John Carpenter Frwy.,
 75063
(214) 929-4500, (800) 922-9222

Holiday Inn DFW Airport North
4441 Hwy. 114 & Esters Blvd.,
 75063
(214) 929-8181, (800) 465-4329

Marriott Hotel DFW Airport
8440 Freeport Pkwy., 75063
(214) 929-8800, (800) 228-9290

Sheraton Grand Hotel at DFW
 International Airport
Hwy. 114 & Esters Blvd., 75063
(214) 929-8400, (800) 325-3535

Love Field Airport Area

Dallas

Clarion Hotel
1241 W. Mockingbird Ln., 75247
(214) 630-7000, (800) 442-7547

Embassy Suites Hotel Dallas
Love Field
3880 W. Northwest Hwy., 75220
(214) 357-4500, (800) 362-2779

Hilton Inn Dallas
5600 N. Central Expy., 75206
(214) 827-4100

Ramada Hotel Love Field
3232 W. Mockingbird, 75235
(214) 357-5601, (800) 228-2828

Houston

Adam's Mark Hotel
2900 Briarpark Dr., 77042
(713) 978-7400, (800) 444-2326

Days Inn Downtown
801 Calhoun St., 77002
(713) 659-2222, (800) 465-4329

Doubletree Hotel
2001 Post Oak Blvd., 77056
(713) 961-9300, (800) 528-0444

Embassy Suites Southwest
9090 SW Frwy., 77074
(713) 995-0123, (800) 553-3417

Four Seasons Hotel Houston Center
1300 Lamar St., 77010
(713) 650-1300, (800) 332-3442

Four Seasons Inn on the Park
4 Riverway, 77056
(713) 871-8181, (800) 342-3442

Hilton & Towers Westchase
9999 Westheimer, 77042
(713) 974-1000

Holiday Inn Crowne Plaza
 Galleria Area
2222 W. Loop S., 77027
(713) 961-7272, (800) 327-6213

Houstonian Hotel &
 Conference Ctr.
111 N. Post Oak Ln., 77024
(713) 680-2626, (800) 456-6338

Hyatt Regency
1200 Louisiana, 77002
(713) 654-1234, (800) 233-1234

Luxeford Suites Hotel
1400 Old Spanish Trail, 77054-1913
(713) 796-1000, (800) 336-7517

Marriott Brookhollow Houston
3000 N. Loop W. 77092
(713) 668-0100, (800) 228-9290

Marriott Hotel by the Galleria
1750 W. Loop S., 77027
(713) 960-0111, (800) 228-9290

Ramada Inn Central
4225 North Frwy., 77022
(713) 695-6011, (800) 228-2828

Ramada Kings Inn Hotel &
 Conference Ctr.
1301 NASA Rd. 1, 77058
(713) 488-0220, (800) 255-7345

Ritz-Carlton Houston
1919 Briar Oaks Ln., 77027
(713) 840-7600, (800) 241-3333

Sheraton Astrodome Hotel
8686 Kirby Dr., 77054
(713) 748-3221, (800) 552-0942

Stouffer Greenway Plaza Hotel
6 Greenway Plaza E., 77046
(713) 629-1200, (800) 468-3571

Town & Country Inn
10655 Katy Frwy., 77024-2284
(713) 467-6411

Warwick Hotel
5701 Main St., 77225
(713) 526-1991, (800) 822-4200

Westin Galleria & Westin Oaks
5060 W. Alabama, 77056
(713) 960-8100, (800) 228-3000

Wyndham Hotel Medical Center
6633 Travis St., 77030
(713) 524-6633, (800) 822-4200

Houston Int'l. Airport Area

Doubletree Hotel Houston
15747 JFK Blvd., 77032
(713) 442-8000, (800) 528-0444

Hilton Inn Airport
500 N. Belt Drive E., 77060
(713) 931-0101, (800) 445-8667

Marriott Greenspoint
255 N. Sam Houston Pkwy. E.,
 77060
(713) 875-4000, (800) 228-9290

Sheraton Crown Hotel &
 Conference Center
15700 JFK Blvd., 77032
(713) 442-5100, (800) 325-3535

Sofitel Hotel
425 N. Sam Houston Pkwy. E.,
 77060
(713) 445-9000, (800) 231-4612

Wyndham Greenspoint
12400 Greenspoint Dr., 77060
(713) 875-2222, (800) 822-4200

WASHINGTON

Seattle

Four Seasons Olympic Hotel
411 University St., 98101
(206) 621-1700, (800) 223-8772

Hilton Seattle
P.O. Box 1927, 98111
(206) 624-0500, (800) 426-0535

Holiday Inn Crowne Plaza
6th & Seneca, 98101
(206) 464-1980

Sheraton Hotel & Towers Seattle
1400 6th Ave., 98101
(206) 621-9000, (800) 325-3535

Stouffer Madison Hotel
515 Madison St., 98104
(206) 583-0300, (800) 468-3571

Warwick Hotel
401 Lenora, 98121
(206) 443-4300, (800) 426-9280

Westin Hotel Seattle
1900 5th Ave., 98101
(206) 728-1000, (800) 228-3000

Sea-Tac Int'l. Airport Area

Seattle

Doubletree Inn
205 Strander Blvd., 98188
(206) 246-8220, (800) 528-0444

Radisson Hotel Seattle Airport
17001 Pacific Hwy. S., 98188
(206) 244-6000, (800) 333-3333

Marriott Seattle Sea-Tac Airport
3201 S. 176th St., 98188
(206) 241-2000, (800) 228-9290

Quality Inn at Sea-Tac
300 S. 176th St., 98188
(206) 246-9110, (800) 228-5151

Red Lion Sea-Tac
18740 Pacific Hwy. S., 98188
(206) 433-1881, (800) 547-8010

WISCONSIN
Milwaukee

Grand Hotel
4747 S. Howell Ave., 53207
(414) 481-8000, (800) 558-3862

Holiday Inn Milwaukee City Center
611 W. Wisconsin Ave., 53203
(414) 273-2950, (800) 465-4329

Hyatt Regency Milwaukee
333 W. Kilbourn Ave., 53203
(414) 276-1234, (800) 223-1234

Marc Plaza Hotel
509 W. Wisconsin Ave., 53203
(414) 271-7250, (800) 558-7708

Pfister Hotel
424 E. Wisconsin Ave., 53202
(414) 273-8222, (800) 558-8222

Ramada Inn Downtown
633 W. Michigan St., 53203
(414) 272-8410, (800) 228-2828

Wyndham Milwaukee Center
139 E. Kilbourn Ave., 53202
(414) 276-8686, (800) 822-4200

Speakers Bureaus

Speakers bureaus book seminar leaders who can provide informative programs to their clients. These organizations can be contacted to find out if your topic is appropriate for them and how to become one of the speakers they book.

ARIZONA

Republic Speakers Bureau
8890 S. Grandview
Tempe, AZ 85284
Bill Blades
(602) 470-0699

ARKANSAS

Access Speakers Bureau, Inc.
4 Shackleford Plaza, Suite 201
P.O. Box 22668
Little Rock, AR 72221-2668
Barbara Vogel
Janice Peters
(501) 225-8667, 225-8375 (Fax)

CALIFORNIA

America's Top Performers
6475 E. Pacific Coast Hwy., Suite 403
Long Beach, CA 90803-4296
Diane Titterington
(213) 598-8470

Barnes Management Co.
15510 Rockfield, Suite C
Irvine, CA 92718
Virginia Barnes
(714) 768-2943

Celebrity Speakers & Entertainment
6345 Balboa, #230
Encino, CA 91316
Bruce Merrin
(818) 887-5066, 996-3637 (Fax)

Convention Connection
18133 Coastline Dr., #3
Malibu, CA 90265
Suzanne Hill
(213) 459-0159

Fisher Group/Jostens Speakers Bureau
P.O. Box 503
Danville, CA 94526
Micky Fisher
(415) 831-1229, 820-6371 (Fax)

Golden Gate Speakers Bureau Int'l.
P.O. Box 1336
Mill Valley, CA 94942-0508
William Shear
(415) 383-5426, 383-4829 (Fax)

Keynote Speakers Inc.
210 California Ave., Suite C
Palo Alto, CA 92406
Barbara Foster
(415) 325-8711

Look Who's Talking, Selected
  Speakers
P.O. Box 7665
Newport Beach, CA 92658-7665
Lisa Williams
(714) 759-9304

The Podium Speakers Bureau
P.O. Box 865
Spring Valley, CA 91976-0865
Sandra Schrift
(619) 469-1383

10K Gold Productions
7760 Winding Way, Suite 722
Fair Oaks, CA 95628
Patricia Mills
(916) 965-5738, 965-9317 (Fax)

Walters' International Speakers
  Bureau
P.O. Box 1120
Glendora, CA 91740
Lillet Walters
(818) 335-8069 or 1855,
  355-6127 (Fax)

World Class Speakers Bureau
10747 Wilshire Blvd., Suite 807
Los Angeles, CA 90024-4432
Joe Kessler
(213) 824-3333, 470-2111 (Fax)

CONNECTICUT

Dammah Production
P.O. Box 254
New London, CT 06320
Muwakil Al-uqdah
(203) 443-4278

Goodman Speakers Bureau Inc.
56 Arbor St.
Hartford, CT 06106
Diane Goodman
(203) 233-0460, 236-6674 (Fax)

DISTRICT OF COLUMBIA

Capital Speakers Inc.
655, National Press Bldg.
Washington, DC 20045
Phyllis McKenzie
(202) 393-0772, 393-1418 (Fax)

Cosby Bureau Int'l., Inc.
2162 Wisconsin Ave., NW
Washington, DC 20007
Joseph Cosby
(202) 833-2344, 833-7757 (Fax)

Jamestown Foundation
1528 18th St., NW
Washington, DC 20036
Leigh S. LaMora
(202) 483-8888, 483-8337 (Fax)

Jack Morton Productions Speakers
  Bureau
1850 K St., NW, #370
Washington, DC 20008
Theresa Brown
(202) 296-1860

National Speaker's Forum
1629 K Street, NW, Suite 500
Washington, DC 20006
(202) 293-5508

FLORIDA

Florida Speakers Bureau
75 Meadow Ln.
Wesley Chapel, FL 33544
Rhonda J. Nelson
(813) 973-0705 or 0639

Pageantry, Inc.
7430 SW 59th St.
Miami, FL 33143-1702
V. Neil Wyrick
(305) 665-8686

Speakers Connection
3530 Pine Valley Dr.
Sarasota, FL 34239
Gerry Tausch
(813) 924-3251, 371-4183 (Fax)

GEORGIA

Jordan Int'l. Enterprises
Lenox Square Box 18737
Atlanta, GA 30326-0737
(404) 261-1122

ILLINOIS

Betty Brown Promotions
107 E. Highland Ave.
Elgin, IL 60120
Betty Brown
(312) 888-0737, 695-9684 (Fax)

Joan B. Hall & Associates
2904 Scottlynne Dr.
Park Ridge, IL 60068
Joan Hall
(708) 825-2501, 291-0115 (Fax)

National Speakers Bureau
222 Wisconsin Ave.
Lake Forest, IL 60045
John Palmer
(800) 323-9442, (708) 295-1122,
 295-5292 (Fax)

On the Scene
54 W. Illinois, Suite 1250
Chicago, IL 60610-4305
Eleanor Woods
(312) 661-1440, 661-1182 (Fax)

INDIANA

Agricultural Speakers Network
4040 Vincennes Cir., #500
Indianapolis, IN 46268-3022
Rich Tiller
(317) 875-0139, 875-0507 (Fax)

Charisma Productions
116 West Osage, P.O. Box 683
Greenfield, IN 46140
Judith G. Shepherd
(317) 894-8484, 462-0909 (Fax)

IOWA

Excalibur Int'l. Speakers Bureau
1520 NW 107th St.
Des Moines, IA 50322
Rod Patterson
(516) 226-0783

Heartland Speakers & Seminars
P.O. Box 556
Council Bluffs, IA 51502
Donna Zeph Telpner
(712) 322-7763

KANSAS

Five Star Speakers, Trainers &
 Consultants
8645 College Blvd., Suite 120
Overland Park, KS 66210
Nancy Lauterbach
(913) 469-0550, 648-7502 (Fax)

North American Speakers
 Bureau
6701 W. 64th St. #100
Overland Park, KS 66202
Brad Plumb
(913) 677-1444, 677-1805 (Fax)

MARYLAND

Speaker's Guild Inc.
11607 Stonewood Ln.
Rockville, MD 20852
(301) 468-7778

Wedgewood Productions, Inc.
1015 Generals Hwy.
P.O. Box 440
Crownsville, MD 21032
James Arth
(301) 621-9600

MASSACHUSETTS

American Program Bureau
9 Galen St.
Watertown, MA 02172
Perry Steinberg
(800) 225-4575, (617) 926-0600,
 926-4526 (Fax)

American Speaker's Bureau, Inc.
850 Boyston St.
Chestnut Hill, MA 02167
(800) 225-4575

Speakers Guild
78 Old King's Hwy.
Sandwich, MA 02563
Ed Larkin
(508) 888-6702, 888-6771 (Fax)

MINNESOTA

Key Seminars Speakers Bureau
5912 Newton Ave. S., Suite 5000
Minneapolis, MN 55419
Michael Podolinsky
(612) 920-2440, 924-9205 (Fax)

MISSOURI

Direct Communication Bureau
1150 Olive Street Rd., Suite 182
Creve Coeur, MO 63017
(314) 567-9277

NEBRASKA

Action Speakers Bureau
12136 Allan Dr.
P.O. Box 37408
Omaha, NE 68137
Pat Steinaur (402) 895-4402
Dick Becklus (402) 895-8656

NEW YORK

Greater Talent Network, Inc.
150 Fifth Ave., Suite 1002
New York, NY 10011
(212) 645-4200

Program Corporation of America
599 W. Hartsdale Ave.
White Plains, NY 10607
Alan Walker
(800) 431-2047, (914) 428-5840,
 428-5356 (Fax)

Royce Carlton, Inc.
866 United Nations Plaza
New York, NY 10017
Carlton S. Sedgeley
(212) 355-7700

NEW JERSEY

Eagles Talent Associates, Inc.
P.O. Box 859
Short Hills, NJ 07078-0859
Esther Eagles
(201) 376-3737, 376-3660 (Fax)

The Leigh Bureau
49-51 State Rd.
Princeton, NJ 08540
(609) 921-6141

OHIO

IMG Bureau
One Erieview Plaza, Suite 1300
Cleveland, OH 44114
Bill Colvin
(216) 522-1200, 522-1145 (Fax)

Speaker's Unlimited
P.O. Box 27225
Columbus, OH 43227
(614) 864-5703

PENNSYLVANIA

Dr. Dooley Speakers Bureau
2946 Sandyford Ave.
Philadelphia, PA 19152
Richard J. Dooley
(215) 624-0955

Showcase Associates, Inc.
911 Cypress Ave.
Philadelphia, PA 19117
(215) 844-6205

Speakers Services
765 Ormond Ave.
Drexel Hill, PA 19026
William D. Thompson
(215) 626-4600

TENNESSEE

Celebrity Speaker's Bureau
P.O. Box 40143
Nashville, TN 37204
(615) 748-9954

Happy Talk Speaking Services
1003 Heritage Village
Madison, TN 37115
Peggy & George Goldtrap
(615) 865-2041, 381-7415 (Fax)

Resource Group of America Inc.
131 Donelson Pike
P.O. Box 140430
Nashville, TN 37214
Charles W. Whitnel, Jr.
(615) 889-4676, 889-1878 (Fax)

TEXAS

American Speakers Association
P.O. Box 6925
Houston, TX 77265
Carol Adkins
(713) 665-1736

The Dallas Speaker's Bureau
P.O. Box 140071
Dallas, TX 75214
(214) 869-0043

Southwest Speakers Bureau, Inc.
14901 Quorum Dr., #210
Dallas, TX 75240
Mary Shiroma
Beverly Shulman
(214) 458-1627, 458-0386 (Fax)

VIRGINIA

Keppler Association, Inc.
4350 N. Fairfax Dr., Suite 700
Arlington, VA 22203
Jim Keppler
(703) 518-4000, 516-4819 (Fax)

Washington Speakers Bureau
310 S. Henry St.
Old Town Alexandria, VA 22314
Bernie Swain
(703) 684-0555, 684-9378 (Fax)

WASHINGTON

Barnard Speakers Bureau
2366 Eastlake Ave. E., #212
Seattle, WA 98102
Carol Barnard
(206) 325-0371, 324-3705 (Fax)

C.B.C.S. Ltd.
P.O. Box 4202
Seattle, WA 98104
Charlotte Benson
(206) 874-5501, 932-6816 (Fax)

WISCONSIN

Associated Speakers, Inc.
12700 W. Bluemound Rd.
Elm Grove, WI 53122
Jack Pachuta
(414) 782-9020, 782-4759 (Fax)

AUSTRALIA

International Celebrity
Management Pty. Ltd.
187 Greville St.
Prahran, Victoria 3181
Karen Williams
61-3-529-3711, 529-4573 (Fax)

Harry M. Miller Speakers Bureau
P.O. Box 313, Kings Cross
Sydney NSW 2011
Harry M. Miller
61-2-357-3077, 356-2880 (Fax)

Ovations
423 Harris St.
Ultimo, NSW 2007
Leanne Harrison
61-2-692-8977, 552-2089 (Fax)

Joan Saxton Speakers Agency
6 Ellingworth Parade
Box Hill, Victoria 3128
Joan Saxton
61-3-899-5724,
  899-5730 (Fax)

CANADA

Can Speak Presentations, Ltd.
1260 Hornby St., #104
Vancouver, B.C. V6Z 1W2
Pauline Price
(604) 687-6868, 683-9114 (Fax)

Contemporary Communications
  Ltd.
2605 Alma St.
Vancouver, B.C. V6R 3S1
Wendy Martynluk
(604) 224-2384, 224-8906 (Fax)

Idea Connection Ltd.
871 Chemong Rd.
Peterborough, Ontario K9H 5Z5
Susan LePage
(705) 743-5066, 745-4121 (Fax)

Speakers Bureau Int'l.
961 Eglinton Ave. E, Suite 200
Toronto, Ontario M4G 4B5
Barbara L. Kincaide
(418) 424-1673 or 1974,
  424-3488 (Fax)

ENGLAND

Celebrity Speakers Int'l.
Studio 230 Canalot
222 Kensal Rd.
London W10 58N
Alex Krywald
44-1-969-9419, 960-2965 (Fax)

Prime Performers
The Studio
5 Kidderpore Ave.
London NW3 7SX
Barbara Kelly
44-1-431-0211, 431-3813 (Fax)

Premier Speakers Ltd.
30 Ives St.
London SW3 2ND
Tony Salisbury
44-1-225-2584 or 2585,
  589-7144 (Fax)

Corporate Training Companies

The following companies specialize in presenting in-house seminars, primarily to corporate clients. These companies represent a large share of the multibillion dollar training business. Most of these companies rely on qualified seminar leaders to present their programs. You can contact them to get more information about their programs and organizations.

CALIFORNIA

Stuart Atkins, Inc.
8383 Wilshire Blvd., Suite 920
Beverly Hills, CA 90211
(213) 655-5436

The Bay Group
10000 Fourth St., Suite 400
San Rafael, CA 94901
(415) 454-6144

Blanchard Training and
  Development
125 State Pl.
Escondido, CA 92025
(619) 489-5005

Courseware, Inc.
10075 Carroll Canyon Rd.
San Diego, CA 92131
(619) 578-1700

Human Factors
Advanced Technology Group
4340 Redwood Hwy., Suite 26
San Rafael, CA 94903
(415) 492-9190

The Impact Organization
490 Post St.
Penthouse, Suite 1700
San Francisco, CA 94120
(415) 362-2322

Integrated Computer Systems
5800 Hannum Ave.
Culver City, CA 90231-3614
(213) 417-8888

Interact Performance
  Systems, Inc.
300 W. Owens Dr., Suite 350
Santa Ana, CA 92706
(714) 835-3671

Leadership Studies
230 W. 3rd Ave.
Escondido, CA 92025-0312
(619) 741-6595

Learning Tree International
6053 W. Century Rd.
Los Angeles, CA 90045-0383
(213) 417-9700

Omega, Consultants to Bank
 Management
444 Market St., 5th Fl.
San Francisco, CA 94111
(415) 543-1836

Practical Management, Inc.
23801 Calabasas Rd.,
 Suite 2026
P.O. Box 8789
Calabasas, CA 91302
(818) 348-9101

Schrello Direct Marketing, Inc.
555 E. Ocean Blvd., Suite 201
P.O. Box 1610
Long Beach, CA 90801-1610
(213) 437-2230

The U.S. Learning Corporation
1150 Foothill Blvd.
La Canada, CA 91011
(818) 790-9450

University Associates, Inc.
8517 Production Ave.
San Diego, CA 92121
(619) 578-5900

Zenger-Miller, Inc.
1735 Technology Dr., 6th Fl.
San Jose, CA 95110-1313
(408) 452-1244

COLORADO

ARC International Ltd.
5445 DTC Pkwy., Suite 720
Englewood, CO 80111
(303) 220-8777

Colorado State University
Div. of Continuing Education
Rockwell Hall
Fort Collins, CO 80523
(303) 491-5288

Morris Massey Associates, Inc.
34 Pima Court
Boulder, CO 80303
(303) 494-7202, (800) 346-9010

The Tracom Corporation
3773 Cherry Creek North Dr.,
 Suite 950
Denver, CO 80209
(303) 388-5451

CONNECTICUT

Consultative Resources Corp.
20 Thorndal Cir.
Darien, CT 06853
(203) 655-2411

Learning International
P.O. Box 10211
200 First Stamford Pl.
Stamford, CT 06904
(203) 965-8400

Mohr Development, Inc.
30 Oak St.
Stamford, CT 06905
(203) 357-1357

Scandinavian Management
 Development Corp.
P.O. Box 863
Madison, CT 06443-2501
(203) 245-3990

Steffen, Steffen & Associates, Inc.
652 Glenbrook Rd.
Stamford, CT 06906
(203) 359-4100

DISTRICT OF COLUMBIA

Longman Crown
1120 20th St., NW, Suite 500
Washington, DC 20036

FLORIDA

Assessment Designs, Int'l.
2180 West State Rd., #434
Sanlando Center—4140
Longwood, FL 32779
(407) 788-8300

Kaset, Inc.
4014 Gunn Hwy., Suite 162
Tampa, FL 33624
(813) 962-7830, (800) 237-2361

GEORGIA

The Atlanta Consulting Group
2028 Powers Ferry Rd., Suite 190
Atlanta, GA 30339
(404) 952-0382

Atlanta Resource Associates
1708 Peachtree St., NW, Suite 305
Atlanta, GA 30309
(404) 892-2336

The Fortune Group Int'l. Inc.
One Concourse Pkwy., Suite 155
Atlanta, GA 30328
(404) 395-2808

O. D. Resources, Inc.
2900 Chamblee-Tucker Rd.
Building 16
Atlanta, GA 30341
(404) 455-7145

ODR, Inc.
2900 Chamblee-Tucker Rd., #16
Atlanta, GA 30341
(404) 455-7145

ParTraining Corporation
4936 President's Way
Tucker (Atlanta), GA 30084
(404) 493-7188, (800) 247-7188

Thompson-Mitchell & Associates
7 Piedmont Center
3525 Piedmont Rd.
Atlanta, GA 30305
(404) 233-5435, (800) 554-1389

ILLINOIS

Applied Learning
1751 W. Diehl Rd.
Naperville, IL 60540
(312) 369-3000

Bank Administration Institute
60 Gould Ctr.
Rolling Meadows, IL 60008
(313) 228-2383, (800) 323-8552

The Executive Technique
716 N. Rush St.
Chicago, IL 60611
(312) 266-0001

SRA/Pergamon
155 N. Wacker
Chicago, IL 60606
(312) 984-7000

Systema Corporation
60 Revere Dr., Suite 600
Northbrook, IL 60062-1563
(312) 498-9530

Universal Training Systems Co.
255 Revere Dr.
Northbrook, IL 60062
(312) 498-9700

IOWA

Center for Professional and
  Executive Development
Iowa State University
365 Carver Hall
Ames, IA 50011
(515) 294-3657

KANSAS

National Seminars Group
6901 W. 63rd St.
P.O. Box 2949
Shawnee Mission, KS 66201-1349
(913) 432-7755, (800) 258-7246

Padgett-Thompson
P.O. Box 8297
Overland Park, KS 66208
(913) 451-2900, (800) 255-4141

Fred Pryor Seminars
2000 Johnson Dr.
P.O. Box 2951
Shawnee Mission, KS 66201
(913) 384-6400, (800) 255-6139

MARYLAND

BNA Communications, Inc.
9439 Key West Ave.
Rockville, MD 20850-3396
(301) 948-0540, (800) 233-6067

Conceptual Systems, Inc.
1010 Wayne Ave., 14th Fl.
Silver Spring, MD 20910
(301) 589-1800

MASSACHUSETTS

Addison-Wesley Publishing Co.
Jacob Way
Reading, MA 01867
(617) 944-3700

Better Communications
401 Commonwealth Ave.
Boston, MA 02215
(617) 262-5440

The Forum Corporation
One Exchange Pl.
Boston, MA 02109
(617) 523-7300

J. Howard & Associates, Inc.
297 Broadway
Arlington, MA 02174
(617) 646-6580

Innovation Associates, Inc.
3 Speen St., Suite 140
Framingham, MA 01701
(508) 879-8301

LearnCom
215 First St.
Cambridge, MA 02142
(617) 576-3100

Learning Dynamics, Inc.
P.O. Box 8999
Waltham, MA 02254
(617) 889-6262

McBer and Company
137 Newbury St.
Boston, MA 02116
(617) 437-7080

ODI
25 Mall Rd.
Burlington, MA 01803
(617) 272-8040, (800) ODI-INFO

ODT, Inc.
P.O. Box 134
Amherst, MA 01004
(413) 549-1293

Situation Management
  Systems, Inc.
195 Hanover St.
Hanover, MA 02339-2294
(617) 826-4433

Training Concepts, Inc.
140 Wood Rd.
Braintree, MA 02184
(617) 843-9996

Weingarten Publications, Inc.
38 Chauncy St.
Boston, MA 02111
(617) 542-0146

The Whole Brain Corporation
Competence Assurance Systems
University Park at M.I.T.
26 Landsdowne St., Suite 500
Cambridge, MA 02139-4234
(617) 661-9151

MICHIGAN

Achievement Center, Inc.
P.O. Box 261
Rochester, MI 48308
(313) 651-3600

Alamo Learning Systems
37000 Grand River
Farmington Hills, MI 48024
(313) 471-6777

Human Synergistics, Inc.
39819 Plymouth Rd.
Plymouth, MI 48170
(313) 459-1030

Sandy Corporation
1500 W. Big Beaver Rd.
Troy, MI 48084
(313) 649-0800, (800) 521-5378

MINNESOTA

Better Than Money Corp.
9201 E. Bloomington Frwy.
Bloomington, MN 55420
(612) 884-3311

Carlson Learning Companies
12755 State Highway 55
Minneapolis, MN 55441
(612) 559-2322

Golle & Holmes Custom
  Education, Inc.
1600 W. 82nd St.
Minneapolis, MN 55431
(612) 885-5500

McLagan International
300 Rosedale Towers
1700 W. Hwy. 36
St. Paul, MN 55113
(612) 631-2034

National Corrective Training Inst.
1601 East Hwy. 13, Suite 201
Burnsville, MN 55337
(612) 890-1067

Wilson Learning Corp.
7500 Flying Cloud Dr.
Eden Praire, MN 55344
(612) 944-2880

MISSOURI

Telephone Doctor
12119 St. Charles Rock Rd.
St. Louis, MO 63044
(314) 291-1012, (800) 882-9911

NEW HAMPSHIRE

LMA, Inc.
365 Melendy Rd.
Milford, NH 03055
(603) 672-0355

NEW JERSEY

Blessing/White, Inc.
900 State Rd.
Princeton, NJ 08540
(609) 924-2080

Block Petrella Weisbord Designed
  Learning, Inc.
1009 Park Ave.
Plainfield, NJ 07060
(201) 754-5100

Industrial Training Systems
  Corp.
20 W. Stow Rd.
Marlton, NJ 08053
(609) 983-7300

Kepner-Tregoe Inc.
P.O. Box 704
Research Rd.
Princeton, NJ 08542
(609) 921-2806

Training House
P.O. Box 3090
Princeton, NJ 08543
(609) 452-1505

NEW YORK

Ambrose Video Publishing
381 Park Ave. S., Suite 1601
New York, NY 10016
(212) 696-4545

American Management
  Association
135 W. 50th St.
New York, NY 10020
(212) 586-8100

American Management Association
P.O. Box 319
Saranac Lake, NY 12983-9988
(518) 891-1500

Berlitz International, Inc.
257 Park Ave. S., 6th Fl.
New York, NY 10010
(212) 598-3333, (800) 528-8908

Communispond, Inc.
485 Lexington Ave., 23rd Fl.
New York, NY 10017
(212) 687-8040

Cornell University-School of
  Industrial & Labor Relations
Conference Center—ILR
Ithaca, NY 14853
(607) 255-3276

Drake Beam Morin, Inc.
100 Park Ave., Suite 1050
New York, NY 10017
(212) 692-7700

Dun & Bradstreet
Business Education Services
100 Church St.
New York, NY 10007
(212) 312-6861

Management Development Inst.
Hagan School of Business
Iona College
New Rochelle, NY 10801-1890
(914) 633-2256

Manus Associates
The Flatiron Building
175 Fifth Ave., Suite 712
New York, NY 10010-77012
(212) 475-0404

M. R. Communication
  Consultant Inc.
237 Park Ave., Suite 2100
New York, NY 10017
(212) 551-3566

Negotiation Institute Inc.
230 Park Ave.
New York, NY 10169
(212) 986-5555

TBA Resources, Inc.
1317 3rd Ave., 9th Fl.
New York, NY 10021
(212) 288-1897

NORTH CAROLINA

Center for Creative Leadership
P.O. Box P-1
5000 Laurinda Dr.
Greensboro, NC 27402-1660
(919) 288-7210

OHIO

Carew Positional
  Selling Systems, Inc.
8280 Montgomery Rd.
Cincinnati, OH 45236
(513) 891-2662, (800) 227-3977

DPEC, Inc.
4588 Kenny Rd.
Columbus, OH 43220
(614) 457-0577, (800) 223-3732

Philip Office Associates, Inc.
750 Talbott Tower
Dayton, OH 45402
(513) 461-1300

OREGON

Pacific Learning Systems, Inc.
815 SW 2nd Ave., Suite 200
Portland, OR 97204
(503) 227-7272

PENNSYLVANIA

Cresheim Management Consultants
803 E. Willow Grove Ave.
P.O. Box 27785
Philadelphia, PA 19118
(215) 836-1400

Development Dimensions Int'l.
1225 Washington Pike
P.O. Box 13379
Pittsburgh, PA 15243-0379
(412) 257-0600

Strategic Management Group, Inc.
3624 Market St.
Philadelphia, PA 19104
(215) 387-4000

TENNESSEE

Paul C. Green, Ph.D., P.C.
6260 Poplar Ave.
Memphis, TN 38119
(901) 761-4120

TEXAS

Action Management
 Assoc., Inc.
12202 Merit Dr., Suite 950
Dallas, TX 75251
(214) 386-5611

Action Systems, Inc.
5005 LBJ Frwy., Suite 1400
Dallas, TX 75244
(214) 385-0680

Booher Writing Consultants, Inc.
12337 Jones Rd., Suite 242
Houston, TX 77070-4844
(713) 955-2525

Employee Development
 Systems, Inc.
3730 Kirby Dr., Suite 415
Houston, TX 77098-3913
(713) 524-2982

The Evans Group
7616 LBJ Frwy., Suite 407
Park Central 1
Dallas, TX 75251
(214) 788-4424

T. J. Hansen Co.
6711 Meadowcreek Dr.
Dallas, TX 75240
(214) 233-1232

HBJ Leadership
10101 Reunion Pl., Suite 200
San Antonio, TX 78216
(800) 622-3231

Teleometrics International
1755 Woodstead Court
The Woodlands, TX 77380
(713) 367-0060, (800) 527-0406

UTAH

The Charles R. Hobbs Corp.
4505 S. Wasatch Blvd., Suite 200
Salt Lake City, UT 84124
(801) 278-5381

VIRGINIA

Factor Learning Design, Inc.
107 London St.
P.O. Box 1420
Leesburg, VA 22075
(703) 777-6988

Industrial Training Corp.
13515 Dulles Technology Dr.
Herndon, VA 22071-3416
(703) 471-1414

NTL Institute for Applied
 Behavioral Science
1240 N. Pitt St., Suite 100
Alexandria, VA 22314
(703) 548-1500, (800) 777-LABS

WISCONSIN

Marquette University
Continuing Education
1918 W. Wisconsin Ave.
Milwaukee, WI 53233
(414) 224-7118

BERMUDA

International Publications Ltd.
P.O. Box HM 1372
Hamilton, Bermuda HM

CANADA

Friesen, Kaye and Associates
3448 Richmond Rd.
Ottawa, Ontario K2H 8H7
(613) 829-3412

Perform Learning & Management
 Systems, Inc.
19 W. Le Royer, Suite 200
Montreal, Quebec H2Y 1W4
(514) 282-0884

Professional Associations for Networking and Education

Professional associations are valuable for three reasons. First, they allow you to network with other professionals who are presenting programs. You will be able to enhance both your marketing skills and your presentation techniques by speaking with colleagues. Second, you will be able to network with your particular audience. This will enable you to learn more about their needs and to meet your potential audience face-to-face. Finally, almost every association has an educational component. You can market your seminar directly to the association that has your target audience as members. Your seminar might be a perfect addition to their regular programming or annual meeting.

Here are some of the most prominent associations related to the seminar business and those who are committed to comprehensive educational programming. Additional associations are mentioned throughout the book, and comprehensive lists of associations can be found in the reference resources described in Chapter 13.

AM stands for "annual meeting."

Administrative Management Society (AMS)
4622 Street Rd.
Trevose, PA 19047
(215) 953-1040
Membership: Office managers.
AM: Spring

200

American Association for Adult and Continuing Education (AAACE)
1112 16th St., NW, Suite 420
Washington, DC 20036
(202) 463-6333

Membership: Adult education organizations and adult education professionals.
AM: Fall

American Education Research Association (AERA)
1230 17th St., NW
Washington, DC 20036
(202) 223-9485

Membership: Educators and behavioral scientists.
AM: Spring

American Management Association (AMA)
135 West 50th St.
New York, NY 10020
(212) 903-8234

Membership: Provides a wide variety of management development programs.
AM: Fall

American Psychological Association (APA)
1200 17th St., NW
Washington, DC 20036
(202) 955-7600

Membership: Has a division devoted to educational psychology.
AM: Summer

American Seminar Leaders Association (ASLA)
899 Boulevard E., Suite 6A
Weehawken, NJ 07087
(800) 735-0511

Membership: Seminar leaders, speakers, consultants, and suppliers to the seminar business. Has professional development programs, publications, and a certification program.
AM: Spring

American Society for Healthcare Education and Training (ASHET)
840 N. Lake Shore Dr.
Chicago, IL 60611
(312) 280-6113

Membership: Educators and trainers for healthcare, wellness, and health-promotion professionals.
AM: Summer

American Society for Healthcare Human Resource Adminstration
 (ASHHRA)
840 N. Lake Shore Dr.
Chicago, IL 60611
(312) 280-4152

Membership: Dedicated to the education and professional development of
hospital personnel administrators.
AM: Summer

American Society for Quality Control (ASQC)
310 W. Wisconsin Ave.
Milwaukee, WI 53203
(414) 272-8575

Membership: Promotes the art of quality control and its application to industry.
AM: Spring

American Society for Training and Development (ASTD)
1630 Duke St.
P.O. Box 1443
Alexandria, VA 22313
(703) 683-8100

Membership: Trainers, consultants, and human resource development professionals.
AM: Fall

Association for Behavior Analysis (ABA)
Department of Psychology
Western Michigan University
Kalamazoo, MI 49008-5052
(616) 383-1629

Membership: Individuals interested in the applied experimental and theoretical analysis of the information and image-management industry.
AM: Spring

Association for Continuing Higher Education (ACHE)
Indiana University
620 Union Dr., Rm. 143
North Wing
Indianapolis, IN 46202-5171
(312) 274-2637

Membership: Individuals committed to continuing education and accredited
institutions who offer continuing education programming.
AM: Fall

Association for Educational Communications and Technology (AECT)
1025 Vermont Ave., NW, Suite 820
Washington, DC 20005
(202) 347-7834

Membership: Professionals, such as microcomputer and audiovisual specialists, media services directors, and television producers, who require expertise in instructional technology.
AM: Winter

Association for Graphic Arts Training (AGAT)
One Lomb Memorial Dr.
P.O. Box 9887
Rochester, NY 14623
(716) 475-7175
Membership: Individuals involved in graphic arts training within the graphic industry including printing companies, equipment manufacturers, and the film business.
AM: Fall

Association for Information and Image Management (AIIM)
1100 Wayne Ave., Suite 1100
Silver Spring, MD 20910
(301) 587-2711
Membership: Users and manufacturers of equipment, supplies, and services for the information and image-management industry.
AM: Spring

Association for Multi-Image International, Inc. (AMI)
8019 N. Himes Ave., Suite 401
Tampa, FL 33614
(813) 932-1692
Membership: Individuals who are actively involved in the field of multi-image production utilization.
AM: Summer

Association for Quality Participation (AQP)
801-B W. 8th St., Suite 501
Cincinnati, OH 45203
(513) 381-1959
Membership: Promotes quality circles and participatory management with training programs, national and regional conferences, resource materials, publications, and local chapters.
Semi-AM: Spring and fall

Association for Supervision and Curriculum Development (ASCD)
1250 N. Pitt St.
Alexandria, VA 22314-1403
(703) 549-9110
Membership: Curriculum coordinators and consultants, professors of education, educational administrators, principals, and teachers.
AM: Spring

Association for the Development of Computer-Based Instructional
  Systems (ADCIS)
229 Ramseyer Hall
29 W. Woodruff Ave.
Columbus, OH 43210-1177
(614) 292-4324

Membership: Professionals who are actively involved in computer-based instructional technologies.
AM: Fall

Association of Audiovisual Technicians (AAVT)
2378 S. Broadway
Denver, CO 80210
(303) 698-1820

Membership: Audiovisual technicians in schools, industry, and service shops.
AM: Winter

Association of Human Resources Systems Professionals (HRSP), Inc.
P.O. Box 801646
Dallas, TX 75380-1646
(214) 661-3727

Membership: Data processing and other professionals concerned with the development, maintenance, and operation of human resources systems.
AM: Spring

Association of Outplacement Consulting Firms, Inc. (AOCF)
364 Parsippany Rd.
Parsippany, NJ 07054
(301) 887-6667

Membership: Promotes standards of professional practice in the outplacement business.
Semi-AM: Spring and fall

Association of Visual Communicators (AVC)
15125 Califa St., Suite E
Van Nuys, CA 91406
(818) 787-6800

Membership: Audiovisual professionals using the media of film, video, slides,
filmstrips, multi-image and video disks to communicate information.
AM: Fall

Council of Hotel and Restaurant Trainers (CHART)
c/o Mike Landram
Rax of Indiana
9025 Coldwater Rd., Suite 100
Fort Wayne, IN 46825
(219) 489-2997

Membership: Trainers who develop and train members of the hotel and restaurant industries.
AM: Summer

Employee Assistance Professionals Association (EAPA)
4601 Fairfax Dr., Suite 1001
Arlington, VA 22203-1516
(703) 522-6272

Membership: Professionals who are involved in employee assistance programs and provide a variety of educational programs.
AM: Fall

Hotel Sales and Marketing Association International (HSMAI)
1300 L St., NW, Suite 800
Washington, DC 20005
(202) 789-0089

Membership: Sales and marketing professionals for the hotel industry.
AM: Winter

Human Resource Professionals Association of Ontario
2 Bloor St. West, Suite 600
Toronto, Ontario, M4W 3E2
Canada
(416) 923-2324

Membership: Individuals who deliver human resource services.
AM: Spring

Human Resource Planning Society (HRPS)
228 E. 45th St., 14th Fl.
New York, NY 10017
(212) 490-6387

Membership: Planning and development specialists, staffing analysts, business planners, and others concerned with planning for employee recruitment, development, and utilization.
AM: Winter

Instructional Systems Association (ISA)
P.O. Box 1196
Sunset Beach, CA 90742
(714) 846-6012

Membership: Organizations that design and deliver training programs.
AM: Winter

Insurance Conference Planners Association (ICPA)
2801 Woodbine Dr.
N. Vancouver, B.C.
Canada U7R 2R9
(604) 988-5401

Membership: Meeting planners from the insurance industry.
AM: Fall

Interactive Multimedia Association (IMA)
800 K St., NW, Suite 440
Washington, DC 20001
(202) 408-1000

Membership: Companies, individuals, and institutions involved in producing and using interactive multimedia technology.
AM: None

International Association for Continuing Education and Training
(IACET)
1101 Connecticut Ave., NW, Suite 700
Washington, DC 20036
(202) 857-1122

Membership: Educational institutions, hospitals, professional societies, and others providing continuing medical education.
AM: Fall

International Association of Business Communicators (IABC)
One Hallidie Plaza, Suite 600
San Francisco, CA 94102
(415) 433-3400

Membership: Communications and public relations professionals.
AM: Spring

International Customer Service Associates (ICSA)
111 E. Wacker Dr.
Chicago, IL 60601
(312) 644-6610

Membership: Customer service management professionals.
AM: Fall

International Federation of Training and Development Organizations
(IFTDO)
22, Sapperton
Near Cirencester, Gloustershire
GL 7 6LQ
United Kingdom
011 44 285 76305

Membership: International training and development associations.
AM: Summer

International Mass Retail Association (IMRA)
1901 Pennsylvania Ave., NW, 10th Fl.
Washington, DC 20006
(202) 861-0774

Membership: Mass market retailers and their suppliers.
AM: Spring

International Personnel Management Association (IPMA)
1617 Duke St.
Alexandria, VA 22314
(703) 549-7100

Membership: Personnel managers and administrators.
AM: Fall

International Society for Intercultural Education, Training, and Research
 (SIETAR)
733 15th St., NW, Suite 900
Washington, DC 20005
(202) 737-5000

Membership: Students, researchers, professors, and human resource directors involved in intercultural education.
AM: Spring

International Teleconferencing Association (ITCA)
1150 Connecticut Ave., NW, Suite 1050
Washington, DC 20036-4104
(202) 833-2549

Membership: A clearinghouse for the exchange of information between users and providers in the field of teleconferencing.
AM: Summer

International Television Association (ITVA)
6311 N. O'Connor Rd., LB-51
Irving, TX 75039
(214) 869-1112

Membership: Individuals in nonbroadcast video who use videotape and video equipment in organizational settings to write and edit video programs.
AM: Spring

National Association for Industry-Education Cooperation (NAIEC)
235 Hendricks Blvd.
Buffalo, NY 14226-3304
(716) 834-7047

Membership: Members dedicated to improved coordination between industry and education in school improvement, career education, and human-resource development.
AM: Spring

National Association of Government Training and Development Directors
 (NAGTADD)
Council of State Governments
Iron Works Pike, P.O. Box 11910
Lexington, KY 40578-1910
(606) 252-2291

Membership: Individuals who direct training and development programs for any government employees.
AM: Fall

National Community Education Association (NCEA)
801 N. Fairfax St., Suite 209
Alexandria, VA 22314-0161
(703) 683-6232

Membership: Sponsors and supports community involvement in public education and lifelong learning opportunities.
AM: Fall

National Home Study Council (NHSC)
1601 18th St., NW
Washington, DC 20009
(202) 234-5100

Membership: A federally recognized accrediting agency and trade association for home study schools.
AM: Winter

National Management Association (NMA)
2210 Arbor Blvd.
Dayton, OH 45439
(513) 294-0421

Membership: Middle-level and supervisory management personnel dedicated to professional management.
AM: Fall

National Society for Performance and Instruction (NSPI)
1300 L St., NW, Suite 1250
Washington, DC 20005
(202) 408-7969

Membership: Dedicated to increasing productivity in the workplace through the application of performance and instructional technologies.
AM: Spring

National Society of Sales Training Executives (NSSTE)
203 E. 3rd St.
Sanford, FL 32771
(407) 322-3364

Membership: Sales and management trainers.
AM: Fall and spring

National Speakers Association (NSA)
3877 7th St., Suite 350
Phoenix, AZ 85014
(602) 265-1001

Membership: Provides professional development for professional speakers and trainers.
AM: Summer

National Training Systems Associations (NTSA)
2425 Wilson Blvd., Suite 457
Arlington, VA 22201
(703) 243-1655

Membership: Companies in the simulation and training industry and their support services.
AM: June

National University Continuing Education Association (NUCEA)
One Dupont Circle, Suite 615
Washington, DC 20036-1168
(202) 659-3130

Membership: Accredited universities with continuing higher education programs and professional staff.
AM: Spring

Ontario Society for Training and Development
111 Queen St. E., Suite 302
Toronto, Ontario, Canada M5S 1S2
(416) 367-5900

Membership: Trainers, consultants, and human resource professionals.
AM: Fall

Professional Services Management Association (PSMA)
4226 Park Rd., Suite A
Charlotte, NC 28209-3218
(704) 521-8890

Membership: Business managers of professional services firm seeking to exchange ideas and information.
AM: Fall

Quality and Productivity Management Association (QPMA)
300 N. Martingale Rd., Suite 230
Schaumberg, IL 60173
(708) 619-2909

Membership: Companies with corporatewide quality and productivity improvement efforts.
Semi-AM: Spring and fall

Society for Applied Learning Technology (SALT)
50 Culpepper St.
Warrenton, VA 22186
(703) 347-0055

Membership: Industrial, military, and academic managers involved in the design, production, or use of technology-based education.
AM: Winter

Society for Human Resource Management (SHRM)
606 N. Washington St.
Alexandria, VA 22314
(703) 548-3440

Membership: Personnel and industrial relations executives and human-resource managers.
AM: Spring

Society of Incentive Travel Executives
21 W. 38th St., 10th Fl.
New York, NY 10018
(212) 575-0910

Membership: Corporate users—airlines, tourists boards, cruise lines, destination management companies; consultants—hotels and travel agents.
Semi-AM: Spring and fall

Society of Insurance Trainers and Educators (SITE)
P.O. Box 513
Cary, IL 60013
(312) 516-1921

Membership: Education and training personnel directors and those responsible for the training function in insurance.
AM: Summer

Speech Communication Association (SCA)
5105 Backlick Rd., Suite E
Annadale, VA 22003
(703) 750-0533

Membership: Teachers involved in all levels and all aspects of communication arts and sciences, media communications consultants, students, libraries, and persons in theater production.
AM: Fall

The Organization Development Institute (The O.D. Institute)
6501 Wilson Mills Rd., Suite K
Cleveland, OH 44143
(216) 461-4333

Membership: Organized to disseminate information about organization development training in conflict resolution and the technologies of effective management.
Semi-AM: Spring and fall

Toastmasters International (TI)
P.O. Box 9052
Mission Viejo, CA 92690
(714) 858-8255

Membership: Individuals who want to develop public speaking skills. Weekly local meetings are held throughout the U.S.
AM: Summer

Training Media Association (TMA)
198 Thomas Johnson Dr., Suite 206
Frederick, MD 21701
(301) 662-4268

Membership: Individuals concerned with preventing unauthorized copying of training media, especially films, videotapes, and printed media.
Semi-AM: Winter and spring

World Computer Graphics Association, Inc. (WCGA)
2033 M St., NW, Suite 399
Washington, DC 20036
(202) 775-9556

Membership: Serving the needs of the global computer graphics community through sponsoring exhibitions, conferences, and seminars internationally.
AM: 15 per year

World Future Society (WFS)
4916 St. & Elmo Ave.
Bethesda, MD 20814
(301) 656-8274

Membership: Scientists, educators, government officials, and others interested in social and technological developments of the future.
AM: Quadrennial meetings

Public Seminar Companies

The following list will help give you an overview of the public seminar business. You can write or call and get brochures to become more familiar with direct mail seminar brochures.

You also might want to attend some of these programs. There is no better way to learn about such matters as seminar design, format, handouts, and back-of-the-room sales. This list is also valuable to you if you are interested in becoming a presenter for an established public seminar company.

Advanced Professional Development Institute
1206 Bank St.
Ottawa, Ontario KIS 3Y1
Canada
(613) 523-3333
No. Seminars/Year: 11 in English and 11 in French.
Where: Ottawa, Toronto, Montreal, and Quebec.
Topics: Writing skills (professional and advanced); management skills; project management; strategic management; speaking, interviewing, and presentation skills; effective communications; time management; assertiveness skills and effective leadership; government policy-making and issues management.
Industry: Government and most industries.
Faculty: Staff and consultants.
Contact: Alain Martin.

Algonquin Management Center
200 Elgin St., 10th Fl.
Ottawa, Ontario K2P 1L5
Canada
(613) 232-0090
No. Seminars/Year: 120.

Where: Ottawa.
Topics: Support, clerical, and secretarial staff; lower- and some middle-level management.
Industry: Mostly government, manufacturing, and hi-tech.
Faculty: Consultants.
Comments: Also does 3–5 conferences; uses outside speakers.
Contact: Frank Picciano.

American Arbitration Association
140 W. 51st St.
New York, NY 10020
(212) 484-3233
No. Seminars/Year: More than 100 (50 in Puerto Rico and St. Thomas)
Where: Nationwide.
Topics: Construction advocacy, unions, labor-management relations, advanced advocacy, and drug and alcohol problems in the workplace.
Industry: Unions and labor management.
Faculty: Panel of speakers from company; some outside speakers.
Contact: Allen Silberman, Vice President, Training.

American Business Consultants, Inc.
1540 Nuthatch Ln.
Sunnyvale, CA 94087
(408) 738-3011
No. Seminars/Year: 52.
Where: Nationwide.
Topics: Valuing, buying, and selling businesses.
Industry: All businesses.
Faculty: Will Tetreauld, President.

American Biographical Institute, Inc.
5126 Bur Oak Cir.
P.O. Box 31226
Raleigh, NC 27622
(919) 781-8710
No. Seminars/Year: 1.
Where: Kenya, Toronto, Singapore, and Washington, DC.
Topics: Specific topics related to speaker's expertise.
Industry: No particular industry.
Faculty: Speakers who appear in *American Biography*.
Comments: Publishes a book of biographies and holds an annual conference at which speakers featured in *American Biography* make presentations.

American Compensation Association
14040 N. Sight Blvd.
Scottsdale, AZ 85260
(602) 951-9191
No. Seminars/Year: 300.
Where: 68 locations in major cities.
Topics: 24 different compensation and benefits programs.
Industry: All industries and the public sector.

Faculty: Members of association and outside consultants.
Contact: Jeff Smith.

American Management Association
135 W. 50th St.
New York, NY 10020
(212) 903-7915
No. Seminars/Year: 4167.
Where: Management centers in New York; Atlanta; Washington, DC; and international locations.
Topics: Finance, research and design, sales and marketing, insurance risk management, and manufacturing.
Faculty: Consultants and independent contractors.
Contact: Patricia Conway.

American Marketing Association
250 S. Wacker Dr.
Chicago, IL 60606-5819
(312) 648-0536
No. Seminars/Year: 25–30.
Where: Toronto, Orlando, New Orleans, Phoenix, southern California, and Hawaii.
Topics: Research, services, new products, sports marketing, and marketing education.
Industry: All industries specifically for the marketing department.
Faculty: Outside speakers. Each conference has a committee of volunteer members. Speakers are usually volunteers.

American Productivity and Quality Center
123 N. Post Oak Ln.
Houston, TX 77024
(713) 681-4020
No. Seminars/Year: 100.
Where: Nationwide. Regional locations include Raleigh, NC and Colorado Springs, CO.
Topics: Total quality management, benchmarking, customer satisfaction, and zero defects.
Industry: All industries—upper- and middle-level management, including health care and accounting.
Faculty: Staff and subcontractors.

Association of National Advertisers, Inc.
155 E. 44th St.
New York, NY 10017
(212) 697-5950
No. Seminars/Year: Four course seminars scheduled every month.
Where: Westchester, NY.
Topics: Publications.
Industry: Publishing and advertising.
Contact: Renee Paley.

Association for Quality and Participation
801-B W. 8th St., Suite 501
Cincinnati, OH 45203
(513) 381-1959
No. Seminars/Year: 4; cosponsor 2.
Where: Nationwide.
Topics: Employee involvement and total quality management.
Industry: All industries, especially manufacturing, services, and aerospace.
Faculty: Program design committee issues a call for papers or presentations.

Battelle Professional Development Center
P.O. Box C-5395
4000 NE 41st St.
Seattle, WA 98105-5428
(206) 528-3402
No. Seminars/Year: 60.
Where: Western U.S. and Ohio.
Topics: Management, leadership, and project management as they relate to total quality.
Industry: Manufacturing, services, government, and industries implementing total quality.
Faculty: Specialists who have done research in the area.
Comments: One of the largest research and development corporations in the world. It does consulting on organization management.
Contact: Jody Greengo or Cheryl Waale, Director of Program Development.

Beals Advertising and PR
4679 Vista St.
San Diego, CA 92116
(619) 284-1145
No. Seminars/Year: 12–20.
Where: Nationwide.
Topics: Marketing, advertising, public relations, and speaking skills.
Industry: All industries and small business personnel. (Those using seminars as a way to put their companies on the map.)
Faculty: Gary Beals, President.
Comments: One-person company.

Bear Tribe Medicine Co.
P.O. Box 9167
Spokane, WA 99209
(509) 326-6561
No. Seminars/Year: 15 educational programs and 8 medicine-wheel gatherings.
Where: Nationwide and international.
Topics: Medicine wheel, getting in touch with self, and Native American spirituality and how it relates to the planet today.
Industry: People who have read Sun Bear's books and magazine, *Wildfire*.
Faculty: Staff, people in the community, and students of Sun Bear.
Comments: Formed by medicine man Sun Bear, a Chippewa Native American.

Brookings Institution
Center for Public Policy Education
1775 Massachusetts Ave., NW
Washington, DC 20036
(202) 797-6000
No. Seminars/Year: 100.
Where: Most in Washington, DC. Overseas: South Korea, Republic of China, Soviet Union, Mexico, Argentina, and Belgium.
Topics: Conferences on public policy and executive education seminars.
Industry: Corporations and governments dealing with telecommunications, oil, automotive industry, or any corporation dealing with government regulations and trade policy.
Comments: This is a think tank, the oldest institute in Washington, DC.
Contact: Joan Mylin.

Bryant College
The Center for Management Development
450 Douglas Pike
Smithfield, RI 02917-1283
(401) 232-6200
No. Seminars/Year: 45 offerings, which are given 3–4 times per year.
Where: Bryant College and hotels in Massachusetts; New Hampshire; Avon, CT; Nashua, NH; and Newport, RI.
Topics: Business topics: 1-, 2-, and 3-day programs. Institute for Training Trainers: management, computers, sales, and marketing.
Industry: All industries.
Faculty: Consultants for the college.
Contact: Rosemary D'Arcy.

The Burke Institute
800 Broadway
Cincinnati, OH 45202-1303
(800) 544-7373
No. Seminars/Year: 150.
Where: Cincinnati, Chicago, New York, Boston, and San Francisco.
Topics: More than 30 topics relating to marketing.
Industry: Consumer, industrial, health care, and all industries involved with marketing.
Faculty: Staff.

Business and Professional Research Institute
31 Main St.
Wills River, VT 05081
(800) 222-2921
No. Seminars/Year: More than 1000.
Where: Major cities in the U.S., Canada, and Europe.
Topics: 15 seminar topics, including newsletters, desktop publishing, and accounts receivable.
Industry: A wide variety of industries.
Faculty: Staff and consultants.
Contact: Julie Moss.

Business Women's Training Program
P.O. Box 12566
Shawnee Mission, KS 66212
(800) 423-6540
No. Seminars/Year: 200.
Where: U.S. and abroad.
Topics: All topics of interest to businesswomen.
Industry: All.
Faculty: Outside female seminar leaders.

California Institute of Technology
Industrial Relations Center
1-90
Pasadena, CA 91125
(818) 356-4046
No. Seminars/Year: 93 (about 8 per month).
Where: Pasadena.
Topics: All courses focus on technology. Middle-management programs. Skills courses focus on management and leadership issues for technical professionals. Executive programs—2-day courses on strategic planning, management of technology, manufacturing strategy, marketing of technology-based products, and total quality management.
Industry: A variety: medical, aerospace, food, chemicals, oil, utilities, and computers.
Faculty: Outside consultants in particular.
Contact: Ann Campbell or Valerie Hood.

CareerTrack
3085 Center Green Dr.
Boulder, CO 80301-5408
(303) 447-2323
No. Seminars/Year: 6500, including public and in-house.
Where: Major and secondary cities (with a population of more than 50,000) throughout the U.S.
Topics: Management issues, consumer issues, communications, and motivation.
Industry: All industries, government agencies, nonprofit associations, and the general public.
Faculty: Contract workers—experts in the topic or issue. Speakers provide 2–3 topics each. Approximately 110 different speakers are used.
Contact: Jeff Hildebrandt.

Center for Accelerated Learning
1103 Wisconsin St.
Lake Geneva, WI 53147
(414) 248-7070
No. Seminars/Year: 9–10.
Where: Orlando; Washington, DC; London; Chicago; Toronto; and San Diego.
Topics: Accelerated training.
Industry: All industries interested in training.
Faculty: David Meier, and faculty members of the center.

Comments: David Meier is a pioneer in the field of accelerated learning for corporations in the U.S. and Europe.

Center for Business Development
2409 Villa Ln.
McHenry, IL 60050-2969
(815) 344-2500
No. Seminars/Year: Limited, mostly in-house.
Where: Worldwide.
Topics: Time management, delegation, performance appraisal, performance management, counseling, listening, achieving excellence, basics of supervision, and training trainers.
Industry: Training community; broad-based industries.
Faculty: 11 subcontractors.
Contact: Dr. Larry Kakklenberg.

Center for Creative Leadership
5000 Laurinda Dr.
Greensboro, NC 27410
(919) 288-7210
No. Seminars/Year: 152.
Where: Greensboro, NC; University of Maryland; Colorado Springs, CO; and Brussels, Belgium.
Topics: Leadership development programs.
Industry: CEOs and managers from both the for-profit and nonprofit sectors.
Faculty: Staff, consultants, and outside speakers.
Contact: Melody Cranberg.

Center for Creative Learning
6040 Lisbon Ave.
Milwaukee, WI 53210
(414) 873-6040
No. Seminars/Year: More than 150.
Where: Wisconsin.
Topics: Personal growth, self-esteem, relationships, money, and goal setting.
Industry: Profit and nonprofit organizations.
Faculty: Independent contractors.
Comments: Intensive weekend programs; emotional process work. Center is an associate of the Funeral Service Institute for funeral directors.

Center for Entrepreneurial Management, Inc.
180 Varick St., Penthouse
New York, NY 10014-4606
(212) 633-0060
No. Seminars/Year: 5.
Where: New York City, the West Coast, and Texas.
Topics: Management course for CEOs, family businesses, and the power of persuasion.
Industry: Entrepreneurs; all businesses.

Faculty: Members of the center; experts in the field.
Comments: This association is an organization of entrepreneurs.
Contact: Joe Mancuso.

Center for Inventory Management
941 Carlisle Rd.
Stone Mountain, GA 30083-4798
(404) 296-6020
No. Seminars/Year: 4.
Where: Atlanta.
Topics: Inventory management, material requirements planning, and inventory record accuracy.
Industry: Manufacturing and distribution.
Faculty: Hank Jordan, President.
Comments: One-person operation.

Center for Studies of the Person
1125 Torrey Pines Rd.
La Jolla, CA 92037
(619) 459-3861
No. Seminars/Year: Two 10-day programs.
Where: University of California, San Diego, and Europe.
Topics: Living now—diversity by design, not by default.
Industry: Psychologists.
Faculty: Facilitators who are members of the center and the director.
Comments: Psychological assistance program.

Clemson University College of Commerce and Industry Professional
  Development
P.O. Drawer 912 Clemson, SC 29633
(803) 656-3981
No. Seminars/Year: 600.
Where: Nationwide, especially southeast U.S.
Topics: Management, personal development, and technical subjects.
Industry: Textiles and computers.
Faculty: Staff and outside seminar leaders.
Contact: Helena Douglas.

College of St. Thomas
The Management Center
Mail Station 5058
St. Paul, MN 55105
(612) 647-5219
No. Seminars/Year: 20–24.
Where: St. Paul, MN.
Topics: Personal improvement, basic supervision, writing, and quality management.
Industry: Manufacturing and service companies; all areas of business, finance, and accounting.
Faculty: Faculty from the School of Business. Outside consultants with expertise in management.

Columbia Executive Programs
Columbia University
324 Uris Hall
New York, NY 10027
(212) 854-3395
No. Seminars/Year: 1000 (17 different programs given multiple times each year).
Where: Conference facilities of Columbia Executive Programs—Arden House and Harrison House, California, and Europe.
Topics: Marketing analysis.
Industry: All industries—middle- to senior-level executives.
Faculty: Business School faculty and experts in a given field.

Computer Security Institute
600 Harrison St.
San Francisco, CA 94107
(415) 905-2380
No. Seminars/Year: 12–15, plus 2 conferences.
Where: Major hub cities.
Topics: Computer security: awareness, microcomputers, viruses, and local-area networks.
Industry: Computer.
Faculty: 2 teachers of regional seminars and contract speakers on computers.

Conference Board
845 Third Ave.
New York, NY 10022
(212) 759-0900
No. Seminars/Year: 75.
Where: Brussels, Belgium; Ottawa, Canada; New York; Chicago; Houston; Pittsburgh; Los Angeles; Phoenix; Philadelphia; and Washington, DC.
Topics: Compensation, management development, communications, marketing, quality, human resources, strategic management, financial briefings and conferences, and business ethics.
Industry: Fortune 500 companies.
Faculty: Consultants—directors select speakers based on expertise.

Cornell University
New York State School of Industrial and Labor Relations
15 E. 26th St., 4th Fl.
New York, NY 10010
(212) 340-2800
No. Seminars/Year: More than 200.
Where: New York City.
Topics: Labor relations studies, human resources, collective bargaining, EEO programs, Latino leadership studies program, and trade union women's study program.
Faculty: Faculty of Cornell University and consultants.
Contact: Hector Riveria.

Creative Training Techniques
7251 Flying Cloud Dr.
Eden Prairie, MN 55344
(612) 829-1954
No. Seminars/Year: More than 100.
Where: Nationwide.
Topics: Training the trainer, needs assessment and evaluation, and making training stick.
Industry: Any industry involved in training and human resources.
Faculty: Bob Pike and six trainers.
Contact: Bob Pike.

Data-Tech Institute
Lakeview Plaza
P.O. Box 2429
Clifton, NJ 07015
(201) 478-5400
No. Seminars/Year: 25–30 topics: 70–100 per month and 900–1200 per year.
Where: North America.
Topics: Telecommunications, data communications, microcomputers, networking, and finance.
Industry: Computer industry, government, and services.
Faculty: Staff.

Delphi II Foundation Institute
4265 SW 8th St., Suite 200
Miami, FL 33134
(305) 666-3502
No. Seminars/Year: 61 9-week programs.
Topics: Annual conference for teachers and self-esteem, communications, discipline, team building, and cooperative discipline. Programs on handling conflict and peer pressures.
Industry: Educators and those interested in education.
Faculty: 32 bilingual teachers offering courses in English and Spanish.
Contact: Linda Jalenis, Program Director.

Designetics International, Inc.
P.O. Box 158
Waterloo, Ontario N2J 3Z9
Canada
(519) 741-9665
No. Seminars/Year: 12.
Where: Canada—Montreal, Calgary, and Vancouver.
Topics: Project management and priorities and performance.
Industry: Technical.
Faculty: Outside consultants.
Contact: Sid Love.

Development Communications, Inc.
312 Montgomery, Suite 209
Alexandria, VA 22314
(703) 683-3100
No. Seminars/Year: 21 seminars and 2–5 quarterly workshops.
Where: Alexandria, VA.
Topics: Video production: scripting, editing, field production, camera techniques, music, and audio.
Industry: Government agencies who want to learn about making videos and training films.
Faculty: Staff and free-lancers.

Digital Consulting, Inc.
6 Windsor St.
Andover, MA 01810
(508) 475-6990
No. Seminars/Year: 150.
Where: U.S., Canada, and Europe.
Topics: Software and M.I.S.
Industry: All industries.
Faculty: Staff and outside consultants.
Contact: Marney Peabody.

Dimensional Reading, Inc.
98 Main St., Suite 539
Tiburon, CA 94920
(415) 435-3875
No. Seminars/Year: 5.
Where: Worldwide, especially Asia.
Topics: Speed writing, presentation skills, and communications concepts.
Industry: All businesses.
Faculty: Joyce Turley and 5 teachers.

Disney World Seminar Productions
P.O. Box 10,000
Lake Buena Vista FL 32830-1000
(407) 824-7997
No. Seminars/Year: 12 per topic per year or upon request.
Where: Walt Disney World hotels and grounds.
Topics: Business management: Disney's approach to people management, quality service, and creativity. Teachers/educators: graduate credits and teacher certification. Young people's programs. Group convention workshops.
Industry: All industries involving management and teaching.
Faculty: Staff of Disney World and Florida State University faculty.
Contact: Janet Bruillard.

Douglis Visual Workshops
212 S. Chester Rd.
Swarthmore, PA 19081
(215) 544-7977
No. Seminars/Year: 27 one-day seminars on travel photography.

Where: Nationwide.

Topics: Communicating with pictures; travel safaris—travel and wildlife photos; visual creativity; photo editing, layout, and design; editorial photography; and personal photography.

Industry: Public relations, communications, general public, corporate communications, and editorial specialists.

Faculty: Philip Douglis.

Comments: One-person business promoting concept of visual literacy in communications.

Dun & Bradstreet Corporation Foundation
Business Education Service
P.O. Box 3734 New York, NY 10008-3734
(212) 312-6880

No. Seminars/Year: 4000.

Where: U.S. and Canada.

Topics: 35–40 different topics: finance, computer, and supervisory training.

Industry: Lower- and middle-level management in all industries.

Faculty: Outside consultants who are experts in a given area.

Contact: Greg Becker.

Dynamics of Human Behavior
3 Waters Park Dr., Suite 228
San Mateo, CA 94403
(415) 574-1013

No. Seminars/Year: 8.

Where: U.S., Republic of China, India, and Soviet Union.

Topics: Management skills, leadership, memory, and listening skills.

Industry: All.

Faculty: Madelyne Burley-Allen, Founder.

Comments: Consulting is offered to companies who want to set up their own programs.

Contact: Arlene Blackton.

Evolving Technology Institute
P.O. Box 60010
San Diego, CA 92106-2095
(800) 325-1289

No. Seminars/Year: 100.

Where: Nationwide.

Topics: Automatic control systems.

Industry: Aerospace and electronics.

Faculty: Staff.

Contact: Dan Rowe.

Executive Enterprises, Inc.
22 W. 21st St.
New York, NY 10010-6904
(212) 645-7880

No. Seminars/Year: 400–439.

Where: Major cities in U.S. and Canada.

Topics: Environment, energy, corporate accounting and reporting, banking, insurance, labor relations, and municipal financing.
Industry: Many industries, corporations, attorneys, CPAs, and related consultants.
Faculty: Expert speakers on topics.
Comments: Publishers of periodicals and professional books in the areas of environment and energy.
Contact: Jim Slabe.

Federal Publications, Inc.
1120-20 St., NW
Washington, DC 20036
(202) 337-7000
No. Seminars/Year: 500.
Where: Nationwide: Washington, DC; Boston; Orlando; San Diego; Las Vegas; San Francisco; and Seattle.
Topics: Government contract law, construction law, and environmental law.
Industry: Companies dealing with the government.
Faculty: 600 lecturers or instructors from law firms.

Foundation for Credit Education
RD #1
692 Brandywine Rd.
Nazareth, PA 18064
(215) 759-5367
No. Seminars/Year: 50.
Where: Worldwide.
Topics: Accounts receivable, credit, and collection.
Industry: CPA trade associations.

Fournies & Associates, Inc.
129 Edgewood Dr.
Bridgewater, NJ 08807
(201) 526-2442
No. Seminars/Year: A few.
Where: All over U.S. and Canada.
Topics: Coaching for improved work performance.
Industry: All.
Faculty: Ferdinand Fournies and Sandra Fournies.

Friesen, Kaye & Associates
3448 Richmond Rd.
Ottawa, Ontario K2H 8H7
Canada
(613) 829-3412
No. Seminars/Year: 100.
Where: Ontario, Los Angeles, and Fort Lauderdale.
Topics: Training trainers—9 different programs.
Industry: All companies that do training.

Faculty: Instructors on staff.
Comments: 25-year-old customized course-development service.

Government Institutes, Inc.
966 Hungerford Dr., Suite 24
Rockville, MD 20850-1714
(301) 251-9250
No. Seminars/Year: 115.
Where: Nationwide including Philadelphia, San Francisco, and Chicago.
Topics: Environmental health and safety and hazardous waste.
Industry: Oil and petroleum and corporations having to comply with EPA standards.
Faculty: Members of major law firms and presidents of major chemical companies (depending on course).

Haerr and Company
6919 N. Knoxville
Executive Plaza
Peoria, IL 61614
(309) 692-5520
No. Seminars/Year: As demand dictates.
Topics: How to treat employees nicely, business management for smaller firms, and corporate strategic planning.
Industry: All.
Faculty: Owner of company.
Comments: One-person business. Seminars sponsored by chambers of commerce, colleges, and universities.

Heaton & Associates
P.O. Box 205
905 Corydon
Winnipeg MAN R3M 3S7
Canada
(204) 475-9810
No. Seminars/Year: 25.
Where: Western and eastern Canada.
Topics: Supervisory and management skills, collective bargaining, and project management.
Industry: All.
Faculty: Outside consultants.

The Ned Hermann Group
2075 Buffalo Creek Rd.
Lake Lure, NC 28746
(704) 625-9153
No. Seminars/Year: 17.
Where: Lake Lure (near Charlotte).
Topics: Whole-brain technology, applied creative thinking, and creative problem solving.
Industry: Any corporation interested in problem-solving creativity.
Faculty: 15 trained in brain-dominance workshops.

Human Dynamics
P.O. Box 7241
Greensboro, NC 27417
(919) 854-0120
No. Seminars/Year: 50.
Where: Southeastern states and Mid-Atlantic states (New York to Florida).
Topics: Selected management topics, advanced leadership, leadership development for female managers, and strategic planning.
Industry: Service manufacturing, health care, and government.
Faculty: On-site faculty and contractual consultants (educators under contract).

The Humor Project, Inc.
110 Spring St.
Saratoga Springs, NY 12866
(518) 587-8770
No. Seminars/Year: Annual international conference, 2 annual seminars, and 100 programs.
Where: Saratoga Springs.
Topics: Humor as a positive power and humor in business.
Industry: Health care education and business.
Faculty: Dr. Joel Goodman plus presenters for annual conference.
Contact: Dr. Joel Goodman.

Idea Seminars
P.O. Box 369
Omaha, NE 68101
(402) 342-4221
No. Seminars/Year: On request; as many as 50.
Where: Nationwide and Europe.
Topics: Copy preparation.
Industry: Graphic arts.
Faculty: None.
Comments: One-person operation; semiretired.
Contact: Walter B. Graham.

Information Mapping
275 Wyman St.
Waltham, MA 02154
(617) 890-7003
No. Seminars/Year: 15.
Where: International.
Topics: Report writing, creating documentation, and software for the brain.
Industry: All, especially those with complex information needs, such as the Fortune 1000 companies.
Faculty: Subcontracted instructors to train the trainer.
Comments: Unique methodology for presenting information.
Contact: Douglas Gorman, President.

Innovation Associates, Inc.
P.O. Box 2008
Framingham, MA 01701
(508) 879-8301
No. Seminars/Year: 24 with 40 attendees each.
Where: Boston, San Diego, and Toronto.
Topics: Total quality, partnering in total quality, SEMATECH, organizational change, team building, and systems thinking.
Industry: Finance, advertising, computer, manufacturing, and any industry undergoing change.
Faculty: Principals and consultants of company.
Comments: Enables companies to become learning organizations.

Institute for Professional Education
P.O. Box 756
Arlington, VA 22216
(703) 527-8700
No. Seminars/Year: 250.
Where: Washington, DC; San Francisco; Chicago; Phoenix; Denver; Atlanta; Lancaster, PA.
Topics: Statistics, management, research design, simulation modeling, forecasting, and the applied art of artificial intelligence.
Industry: All.
Faculty: Consultants.
Contact: Fred Karch, President.

Interaction Associates
185 Berry St., Suite 150
San Francisco, CA 94107
(415) 777-0590
No. Seminars/Year: 25.
Where: U.S.
Topics: Management facilitation and leadership.
Industry: Community groups, school systems, corporations, nonprofit organizations, and government.
Faculty: Specialists in organizational development, strategic planning, and business development.
Comments: Founders published *How to Make Meetings Work.* Interaction method.
Contact: Kathleen Erickson-Frunen.

The Interface Group, Inc.
300 First Ave.
Needham, MA 02194
(617) 449-6600
No. Seminars/Year: 11 conferences at trade shows.
Where: West: Las Vegas and San Francisco.
Topics: High-tech and computers.
Industry: High-technology.
Faculty: Keynoters and outside speakers.

Comments: Independent producers of conferences and expositions.
Contact: Steve Merkman.

International Business Information Services
Drawer 4082
Irvine, CA 92716-4082
No. Seminars/Year: More than 120.
Where: U.S. and Canada.
Topics: The needs of entrepreneurs and small company managers dealing with practical business matters.
Industry: Manufacturing, service, and distribution.
Faculty: In-house faculty supported by outside lecturers as appropriate.
Comments: Also publishes special reports and regular syndicated columns on business topics of current interest.
Contact: Botha Chamberlain, Director of Services.

International Business & Management Institute (IBMI)
P.O. Box 3172
Tustin, CA 92681-3271
(714) 552-8494
No. Seminars/Year: Numerous public, corporate, in-house, and academic programs.
Where: U.S. and abroad.
Topics: Management topics focusing on international operations and developments.
Industry: Most industry and professional groups.
Faculty: Mostly IBMI associates; occasionally also outside senior experts practicing in various disciplines.
Comments: Also publishes management books, monographs, and special reports.
Contact: Dr. C. A. Hacapes, Associate Director, Management Education.

International Registry of Organization Development Professionals
11234 Walnut Ridge Rd.
Chesterland, OH 44026
(216) 461-4333
No. Seminars/Year: 2 conferences.
Where: U.S. and abroad.
Topics: Organization and management development.
Industry: All.
Faculty: Members of the organization.
Contact: Dr. Donald W. Cole.

Investment Seminars, Inc.
1543 2nd St.
Githler Building
Sarasota, FL 34217
(813) 955-0323
No. Seminars/Year: 10–20.
Where: U.S. and abroad.
Topics: Investing.

Industry: All.
Faculty: Outside consultants.
Contact: Kim Githler.

Karrass Negotiating, Management, & Sales Seminars, Inc.
1625 Stanford St.
Santa Monica, CA 90404
(213) 453-1806
No. Seminars/Year: 200 (600,000 participants).
Where: U.S. and abroad, including Canada, London, and Copenhagen.
Topics: Negotiating and purchasing.
Industry: Major oil companies and Fortune 500 companies.
Faculty: Staff trained by Dr. Chester Karrass.
Contact: Marilyn Thomas.

J. L. Kellogg Graduate School of Management
Northwestern University
James L. Allen Center
2169 Sheraton Rd.
Evanston, IL 60208-2800
(708) 491-3308
No. Seminars/Year: 3 on general management (broken into 3 levels) and 25–30 other programs.
Where: Evanston, IL—Allen Center.
Topics: Business and general management.
Industry: All—profit and nonprofit.
Faculty: Staff of Kellogg School.
Contact: Cynthia Garrels.

Ken Keyes College
The Vision Foundation, Inc.
790 Commercial Ave.
Coos Bay, OR 97420
(503) 267-6412
No. Seminars/Year: 60–100 (some given several times).
Where: Coos Bay, OR; Florida; New York; California; and Ohio.
Topics: Personal growth, power of unconditional love, and healing yourself.
Industry: Broad spectrum of participants.
Faculty: 8–10 trainers.
Comments: Ken Keyes is author of books on personal growth.
Contact: Walley Hill.

Kepner-Tregoe, Inc.
Research Rd.
P.O. Box 704
Princeton, NJ 08542
(609) 921-2806
No. Seminars/Year: 75 three-day seminars.
Where: U.S. and Canada.
Topics: Technology, training the trainer, problem solving, people management, management involvement, and project management.

Industry: Broad spectrum of those who can use technology: automotive, banking, and finance.
Faculty: 25 contract instructors and 60 field people who sell and deliver.
Comments: Geared to upper-level managements.
Contact: Ginny Nelson, Manager of Public Sessions.

Kessler Management
10747 Wilshire Blvd., Suite 807
Los Angeles, CA 90024-4432
(213) 824-3333
No. Seminars/Year: 36.
Where: Worldwide.
Topics: Self-improvement.
Industry: General public.
Faculty: Experts in field.
Comments: Manager and speakers bureau.
Contact: Joseph I. Kessler.

Keye Productivity Center
P.O. Box 27-480
Kansas City, MO 64180
(800) 821-3919
No. Seminars/Year: 4000.
Where: U.S. and abroad.
Topics: Management, supervision, secretarial science, human resources, and niche markets.
Industry: All.
Faculty: Independent contractors trained by the center; outside seminar leaders.

Knowledge Industry Publications, Inc.
701 Westchester Ave.
White Plains, NY 10604
(914) 328-9157
No. Seminars/Year: 6 trade shows with seminar programs.
Where: San Francisco; Los Angeles; Chicago; Washington, DC; and New York.
Topics: Video field production, scripting, lighting, directing, and computer graphics.
Industry: Computer graphics and professional video.
Faculty: Authors of books on topics.
Comments: Set up trade shows and hire speakers. Write seminars and do promotion. Also publish books.
Contact: Debra Rotalo, Trade Show Manager.

Kroeger Associates
3605-C Chain Bridge Rd.
Fairfax, VA 22030
(703) 591-6284
No. Seminars/Year: 2 per month.
Where: Fairfax, VA and California.
Topics: Personality and management styles.

Industry: Religion, government, medicine, banking, and universities.
Faculty: Independent contractors.
Contact: Connie Ridge.

Lakewood Conferences
50 South 9th St.
Minneapolis, MN 55402
(612) 333-0471
No. Seminars/Year: 12.
Where: U.S. and abroad.
Topics: Training and development, customer-service training, and human resources.
Industry: All.
Faculty: Consultants.
Comments: Publishers of *Training* magazine.

Langevin Learning Systems
1990 River Rd.
Manotick Ontario K0A 2N0
Canada
(613) 692-6382
No. Seminars/Year: 60.
Where: Toronto, Montreal, Calgary, New York, Chicago, Atlanta, San Francisco, and Los Angeles.
Topics: Training trainers, instructional design, and needs assessment.
Industry: All.
Faculty: Staff.
Comments: Specialized.

Leadership Development Associates
99 Kinderkamack Rd.
Westwood, NJ 07675
(201) 666-9494
No. Seminars/Year: 35.
Where: New York area; Jacksonville, FL; Amelia Island, FL.
Topics: Leadership development.
Industry: All businesses, especially utilities, government, manufacturing, and banking.
Faculty: Joe Mastronerio, President; consultants as needed.

Leadership Development Center
4541 N. Prospect Rd., Suite One
Peoria, IL 61614
(309) 685-1900
No. Seminars/Year: 30.
Where: Peoria, IL; Chicago; and St. Louis.
Topics: Managing for commitment, the human side of business, leadership development, and helping people work effectively.
Industry: Wide variety concerned with people issues.
Faculty: One full-time faculty, current CEOs, college professors under contract.
Comments: Practical approach to leadership theories. Practitioners are actu-

ally linked to Center for Creative Leadership, Greensboro, NC. Geared to managers and staff specialists.
Contact: Robert O. Farquhar, President.

Leadership Dynamics
29 Lansing Rd.
West Newton, MA 02165
(303) 440-0909
No. Seminars/Year: As needed.
Where: Colorado.
Topics: Facilitation training: skills of being a facilitator of problem-solving groups, training the trainer, team development, leadership development, and total quality management.
Industry: All.
Faculty: Principal/owner, Dr. Lois Hart.

Learning Dynamics, Inc.
29 Lansing Rd.
West Newton, MA 02165
(617) 332-7070
No. Seminars/Year: 100.
Where: U.S. and Canada.
Topics: Management, supervision, communications skills, customer service, and sales.
Industry: All: High-tech, government, finance, and manufacturing.
Faculty: Independent staff of consultants.
Contact: Allen Cannie.

Learning International
225 High Ridge Rd.
Stamford, CT 06905
(203) 965-8400
No. Seminars/Year: More than 100.
Where: International.
Topics: Sales, sales management, and customer service.
Industry: All.
Faculty: Outside consultants.

Levinson Institute, Inc.
375 Concord Ave.
Belmont, MA 02178
(617) 489-3040
No. Seminars/Year: 6.
Where: Bedford, MA.
Topics: Leadership (weeklong immersion seminar), personality, psychological contract, managing stress and change, and practice leading.
Industry: All: executive officers, twice yearly; general managers, four times yearly.
Faculty: Members of Levinson and private psychologists and psychiatrists.
Contact: Melinda Flood.

Lifecycle Learning
1320 Centre St., Suite 305
Newton, MA 02159
(617) 964-5050
No. Seminars/Year: 100.
Where: U.S. and Canada.
Topics: Personal and professional growth, mental health education, and adult children of alcoholics.
Industry: Mental health practitioners. (Seminars are accredited for continuing education.)
Faculty: Guest speakers who are nationally known authors, lecturers, and presenters.
Contact: Dr. Robert Aylmer, President.

Lighthouse Communications, Inc.
233 W. Central St.
Natick, MA 01760-3714
(508) 650-1001
No. Seminars/Year: 4.
Where: Nationwide, especially New York; Washington, DC; Boston; and southern California.
Topics: Magazine management and circulation.
Industry: Magazine.
Faculty: Staff—principals of company.
Comments: Division of Lighthouse Communications, Inc.

Mail Advertising Service Association Int'l.
1421 Prince St., Suite 200
Alexandria, VA 22314-2814
(703) 836-9200
No. Seminars/Year: 6.
Where: Nationwide.
Topics: Technical seminars on machines used in lettershops.
Industry: Mail advertising.
Faculty: Representatives from companies and outside seminar leaders.
Comments: Trade association.
Contact: Director of Conferences

Management Directions
1250 Old Henderson Rd.
Columbus, OH 43220
(614) 457-1700
No. Seminars/Year; 12.
Where: Columbus, OH.
Topics: Presentation skills, team building, supervision, and stress management.
Industry: All.
Faculty: Staff.
Contact: Bonnie Mathews.

Manuals Corporation of America
152 Chestnut Hill Rd.
Coopersburg, PA 18036
(215) 967-2005
No. Seminars/Year: 30–40.
Where: Major cities in U.S. and Canada.
Topics: Manuals development course, layout and design, advanced manuals workshop, and manuals design.
Industry: All.
Faculty: President of company, consultants from business-run programs, and outside seminar leaders.
Comments: Charles H. Lutz, Jr.

Market Data Retrieval
16 Progress Dr.
Shelton, CT 06484
(800) 243-5538
No. Seminars/Year: 4.
Where: Major cities in U.S.
Topics: Direct marketing for educational marketing; how to design a promotional piece; education marketing in the 1990s—selling materials to educational facilities; and integrating various marketing arms to work together.
Industry: Direct marketing for direct mail.
Faculty: Outside consultants.
Contact: Michael Shields.

MTS Systems Corp.
P.O. Box 24012
Minneapolis, MN 55424
(612) 937-4335
No. Seminars/Year: 10 in-house.
Topics: Computer topics based on current business needs.
Industry: All.
Faculty: Staff seminar leaders and outside consultants.
Contact: Kitty Warner.

National Association of Credit Management (NACM)
8815 Centre Park Dr., Suite 200
Columbia, MD 21045-2117
(301) 740-5560
No. Seminars/Year: National annual convention. Conferences designed to meet specific needs of members of the trade association.
Where: Major cities in U.S. (varies each year).
Topics: Credit management.
Industry: All.
Faculty: Graduate school facilities run by NACM, Baylor, Santa Clara.
Comments: Trade association representing business credit executives.
Contact: Sandy Segrist.

National Crisis Prevention Institute
3315-K N. 124th St.
Brookfield, WI 53005-9932
(414) 783-5787
No. Seminars/Year: 81.
Where: 27 metropolitan U.S. cities and Canada.
Topics: Nonviolent crisis intervention.
Industry: Mental health, education, law enforcement, and human services.
Faculty: Staff.
Contact: Lisa Keehn.

National Graduate University
1101 N. Highland St.
Arlington, VA 22201
(703) 527-4800
No. Seminars/Year: About 100.
Where: 45 major U.S. cities.
Topics: Human resources management, personnel administration, federal grants and contracts, and federal regulations in procurement buying (government purchasing).
Industry: All public and private industries.
Faculty: Speakers associated with the University's adjunct instructor.
Comments: Donna Smith.

National Seminars Group
6901 W. 63d St.
Shawnee Mission, KS 66202-4007
(913) 432-7755
No. Seminars/Year: 4800.
Where: Canada, U.S., Great Britain, and the Netherlands.
Topics: 25 different topics, including communications, leadership, productivity, and lifestyle.
Industry: Entry- to upper-level personnel in small- to medium-sized training businesses.
Faculty: Professional speakers with expertise on topics.
Comments: National career workshop; national businesswomen's leadership; and national press publications: books, tapes, and videos on same topics as seminars.
Contact: Gary Weinberg.

Negotiation Institute, Inc.
230 Park Ave.
New York, NY 10169
(212) 986-5555
No. Seminars/Year: 30.
Where: U.S. and abroad.
Topics: Negotiations.
Industry: All.
Faculty: Lawyers or business people with extensive experience in negotiating.
Contact: E.B. Murray.

New York State Society of CPAs
200 Park Ave.
New York, NY 10166-0010
(212) 973-8376
No. Seminars/Year: 750–800 presentations covering 350 topics.
Where: New York.
Topics: Accounting and auditing, advisory services, management and personnel development, specialized knowledge, taxation, and microcomputer applications.
Industry: CPAs.
Faculty: All CPAs or proven experts in specific topic.

New York University School of Continuing Education
Center for Direct Marketing
48 Cooper Sq.
New York, NY 10003
(800) FIND-NYU
No. Seminars/Year: 30–50.
Where: New York, Los Angeles, and San Francisco.
Topics: Real estate, tax, law, finance, banking, information technology, hospitality, and careers.
Industry: All.
Faculty: Adjunct instructors in the industry.
Contact: Ken Connors.

North Carolina Outward Bound School
121 N. Sterling St.
Morgantown, NC 28655
(704) 437-6112, (800) 627-5971
No. Seminars/Year: 250 as well as year-round courses.
Where: Western N. Carolina; Florida Everglades; and Atlanta, GA.
Topics: Experiential education using wilderness setting for personal growth and physical challenge.
Industry: All.
Faculty: Staff.
Contact: Merrilee Kaufman.

Northwestern University
The Transportation Center
1936 Sheridan Rd.
Evanston, IL 60208-4040
(708) 491-3741
No. Seminars/Year: 6–7.
Where: Evanston, IL.
Topics: Executive seminars on transportation and energy issues.
Industry: Transportation, energy, and logistics.
Faculty: Northwestern University faculty; specialists in the field of transportation and energy.
Contact: Barbara Duggan.

Novations Consulting Group
2155 N. 200 West, Suite 201
Provo, UT 84604
(801) 375-7525
No. Seminars/Year: 100.
Where: U.S., the Far East, Europe, Canada, and Latin America.
Topics: Career development, strategic alignment, self-directed work teams, and internal consulting/consulting skills for senior management.
Industry: All.
Faculty: Staff and contract consultants.
Comments: Book available on career development.
Contact: Ron Olphius.

NTL Institute
1240 N. Pitt St.
Alexandria, VA 22314-1403
(703) 548-1500
No. Seminars/Year: 100.
Where: Bethel, ME; San Diego; Tampa; Washington, DC; Colorado; and other U.S. sites.
Topics: Human relations training, management and personal development, consultation skills, organization development, and training of trainers.
Industry: All: large and small, public and private.
Faculty: NTL professional members: consultants, trainers, psychologists, educators, and organization development practitioners.
Contact: Emily Hickey.

Oasis Center for Human Potential
7463 N. Sheridan
Chicago, IL 60626
(312) 274-6777
No. Seminars/Year: 500.
Where: Chicago.
Topics: Personal development and training in people-helping skills.
Industry: All adults in helping fields.
Faculty: Contract with consultants.
Contact: Delacy Sarantos.

The Ohio State University Public Management Programs
School of Public Policy
210 Haggerty Hall
1775 College Rd.
Columbus, OH 43210-1399
(614) 885-0262
No. Seminars/Year: 40.
Where: Fawcett Center for Tomorrow in Columbus.
Topics: Public management, coaching skills for management, and statistics.
Industry: Middle-level management in the public sector.
Faculty: School of Public Policy and Management, College of Business, other

colleges within Ohio State University, private consultants, and faculty from other universities.

Comments: Program sells membership in the MAPS series.

Contact: Louise Hopkins.

The William Oncken Corporation
18601 LBJ Frwy., Suite 315
Mesquite, TX 75150
(214) 613-2084

No. Seminars/Year: 80.

Where: Major cities in U.S., Canada, and Europe.

Topics: Management and organizational development.

Industry: All, especially government, medicine, health, insurance, real estate, and publishing.

Faculty: Staff instructors.

Contact: Romana Ford, Vice President, Sales and Marketing.

Organizational Consultants, Inc.
55 Child St., #301
P.O. Box 330145
San Francisco, CA 94133
(415) 989-6189

No. Seminars/Year: 4 of each seminar.

Where: San Francisco, Chicago, and Washington, DC.

Topics: Consulting for organizational effectiveness, social-technical systems designed for total quality, and study mission to Japan (world-class Japanese organizations that use social-technical systems).

Industry: Private and public sectors; large and small companies.

Faculty: Staff: John J. Sherwood, William Pasmore, and Paul Tolchinski.

Contact: Jan King.

The PACE Organization
P.O. Box 1378
Studio City, CA 91614
(818) 769-5100

No. Seminars/Year: 6.

Where: Palm Springs and Hilton Head.

Topics: High-performance behavior, self-esteem, goal setting, responsibility, and communications.

Industry: Service, stock brokerage, aerospace, and sales.

Faculty: James W. Newman, Founder.

Contact: Nan Newman.

Padgett Thompson of American Management Association
11221 Row Ave.
Leawood, KS 66211
(800) 255-4141

No. Seminars/Year: More than 6000.

Where: U.S. and abroad.

Topics: Management, supervision, secretarial science, human resources, niche markets, and purchasing.

Industry: All.
Faculty: Independent contractors who are experts in the topic and well-known trainers who do specific seminars.
Comments: All seminars developed internally by training department.

Penn State Executive Programs
310 Business Administration Bldg.
University Park, PA 16801-9975
(814) 865-3435
No. Seminars/Year: 16.
Where: Penn State.
Topics: General management and functional management.
Industry: All.
Faculty: Faculty and outside seminar leaders.
Contact: Dr. Virginia Freeman.

Performance Seminar Group
325 Myrtle Ave.
Bridgeport, CT 06604
(203) 366-2490, (800) 222-2921
No. Seminars/Year: More than 100.
Where: U.S. and Canada.
Topics: Accounts receivable, sales writing, newsletter writing, desktop publishing, buying (general), and buying (printing).
Industry: All.
Faculty: Independent contractors.
Contact: Julie Moss.

Personnel Decisions, Inc.
2000 Plaza VII Tower.
45 S. 7th St.
Minneapolis, MN 55402-1608
(612) 339-0927, (800) 633-4410
No. Seminars/Year: 45.
Where: Minneapolis, New York, and Dallas.
Topics: Management, leadership, and human resources.
Industry: All.
Faculty: Staff only.
Contact: Keith Halpern.

Pfieffer & Co., Inc.
8517 Production Ave.
San Diego, CA 92121
(619) 578-5900
No. Seminars/Year: 50.
Where: San Francisco; Toronto; San Diego; and Washington, DC.
Topics: Team building, applied strategic planning, group dynamics, and organizational development.
Faculty: Staff.
Contact: Dick Roe.

Pope & Associates, Inc.
1313 E. Kemper Rd., Suite 350
Cincinnati, OH 45246
(513) 671-1277
No. Seminars/Year: 21.
Where: Cincinnati and elsewhere in U.S.
Topics: Diversity management training, consulting pairs training, self development, and self-development for women.
Industry: All.
Faculty: Trainers on staff.
Contact: Adrienne Calhoun.

Power & Systems
P.O. Box 388 Prudential Station
Boston, MA 02199
(617) 437-1640
No. Seminars/Year: 100.
Where: Washington, DC; Boston; Chicago; and San Francisco.
Topics: Empowerment in organizations: total system empowerment, middle empowerment skills for middle-level managers, continuous empowerment module, and training the trainer in empowerment.
Industry: All, especially total quality management initiatives.
Faculty: Barry Oshry and other outside consultants.
Contact: Sam Zimmerman.

Prime Learning International
165 W. 400 South
Alpine, UT 84004
(801) 756-5989
No. Seminars/Year: 900.
Where: All major U.S. cities and abroad.
Topics: Secretarial science and computer.
Industry: All.
Faculty: Outside consultants.
Contact: Diane Hartman.

Princeton Research Institute
P.O. Box 2702
Scottsdale, AZ 85252
(602) 994-0016, (609) 396-0305
No. Seminars/Year: 12.
Where: U.S. and Canada.
Topics: Mergers and acquisitions, corporate restructuring, divestiture, and going public.
Industry: All.
Faculty: Staff and practitioners.
Contact: Bill Arnold.

Project Management Mentor Div. AHRD Association, Inc.
2082 Union St.
San Francisco, CA 94123-4103
(415) 922-4706
No. Seminars/Year: 100–150 in-house.
Topics: Project management, information systems, managing multiple projects in the matrix environment.
Faculty: Own staff.

Pryor Resources, Inc.
2000 Shawnee Mission Pkwy.
Shawnee Mission, KS 66208
(913) 722-3990
No. Seminars/Year: 4000.
Where: U.S. and abroad.
Topics: Business skills enhancement.
Industry: Business support staff, high-end managers, middle-level managers, and technical staff.
Faculty: Professionals and experts in the field; staff and contract consultants.
Contact: Janet Turner.

Psychological Associates, Inc.
8201 Maryland Ave.
St. Louis, MO 63105
(314) 862-9300
No. Seminars/Year: 36.
Where: St. Louis.
Topics: Leadership, general management, sales training, and team building.
Industry: Service.
Faculty: Staff and outside consultants.
Comments: Participatory programs.
Contact: Raymond Halagera.

QCI International
1425 Vista
Airport Industrial Park
Red Bluff, CA 96080
(916) 527-6970
No. Seminars/Year: 28–30.
Where: U.S., Australia, Turkey, the Netherlands, and Africa.
Topics: Facilitation training courses and employee involvement arena.
Industry: Quality assurance, trainers, human resources, and management in all industries.
Faculty: Staff and independent contractors.
Comments: Geared toward middle-level management in medium-sized companies.
Contact: Joyce McClelland.

Quantum Educational Discoveries, Inc.
28 Commerce St.
Williston, VT 05495
(802) 864-6186
No. Seminars/Year: More than 100.
Where: Nationwide.
Topics: Accounting Game, Breakthrough (2-day, a model for change), Choices Weekend (3-day self-help workshop), Getting to Know Yourself, Train the Trainer, Accelerated Learning for Course Design — Whole-Brain Theory.
Industry: All.
Faculty: Trains own faculty.
Contact: Marge Berger.

Rice University
Jesse H. Jones Graduate School of Administration
Office of Executive Development
P.O. Box 1892
Houston, TX 77251
(713) 527-6060
No. Seminars/Year: Approximately 85.
Where: Mostly at Jones Graduate School at Rice; the balance at corporate customers' locations.
Topics: Business writing, computer usage, finance and accounting, supervision, sales and marketing management, project management, personal productivity, quality, management development courses for middle- and upper-level managers, and many more.
Industry: Business, government, military, and nonprofit organizations.
Faculty: Mostly Ph.D. faculty of the Jones School and other professionals in their fields from Texas and elsewhere in the U.S.

Richardson Management Associates
2060 Sherbrooke St. W., #102
Montreal, PQ H3H 1G5
Canada
(514) 935-2593
No. Seminars/Year: 40.
Where: Montreal, Toronto, Calgary, Los Angeles, Atlanta, Dallas, and Phoenix.
Topics: Interpersonal skills and communications.
Industry: All.
Faculty: Staff.
Contact: Louise MacDonald.

Schnapper Associates, Inc.
2522 W. Fitch Ave.
Chicago, IL 60645
(312) 262-2113
No. Seminars/Year: 12.
Where: Washington, DC; Chicago; and Philadelphia.

Topics: Job hunting and leadership.
Industry: All.
Faculty: Mel Schnapper, President, and staff.

A. E. Schwartz and Associates
P.O. Box 228
Waverly, MA 02179-9998
(617) 926-9111
No. Seminars/Year: 50.
Where: Primarily East Coast, Midwest, and West Coast.
Topics: Management, sales, and customer service.
Industry: All.
Faculty: Staff seminar leaders and outside consultants; certify trainers for specific programs.
Contact: Andrew E. Schwartz, President.

Scientific Methods, Inc.
P.O. Box 195
Austin, TX 78767
(512) 477-5781
No. Seminars/Year: 24–36.
Where: Major U.S. cities.
Topics: Managerial grid, executive grid, advanced grid, human interaction.
Industry: All.
Faculty: Staff and some outside speakers.
Contact: Carol Howard or Bob Peck.

Seminars International
Division of Business Communications & Information, Inc.
14201 Mur-Len Rd.
Olathe, KS 66062
(913) 780-0020
No. Seminars/Year: 1500.
Where: Continental U.S., Alaska, Hawaii, and Puerto Rico.
Topics: Sales and marketing, decision making, finance, behavioral topics, ethics, and cross-cultural diversity.
Industry: All—private and public corporations of all sizes.
Faculty: 30, plus seminar leaders and outside consultants.
Contact: Robert J. Eckholt, President and CEO.

David Silver Financial Services, Inc.
524 Camino del Monte Sol
Santa Fe, NM 87501
(505) 983-1769
No. Seminars/Year: 8.
Where: Continental U.S.
Topics: Entrepreneurship and saving troubled businesses.
Industry: All.
Faculty: Staff.
Contact: David Silver.

Situation Management Systems, Inc.
195 Hanover St.
Hanover, MA 02339
(617) 826-4433
No. Seminars/Year: 35–40.
Where: Nationwide.
Topics: Influence, negotiation, selling, problem solving, and innovation.
Industry: All.
Faculty: Staff seminar leaders and outside consultants.
Contact: Mr. Kane.

Southern Illinois University
Center for Management Studies
Edwardsville, IL 62026-1251
(618) 692-2668
No. Seminars/Year: 30–40.
Where: St. Louis and Edwardsville.
Topics: Management, management skills, presentation skills, communication, socialization skills, and leadership.
Industry: All.
Faculty: Southern Illinois University plus some contract consultants.
Comments: James F. Miller, Director.

Sroge Publishing
228 N. Cascade Ave., Suite 307
Colorado Springs, CO 80903-1325
(719) 633-5556
No. Seminars/Year: 8–10.
Where: U.S. and Canada.
Topics: How to create successful catalogs and successful direct mail methods.
Industry: Direct mail marketing.
Faculty: Maxwell Sroge.

Success Builders
P.O. Box 27-496
Kansas City, MO 64180
(800) 348-7350
No. Seminars/Year: 300.
Where: U.S. and abroad.
Topics: Single skill-based programs, such as writing and proofreading.
Industry: All.
Faculty: Independent contractors trained by the corporations.

Swan Consultants, Inc.
420 Lexington Ave.
New York, NY 10170
(212) 682-0606
No. Seminars/Year: Varies.
Where: Nationwide.
Topics: Interviewing skills.
Industry: Human resources.

Faculty: Dr. William Swan and staff.
Contact: Dr. William Swan.

Sys-tem-a-tion
2452 S. Trenton Way, Suite L
Denver, CO 80231
(303) 745-1820
No. Seminars/Year: Approximately 200.
Where: Nationwide.
Topics: Systems and management workshops, fast-start systems analysis, project planning, procedure writing, interviewing, and role-playing.
Industry: Junior-level systems managers or developers in banking, insurance, and public utilities.
Faculty: 5 instructors with experience in own business or corporation.
Contact: Paul Ray.

Technology Futures, Inc.
6034 W. Courtyard Dr.
Austin, TX 78730-5014
(512) 343-6468
No. Seminars/Year: 4.
Where: Sea Island, GA, and Castine, ME.
Topics: Innovation by design.
Industry: Telecommunications and other Fortune 500 companies.
Faculty: Staff and outside experts.
Comments: Services in executive development; education; and training, research, and consulting. Specialty is innovation management and organizational change.
Contact: Nancy Beckham.

Teleometrics International
1755 Woodstead Court
The Woodlands, TX 77380
(713) 367-0060
No. Seminars/Year: 7.
Where: Southwest; Houston; Washington, DC; and Detroit.
Topics: Interpersonal communications, management styles, motivational processes, decision making, teamwork, and conflict management.
Industry: All.
Faculty: Staff.
Contact: Lori Nemetz.

Tennant
P.O. Box 1452, M.S. #200
Minneapolis, MN 55440
(612) 424-1369
No. Seminars/Year: 34–40.
Where: Minneapolis, Chicago, and San Diego.
Topics: Quality improvement, strategic quality management, functional analysis, supplier quality, and employee recognition.
Industry: General.

Faculty: Staff.
Contact: Rita Mail.

The Training Clinic
645 Seabreeze Dr.
Seal Beach, CA 90740
(213) 430-2484
No. Seminars/Year: 300.
Where: 14 major cities throughout U.S. and the Netherlands.
Topics: Training the trainer, new-employee orientation, new-trainer survival skills, internal consulting skills for trainers, creative training, effective training coordination, and designing effective training problems.
Industry: All industries with training responsibilities.
Faculty: Staff.
Comments: Programs are highly interactive and practical and model what they teach.
Contact: Richard Barbazette.

Trancorp
20200 Governors Dr.
Olympia Fields, IL 60461
(708) 481-2900
No. Seminars/Year: 40–50.
Where: San Francisco; Atlanta; Miami; New York; Washington, DC; Dallas; Toronto; San José; Phoenix; Vancouver; and Minneapolis.
Topics: Franchising and related topics.
Industry: Anyone interested in franchising.
Faculty: Staff: Chairman, President, Senior Vice President.

Tri-Unity Wellness Center
903 E. Johnson St.
Madison, WI 53703
(608) 256-0080
No. Seminars/Year: 7.
Where: Wisconsin.
Topics: Massage, yoga, relationships, psychic abilities, relaxation, and stress management.
Industry: Personal growth.
Faculty: Staff and specialists in the field.
Comments: Learning the natural way to focus.

Tustin Technical Institute, Inc.
22 E. Los Olivos St.
Santa Barbara, CA 93105
(805) 682-7171
No. Seminars/Year: 50.
Where: Nationwide.
Topics: Environmental engineering, equipment reliability, computer applications, electrostatic discharge training, vibration and noise climatics, hazardous material and waste management, and program and product management.

Industry: Military contractors and installations; industrial and commercial companies.
Faculty: Independent contractors and consultants—known experts in the field.
Comments: Also correspondence courses and satellite transmissions.
Contact: Brian Slattery.

TREC Software Enterprises Corp.
31220 La Baya Dr., Suite 110
Westlake Village, CA 91362
(818) 889-7814
No. Seminars/Year: 1–2.
Where: U.S. and abroad.
Topics: Software support and defense software.
Industry: Government and government contractors.
Faculty: Staff.

United Communications Group
CCMI
1300 Rockville Pike
Rockville, MD 20852-3030
(800) 487-4824
No. Seminars/Year: 40.
Where: Major U.S. cities.
Topics: Telecommunications, health care, government procurement, petroleum and product marketing, military information, and postal regulations.
Industry: Telecommunications.
Faculty: Editor of publication presenting seminar and outside consultants.
Contact: Julie Upton.

University of Arizona
Engineering Professional Development
P.O. Box 9, Harvill Building
Tucson, AZ 85721
(602) 621-3054
No. Seminars/Year: 20–25.
Where: Nationwide.
Topics: Engineering.
Industry: Science and engineering.
Faculty: University faculty.
Contact: Mr. Paul Baltes.

UCLA Extension
10995 LeConte Ave.
Los Angeles, CA 90024
(213) 825-1901
No. Seminars/Year: 4500 seminars; 70 certificate programs.
Where: Westwood, CA, area; San Fernando Valley; West Los Angeles; Highland Park; and other major U.S. cities.
Topics: Arts, business engineering and management, education, health science, and humanities, and social sciences.

Industry: All.
Faculty: UCLA faculty, instructors from outside sources, and consultants.
Contact: John Watson, Marketing Department, Suite 315, UCLA Extension.

University of Chicago
Office of Continuing Education
5835 S. Kimbark Ave. Chicago, IL 60637
(312) 702-1727
No. Seminars/Year: 600.
Where: Chicago, and Vail, CO.
Topics: Publishing, marketing, liberal arts programs geared to individuals, publishing, and business.
Faculty: University faculty.

The University of Michigan
Michigan Business School
Executive Education Center
Ann Arbor, MI 48109-1234
(313) 763-9461
No. Seminars/Year: 170.
Where: Ann Arbor.
Topics: 55 different programs, including general management, finance, marketing, and labor relations.
Industry: All.
Faculty: Faculty from Michigan Business School and peer institutions; consultants and experts in the field.
Contact: Ron Bendersby.

University of Pittsburgh
Joseph M. Katz Graduate School of Business
Center for Executive Education
253 Cathedral of Learning
Pittsburgh, PA 15260
(412) 648-1605
No. Seminars/Year: 70–75.
Where: Pittsburgh and Columbus, OH.
Topics: Assertive management, warehouse operation, accounting, secretaries as managers, financial, marketing, purchasing, and hazardous waste management.
Industry: Major corporations, municipal government, and health.
Faculty: University faculty.
Comments: Affiliated with Penton Learning Systems.
Contact: Regina Lewis.

University of Richmond
Management Institute
E. Claiborne Robins School of Business
Richmond, VA 23173
(804) 289-8019
No. Seminars/Year: 100.
Where: Richmond.

Topics: Leadership, management and supervision, personal and professional development, communications, support-staff programs, organizational development, and global business.
Industry: All.
Faculty: Faculty of Management Institute, university faculty, and adjunct faculty.
Contact: Robin Herst.

University of Wisconsin—Milwaukee
University Outreach
929 N. Sixth St.
Milwaukee, WI 53203
(414) 227-3220
No. Seminars/Year: 300.
Where: Milwaukee area and Midwest.
Topics: Management, supervision, human resources, information management, telecommunications, small business management, microcomputers, real estate, insurance, and professional skills development.
Industry: All.
Faculty: University faculty and instructors experienced in the specific topics offered.
Contact: Patrick Milne.

University of Wisconsin
Management Institute
The School of Business
432 N. Lake St.
Madison, WI 53706-1498
(608) 262-3089
No. Seminars/Year: 150; 300 presentations a year.
Where: Madison and Milwaukee.
Topics: Executive-level management; middle-level management; basic management; people skills; communication; accounting; production operations; quality management; sales and customer service; transportation, warehousing, and logistics; training and development; marketing; procurement; and product-service management.
Industry: Profit and nonprofit businesses.
Faculty: 14 full-time and some ad hoc instructors.
Contact: Bill Capellaro.

Urguhardt II Seminars
2061 Business Center Dr.
Irvine, CA 92715-1107
(714) 752-5544
No. Seminars/Year: 40.
Where: Major U.S. cities.
Topics: Tax aspects of independent contract versus employer.
Industry: Business owners.
Faculty: Principals of company.

Walters Speaker Services
P.O. Box 1120
Glendora, CA 91740
(818) 335-8069
No. Seminars/Year: 12 on each topic.
Where: Glendora area, Chicago, and San Francisco.
Topics: Speak and Grow Rich, How to Be a Better Speaker, and How to Have Audience Involvement.
Industry: Professional speakers.
Faculty: Dotty Walters and Lilly Walters.
Comments: Publishers of *Sharing Ideas*, largest magazine for professional speakers; authors of *Speak and Grow Rich*.

Washington Researchers
2612 P Street, NW
Washington, DC 20007
(202) 333-3499
No. Seminars/Year: 15–20.
Where: Washington, DC; San Francisco; and Atlanta.
Topics: How to find information about any company; practical competitor analysis techniques; benchmarking: competitive analysis technique; how to find information about businesses and private companies; and how to design and implement a competitive management program.
Industry: All.
Faculty: Staff: Latila Knight, President; John Ballori; seminar associates; consultants from Kaiser Associates.
Contact: Charles Palermo.

Waterloo Management Education Center
Suite 619
Waterloo Square
Waterloo, Ontario N2J 1P2
Canada
(519) 886-4740
No. Seminars/Year: 20; 600 presentations a year.
Where: U.S. and Canada.
Topics: Supervision, sales management, presentation skills, collective bargaining, and creative thinking.
Industry: Large corporations.
Faculty: 20 consultants.
Comments: Don Deveral, President.

Thomas Wilds Associates, Inc.
P.O. Box 11120
Greenwich, CT 06830
(212) 986-2515
No. Seminars/Year: 10.
Where: Worldwide.
Topics: Records retention, microfilm and optical discs, and procedure writing.
Industry: All.

Faculty: Outside consultants.
Contact: Thomas Wilds.

World Trade Institute
One World Trade Center
55th Fl.
New York, NY 10048
(212) 435-2900

No. Seminars/Year: 200-300.
Where: Chicago; San Francisco; Dallas; Atlanta; Boston; and Washington, DC.
Topics: International finance and accounting (introductory and advanced), international law, international logistics, marketing (introductory and intermediate), international taxation (introductory, intermediate, advanced), and international training.
Industry: All, including lawyers and accountants.
Faculty: Outside specialists in the field and the industry.
Comments: Founded to develop NY and NJ economic region.
Contact: Charles Best.

Wright State University
College of Continuing and Communications Education
140 E. Monument Ave.
Dayton, OH 45402
(513) 224-8511

No. Seminars/Year: 400.
Where: Nationwide.
Topics: Supervisory development, coaching and counseling, professional writing, writing instructional manuals, writing technical documents, computer courses, preventive maintenance, maintenance for fleet managers, supplier certification and contract management, and purchasing.
Industry: All.
Faculty: Consultants who are experts in the field.
Contact: Roger Herrin.

Robert Yourzak & Associates
7320 Gallagher Dr., Suite 325
Minneapolis, MN 55435
(612) 831-2235

No. Seminars/Year: As requested.
Where: Nationwide.
Topics: Project management in microcomputer area, and motivating and managing the project team.
Industry: High-tech, engineering, construction, government, commercial, utilities, and information management.
Faculty: Staff (12 people).
Contact: Robert Yourzak.

Gary Zeune & Associates
100 S. Third St.
Columbus, OH 43215
(614) 221-6228

No. Seminars/Year: 30–35.
Where: Nationwide; offered through state CPA and bar associations.
Topics: Complete guide to initial public offerings; financing techniques for the uncertain 1990s; and competitive strategies for the uncertain 1990s.
Industry: Legal and accounting (CPAs).
Faculty: Gary Zeune, plus attorney from local city as coinstructor.

Index

About the Author

Paul Karasik is president of the American Seminar Leaders Association. ASLA helps both the beginning and the advanced seminar leader market and deliver seminars more successfully.

Mr. Karasik is a full-time seminar leader and presenter who has shared the platform with such notables as ex-President Ronald Reagan and Dr. Norman Vincent Peale. He is president of the Business Institute, a consulting company that provides sales, management, and motivational programs to America's leading businesses, including such Fortune 500 companies as IBM, AT&T, and Citibank, as well as a variety of professional organizations. He is the author of three books, *Achieving Peak Performance*, *Sweet Persuasion*, and *Sweet Persuasion for Managers*, published by Simon & Schuster.

As an expert in the field of motivation, Mr. Karasik practices what he preaches. He regularly "goes the extra mile" by competing in ultra-marathons of 50 miles and more. Mr. Karasik resides in Weehawken, New Jersey.